Willa Cather and Material Culture

STUDIES IN AMERICAN LITERARY REALISM AND NATURALISM

Willa Cather and Material Culture

Real-World Writing, Writing the Real World

Edited by Janis P. Stout

The University of Alabama Press
Tuscaloosa

Manufactured in the United States of America

Hardcover edition published 2005.
Paperback edition published 2012.
eBook edition published 2009.

Typeface: Minion

Cover photograph: Willa Cather. Photograph by Carl Van Vechten. Courtesy of the Library of Congress, Prints and Photographs Division, Carl Van Vechten Collection.
Cover design: Michele Myatt Quinn

∞

The paper on which this book is printed meets the minimum requirements of American National Standard for Information Science–Permanence of Paper for Printed Library Materials, ANSI Z39.48—1984.

Paperback ISBN: 978-0-8173-5731-3
eBook ISBN: 978-0-8173-8232-2

A previous edition of this book has been catalogued by the Library of Congress as follows:
Library of Congress Cataloging-in-Publication Data
Willa Cather and material culture : real–world writing, writing the real world / edited by Janis P. Stout.
p. cm. — (Studies in American literary realism and naturalism)
Includes bibliographical references (p.) and index.
ISBN 0-8173-1436-9 (alk. paper)
1. Cather, Willa, 1873–1947—Criticism and interpretation. 2. Cather, Willa, 1873–1947—Knowledge—Material culture. 3. Literature publishing—United States. 4. Material culture in literature. 5. Reality in literature. 6. Realism in literature. I. Stout, Janis P. II. Series.
PS3505.A87Z93525 2004
813'.52—dc22

2004008808

Many of the invisible attributes of creating are
themselves objectified and made visible in the
materialized structure of the object world.
—Elaine Scarry, *The Body in Pain*

Contents

Abbreviations

Calendar—Stout, ed., *A Calendar of the Letters of Willa Cather*
DCA—Cather, *Death Comes for the Archbishop*
DCF—Dorothy Canfield Fisher
FG—Ferris Greenslet
LG—Cather, *Lucy Gayheart*
LL—Cather, *A Lost Lady*
MA—Cather, *My Ántonia*
MME—Cather, *My Mortal Enemy*
NRa—Cather, "Neighbour Rosicky" (first book publication)
NRb—Cather, "Neighbor Rosicky" (magazine version)
OD—Cather, *Obscure Destinies* (Scholarly Edition)
ODa—Cather, *Obscure Destinies* (original Knopf version)
OP—Cather, *O Pioneers!*
OW—Cather, *On Writing*
PH—Cather, *The Professor's House*
SL—Cather, *The Song of the Lark*
SR—Cather, *Shadows on the Rock*
WC—Willa Cather
WCIP—L. Brent Bohlke, ed., *Willa Cather in Person*
WCPM—Willa Cather Pioneer Memorial, Red Cloud, Nebraska

Willa Cather and Material Culture

Introduction

For Use, for Pleasure, for Status

The Object World of Willa Cather

Janis P. Stout

William Carlos Williams's dictum "no ideas but in things," usually taken as a position statement relating to the *expression* of ideas in poetry, might equally well be read as an observation about their source—that is, where ideas come from. For if human beings can express themselves only in real, sensuous objects (as Karl Marx once wrote),[1] it is perhaps equally true that we can gain personhood, develop selves to express, only within the context of objects—a process Fredric Jameson describes when he states that external objects "'remind' us of ourselves more profoundly than anything that takes place in the impoverished life of our conscious will" (99). Patricia Yaeger, quoting Jameson, terms this process "introjection," or the use of objects "to find a path into the hieroglyphic tangle of our own drives and desires" (142). We live amid objects from the time we are wrapped, still smeared with our mother's blood, in our first blanket. Hence the importance of the study of material culture: Concrete objects are both ingredients and traces of human identity, human history, and human culture. And it is as both—as ingredients or shaping contexts and as expressive traces—that we will here ponder the importance of material objects to the mind and art of Willa Cather.

Objects are not, of course, *the* ingredients or *the* traces of culture; words, both spoken and written on documents (which can also then be studied as objects), are also powerful ingredients and traces of consciousness, of culture, and of the interaction of individual consciousness with culture. But words have been attended to and studied for so long, and have been so privileged above material objects in the hierarchy of what is worthy of attention, that the more recent interest in objects, not merely as illustrations of meaning but as coequal conveyers of meaning, is a significant corrective. As Richard Millington writes, "we *make* our culture" by making objects ("Where" 38). Or in the words of Jules David Prown, we study "material" in order to understand "culture" because "human-made objects reflect, consciously or unconsciously, directly or indirectly, the beliefs of . . . individuals" and of their society more largely (Prown 1).

Cather is not often spoken of in company with Marx and Williams, nor has she often, until quite recently, been regarded as a person *or* a writer for whom the material world held much importance. Our position here is that—contrary to James Woodress's assertion that "material possessions meant to her only what they could do to make her life unencumbered" for writing (74)—she should be. If one of the main projects in Cather studies in the past two decades has been to reclaim Cather for modernism (to be sure, as a modernist with a difference), an even more hotly disputed one has been to consider her less in exceptionalist terms and more in terms of her involvement in, or even investment in, her culture. Both of these fundamental realignments of our understanding of Willa Cather, a writer more customarily regarded as a nostalgist and an aesthete devoted to Art with a capital A, are mediated by attention to material objects, both the objects among which she lived her own life and the objects that appear in her writings.[2]

One of the primary purposes of this volume is to demonstrate the extent to which Cather did participate in her culture, frequently by way of her enjoyment of the material goods that the burgeoning consumerism of the early twentieth century made available. The evidence afforded by both the biographical and the textual thing-ness of Cather's mind lays to rest the once prevalent conception of idealizing scholars and critics that she lived and wrote as an artist set apart from her culture in a kind of purity of aesthetic aspiration, indifferent alike to politics and to material gain. Another of the primary purposes of this volume is to demonstrate the extent to which her pursuit of her art took place within the commercial constraints and interests of the publishing industry—that is, the extent to which she pursued her writing as a career, as distinct from a disinterested engagement in creating art for the ages. In many ways, in the course of pursuing these ends, we incidentally add our voices to the reclamation of Cather for modernism—a quest one would suppose long since completed were it not for the fact that new castles perilously continue to pop up even as new dimensions of her modernism continue to unfold.

One reason Cather has so often been thought of as being more or less unconcerned with physical reality (Yaeger, in the essay already referred to, being an important but rare exception) is that she herself railed so famously against the cluttering of fiction with *things* invoked merely for documentary purposes. She railed, too, against the consumerism that she saw as taking over society in the 1920s, along with a concomitant cheapening of life and lowering of standards of quality on all fronts. Of course, her concern about the cheapening of things and experiences—she tended to refer to it as "commonness"—might itself be seen as evidence of her affection for objects, else why would she care? But in no way more than this sometimes crotchety hostility to the consumerist society in which she lived does she demonstrate how closely she participates in modernism, with, as Douglas Mao writes, its "reflexive antipathy to the commodity" and conspicuous consumption (4). That antipathy among English and American modernists deepened with post–World War I revelations about the privations and resulting poor health of the lower classes in England and with the appalling spectacle of the Great Depression of the 1930s—a well-documented source of distress and concern to Cather. As Mao continues (in his book *Solid Objects,* a study richly pertinent to our interests here despite the absence of reference to Cather),[3] "modernism shows a reaction against consumption . . . no less decisive for it than its retention of aestheticism's privileging of the life devoted to art" (19). Elevating art to a place significantly above ordinary human interactions, endowing art with a meaning-status or reality-status exceeding that of what we usually call reality itself, modernists, and Cather among them, were "famously allergic to art in the service of propaganda." For that very reason, Mao argues, modernists valued and indeed doted over objects, not as commodities or as symbols of abstract or ideal values, but *as* objects, as ends in themselves, for "what the object world represented for modernists above all was a realm beyond the reach of ideology" (9). Or to paraphrase Archibald MacLeish, objects do not (have to) mean but (can merely) be. In a world where meaning is radically called into question, merely being is a comforting state indeed.

Like Walter Benjamin, when he speaks of a "relationship to objects which does not emphasize their functional, utilitarian value" (*Illuminations* 60, qtd by Mao, 5), modernists such as Virginia Woolf, Wallace Stevens, Louis MacNeice, and others tend to focus on individual, isolated objects (Woolf's plain white table envisioned in the tree or her green shawl swathing the skull on the wall; Stevens's deal dresser, his jar; MacNeice's tangerine pips or the curtains he won't have time to get made before the outbreak of war) for their power to concentrate associated emotions and to convey auras of intrinsic value. (Characteristically, Ezra Pound more grandly invokes, not single objects, but "two gross of broken statues" and "a few thousand battered books," and does so not in affectionate citation but in declamation.) Hence Cather's call in "The Novel Démeublé" for a barer stage on which to play out fictions, a stage furnished not with the accumulation of things that cling, as if with velcro, to our ordinary lives, but with the few selected things that will best convey associated emotions. Like Benjamin, too, we who study "commodities" as "emblems" attempt to "read through objects to the truth of the social totality that produced them" (Mao 6) and the ways in which a given artist or writer may participate in that social totality. Steven Lubar and W. David Kingery complained, in their introduction to the volume *History from Things: Essays on Material Culture,* in 1993, that we "too seldom . . . try to read objects as we read books—to understand the people and times that created them, used them, and discarded them" (viii). They might have less complaint now, a decade later, as the study of material culture has at least begun to pervade literary scholarship, as it earlier pervaded history, anthropology, and folklore studies.

Much of our understanding of the importance of material culture has indeed come out of the discipline of anthropology, which, as Millington writes in his essay "Where Is Cather's Quebec? Anthropological Modernism in *Shadows on the Rock,*" developed in the early twentieth century "a new understanding of culture as a category of human experience" and "central arena of human meaning-making" under the leadership of Franz Boas at Columbia (23, 25). In the process of defining itself as a discipline, anthropology became less preoccupied with language and the preservation of languages thought to be disappearing and more attentive to material objects as components of, or expressions of, cultural meaning. The discipline became increasingly attuned, that is, to the concept of a "culture-complex" or cultural gestalt in which the whole that we call a culture is manifest in a wide range of social practices and beliefs, including the shaping, use, and valuing of objects. These components of culture, anthropologists came to believe, were integrated in such a way that differences in "outer activities" and the objects that accompanied them "reflected differences in beliefs and ideals" (Caffrey 153). Objects became a kind of language (Ruth Benedict saw culture as being "written" in objects), beautiful or useful or pleasurable in their own right, but also both beautiful and useful for constituting and communicating cultural meaning.

As Millington writes, "there is every reason to believe that anyone as actively engaged in New York intellectual life as Cather was during the early decades of the century would have encountered" this "new perspective" (26). The unfolding of modern anthropology was in fact going on practically under her nose. Living in New York after 1906, she had many acquaintances at Columbia University, where Boas, working as the sole professor and head of the department of anthropology with the assistance of a cadre of graduate students, researchers, and financial supporters, was creating modern anthropology. We see the evidence of her interest in the subject most readily, of course, in *The Song of the Lark* and *The Professor's House,* with their artifacts of the ancients in the Southwest. Her correspondence (maddeningly reticent as ever) demonstrates that she knew the Boases.[4] Almost incredibly, it gives no evidence whatsoever of her having known either Benedict or Elsie Clews Parsons, both of whom were living in New York during the same years as Cather, were protégées of Boas, and, like Cather, often directed their interests to the Southwest. If today we as literary scholars take up the interest in material culture that is evident here, it is in part because of the interdisciplinarity that increasingly pervaded the academy in the latter part of the twentieth century, through which literary critics as well as historians came into intellectual conversation with anthropologists, to the enrichment of all.

Shadows on the Rock, the novel Millington reads in demonstration of Cather's anthropological imagination, has also been importantly read by

Ann Romines in her 1992 *The Home Plot* for its enunciation of "domestic ritual." The passage centrally quoted by Romines for how the novel "movingly conveys the irrevocable power of Cécile's domestic conditioning" is also the passage quoted by Millington for its demonstration of this child-hero's realization of how daily activities make cultural meaning: "These coppers, big and little, these brooms and clouts and brushes, were tools; and with them one made, not shoes or cabinet-work, but life itself. One made a climate within a climate; one made the days,—the complexion, the special flavour, the special happiness of each day as it passed; one made life" (*SR* 198). If we think about Willa Cather biographically for a moment, we find that domestic objects like Cécile's dish clouts and brooms and brushes were also prominent in her own object life, as she recorded it in her letters. A partial list would include objects both of use and of domestic beauty or pleasure: the blocks of ice that she carried from the dumbwaiter to the icebox every other day, for a while; the napkins, oyster forks, and ice cream freezer her maid Josephine organized when she returned to service in 1921; the aprons and dish towels Cather's mother sent her for Christmas that year and the steamed pudding Carrie Miner Sherwood sent; the single coal grate she and Edith Lewis were able to keep going in their apartment during the fuel shortage of 1918, the last year of World War I; a satin "quilt" or down comforter sent to her for Christmas by Blanche Knopf, allowing her to bundle her old blanket off to the housekeeper; linens and mattresses at Grand Manan that tended to go moldy when the cottage was shut up; a quilt made for her by Nebraska friends, with squares embroidered with flowers alternating with solid green squares whose fancy quilting she praised; a washing machine she bought Annie Pavelka, which she playfully said should be referred to as Willie's Washer; an accumulation of dishes she had to wash when her housekeeper was ill in 1942; a small tulip-patterned tablecloth and napkins that she said she would use when she made her own late-afternoon tea in the kitchen; tablets for laundering her ecru curtains; a dessert recipe she requested from Irene; dustcloths (or in the language of *Shadows on the Rock*, dust-clouts) she apparently wielded herself when she returned from Maine in the summer of 1943 and found the apartment covered with thick dust, then using her fatigue after the big cleaning as an excuse not to go visit Carrie Miner Sherwood in Red Cloud as she had promised.[5]

Most of the objects I have mentioned are equipment of everyday life, perhaps ornamented (like the tulip-printed cloth or the quilt) or even luxurious (like the satin down comforter, a mark of urban prosperity), but primarily utilitarian. Other objects were strictly for enjoyment. A music box owned by the Cather family, for example, in the form of a hookah-smoking Turkish lady, appears in *O Pioneers!*, where it takes a role as an object belonging to Marie. (The actual music box is pictured in the Scholarly Edition of the novel.) Other objects of pleasure mentioned in Cather's letters include: the marionette a visitor brought to tea one February Friday in 1920, who begged for a cigarette, as well as the cigarettes themselves and the Italian tortoiseshell box where they were kept; Italian flagons sent by the Knopfs for Christmas in 1921; doilies that the Swiss housekeeper Josephine Bourda was pleased to find still in their appointed place when she returned; a china nightingale that sang when wound up.[6] Ornamental plants seem to have been especially important to Cather. Flowers in abundance and sometimes whole potted trees bearing oranges or apples were sent by various friends on gift occasions. Christmas trees belong in somewhat the same category, though more heavily laden with traditional values associated with religion. When she was thirty-two years old she still recalled—and deplored—the inadequate Christmas tree of her first year in Nebraska, a box elder wrapped in green paper snipped to make it look like an evergreen.[7] Clearly, decorating the Christmas tree was an important ritual to Cather. Letters to her Pittsburgh friends the Seibels refer to the festive trimming of their tree, and the bringing home of the Christmas tree, as well as Mr. Shimerda's kneeling before it, are important moments in *My Ántonia*.

Food was always important to Cather, as we can tell from her various complaints when she had to spend time in sanitariums, hotels, or hospitals where the cooking was poor or when she had to cope with food shortages during wartime. On the positive side, we see her enthusiasm ("ecstasies" might almost be the word) over an elaborate dinner in Paris, her numerous tributes to Josephine's French cooking, and her pride in having mastered the art of pastry herself during a visit home when her mother was ill.[8] Friends often sent gifts of food, especially at Christmas. A turkey sent by Zoë Akins in January 1943, when food shortages were making life dreary, was especially appreciated; the last of the leftovers went into hash.[9] Apparently Zoë decided that such a successful gift deserved to be repeated—she sent another turkey at Christmas 1944, which unfortunately never arrived. (One worries a bit about the odor in some post office somewhere.) But this second bird becomes a conveyer of meaning of another kind: a measure of Cather's aging. Although she had rushed out in glee to pick up the first one, this time she confesses that it's just as well it got lost, because she didn't feel up to wrestling with the preparation of something so big.[10]

Cather, in turn, often included food in her Christmas boxes for elderly former neighbors in Nebraska, such as the 1932 box she sent Mrs. Lambrecht, with its oranges and apples, celery, cranberries, prunes, dates, and plenty of Butternut coffee. The list reveals her sensitivity to her old friends' station in life; she sent them items that would be too special for their own grocery budgets but not so luxurious as to be unfamiliar or make them uncomfortable. But when she asked Blanche Knopf to have some groceries shipped to her cottage on Grand Manan in the summer of 1931, the list extended to wild rice and two jars of caviar as well as tomato paste and garlic. She enjoyed some candy Irene Miner Weisz sent her in 1932, which was perfect, she said, for nibbling while reading in bed. A decade later, when such items were scarce in the stores, she appreciated Irene's sending her some jars of orange marmalade, apparently homemade, which made tea time a treat.[11]

Both letters and photographs show that clothes were important to her as well. Her students at Allegheny High School in Pittsburgh remembered her "mannish" but "fashionable" dress, especially her crisp shirtwaists and four-in-hand ties (Hoover 43, 48). She seems to have had a special weakness for hats, some of which, in her pictures, may strike us as just slightly comical. She sounds genuinely pleased when she thanks Zoë Akins and Blanche Knopf for blouses, jackets, and dressing gowns. Her references to various shopping excursions or to her niece Mary Virginia's faithfulness in letting her know about sales sound truly zestful. When we read Stephen Tennant's account of his first meeting of Cather, when she came to the door wearing black satin pajamas with a shocking pink top (Hoare 212), we know we are in the presence of a woman who enjoyed clothes that were striking in their effect and who used them as costume. A more intimate pleasure in clothes is conveyed in a note thanking Irene Miner Weisz for some nice silk undervests that didn't ride up![12] But more typically her interest in clothes was directed toward comfort for hiking or working at her desk or toward the construction of persona when going out in public.

Some of the objects Cather mentions seem to have been important to her as status symbols. The four Persian rugs she told her aunt about, shortly after moving into her Bank Street apartment in 1912, seem to have served in some such way. Admitting that she took pride in them, she pointed out that it was the first time she had had a spacious apartment and one she could afford to fix up. When, almost two decades later, she moved into her Park Avenue apartment (which itself must be seen as a status symbol), she noted that she had French tapestries on her walls. One guesses that even if they were there primarily for her own pleasure or sense of coziness (as she told Zoë Akins) they represented the fact that she had made it, financially, and now had the ability to surround herself with finery. We might put in the same category the splendid crèche from France, with thirty figures, that she mentioned having displayed in her parents' home in Red Cloud, the one time she spent Christmas there after their deaths. Certainly we would include the mink coat that she famously bought with royalties from *The Professor's House*—coming as they did on the heels of a net $9,000 she had received for serial rights to the novel. (She asked Irene not to tell her family about this, lest they think she had a lot of money to spare—for spending on them, would be the implication.) Anyone who thinks Cather was indifferent to the financial rewards of writing should read these letters or the many that she wrote to her publishers about sales figures and how she wished their advertising department would work harder and more effectively.[13]

Cather's immersion in the commercial aspects of publishing and the details of books as objects shows itself over and over, not only in these frettings about sales and royalties but in her comments on bindings and covers and paper. During World War I a shortage of paper kept *O Pioneers!* in short supply even when readers continued to ask for it (not in great numbers; there were apparently some 300 sales in its fourth year), and when *My Ántonia* was in preparation she was very specific as to the kind of paper she wanted for it. Another war meant paper problems again. She complained to Ferris Greenslet in 1940 when she found that *Ántonia* was being printed on paper so thin the ink showed through from one side to the other. Such poor-quality bookmaking, she pointed out, affected the reading experience. She was equally particular about her personal stationery, taking time on numerous occasions to apologize when circumstances forced her to use unattractive paper even for a hurried note. These are only a few examples.[14]

Cather's object world was, of course, not only a part of her personal experience but of her writing. Despite her famous pronouncements about the bare stage for fiction (she cited approvingly, in "The Novel Démeublé," the elder Dumas's dictum that "to make a drama, a man needed one passion, and four walls"), the stages of Cather's novels and stories are not bare. Nor did she want the literal stage to be bare when she went to plays, as if the theater could be a matter of words alone. We see that, for instance, in a note she wrote to Zoë Akins after the opening of Akins's play *The Texas Nightingale,* where she praises the appearance of the leading actress and notes especially her "expressive clothes."[15] But if the stages of Cather's narratives are not literally bare, neither are they crowded with trappings of documentary realism. There are exceptions: *The Song of the Lark* was written in a full style that Cather later conceded was not her own, and the Nebraska sections of *One of Ours* are purposely littered with the detritus of a consumer-oriented family—even more so than the early portions of *The Professor's House,* which Cather said was designedly stuffy and crowded. Both of these deliberate clutterings are done for the purpose of setting up barer sections intended to represent a redemptive freeing from paraphernalia of everyday life that wear down their central characters. Whether we read the novels that way or not, we can recognize the design. But in most of her writing Cather avoids clutter altogether, inserting, instead, only a few selected objects, which are there to convey meanings beyond the merely documentary—that is, to be, as she said of the costumes in Akins's play, "expressive." The reaping machine into which the tramp hurls himself in a gruesome suicide in *My Ántonia,* the bathtub old Mrs. Lee resists using in *O Pioneers!,* the Henshawes' plum-colored curtains in *My Mortal Enemy,* with their faded linings—these are objects that convey essential meanings. And as Mary Chinery's recent essay "Willa Cather and the Santos Tradition in *Death Comes for the Archbishop*" demonstrates, we can often understand those meanings better if we have knowledge of the real-world objects being cited and their cultural significance.

Few aspects of Cather show her affinity with modernism so clearly as her attention to and concern with material objects, as these relate to the culture generally. Although this aspect of Cather has been little examined until recent years, it is an aspect inseparable from others that have a long history of scholarly and critical discussion—for example, her aestheticism, on the one hand, and her involvement in (and investment in) her culture, or the lack of it, on the other. Thus, the present discussion of Cather in relation to the object world she inhabited and that other, but related, object world she created in her writing is by no means an isolated conversation, but one that takes up and continues other conversations that have been going on for some time.[16] And so we walk into this room where men and women are sitting around a fire talking about a rather elusive and, so some say, otherworldly figure, stub our collective toe on a glove full of coins or an ice-cream freezer, and interrupt to protest, "But just look around this room, at all these *things*! How many other living rooms have you visited that had this same Persian lady, if not on a music box then in a picture, this same telephone that keeps ringing at just the wrong time, this same dishclout someone dropped here on the sideboard! Doesn't all that tell you something?"

As presented in the essays in this volume, what all that tells us about is first, of course, Willa Cather herself, but also the culture in which she participated. And as Mary Ann O'Farrell demonstrates in the concluding essay of the volume, attention to the materiality in Cather's fiction and the material conditions under which she wrote it provides us some new and fruitful ways to read texts with which we have long been familiar, including her oft-noted essay "The Novel Démeublé" and the writings of some of her most famous, or infamous, critics.

The essay that appears first, Ann Romines's "Willa Cather: A Life with Quilts," shows how Cather's attachment to this one particular type of object contributed to her sense of well-being or at-homeness. Providing both biograpical information and readings of quilts that were important to Cather and her family, Romines also demonstrates connections with Cather's artistic principles and raises the important issue of individual virtuosity versus (or combined with?) community making (as in group-made quilts). The theme of women's participation in a domestic material culture raised in this opening essay runs through most of the volume. It readily combines with the emergence of an increasingly commodified or consumerist culture emerging around the turn of the twentieth century in Jennifer L. Bradley's essay on Cather's work as editor of the *Home Monthly*, her first editorial job.

Bradley's essay raises, too, the idea of how important a role the business practices of the magazine industry played in setting the parameters within which Cather worked. A case study in the persistence of the magazine industry's influence on Cather's work is provided by Park Bucker, whose study of her accommodation to the conventions of the *Woman's Home Companion* is usefully supplemented by a thematic concordance for the story "Neighbour Rosicky." Both Bradley's and Bucker's essays disabuse us of any lingering notion that Cather the literary artist worked in grand isolation from commercial considerations. Michael Schueth examines commercial considerations that shaped, not the writing of a Cather text, but the reception of its film adaptation together with the "selling" of Cather herself in advertising for the second motion picture based (loosely) on *A Lost Lady*. Material parameters of a different sort that also shaped Cather's fiction in important ways are explored by Anne Raine in her essay on contemporary discussions of nature education and Cather's awareness of these discussions as a context for *The Song of the Lark* and *The Professor's House*.

Honor Wallace continues the exploration of female consumerism in her essay on *A Lost Lady* and *The Professor's House*, two of Cather's novels of the 1920s, proposing a link between female consumerist desire and female sexual desire. Provocative intertextual conversation then arises when Deborah Lindsay Williams explores the relation of female desire to the artifacts discovered in the Southwestern settings of *The Song of the Lark* and *The Professor's House*. Such Southwestern artifacts in *Death Comes for the Archbishop* are seen by Sarah Wilson as "sites of cultural mediation" or exchange. Wilson's argument underscores the intentionality of Cather's interest in physical objects. An exchange of a different sort—the exchanging of gifts as a kind of purchase—occupies Robert K. Miller in his essay on *My Mortal Enemy*. Miller's scrupulously constructed estimate of just how much money Myra Henshawe had tucked away in her gloves, both in 1913 terms and in 2002 terms, and his examination of the amount Myra pays for masses for the dead are unprecedented; they open up our understanding of the text in entirely new ways. Miller's essay might indeed serve as an exemplary model of how reading can be enriched by attentiveness to objects and monetary values.

The closing essay by Mary Ann O'Farrell, "Words To Do with Things: Reading about Willa Cather and Material Culture," ponders not only the foregoing essays (thereby serving as a singularly lively afterword) but the more basic questions of what it means to read Cather materially and what it means for writing to incorporate, or refrain from incorporating, "the materiality with which it is enamored."

Notes

1. Elaine Scarry writes similarly that "the action of the imagination is . . . only disclosed in the material and verbal residues she leaves behind" (*Body in Pain*, 306).

2. The Scholarly Edition of Cather's works, of which six volumes have thus far appeared, is notably contributing to this realignment of our understanding by providing abundant explanatory notes of objects that appear in her texts and by situating her writing within the context of publication business practices. Although the absorption of such painstaking textual work into scholarly and critical practice is necessarily gradual, it can be expected that these attributes of the edition will greatly forward materialist considerations of Cather.

3. Surprisingly, Mao does not refer to Cather even when he writes that modernist novelists "were moving to get out from under the ponderous concretions of those writers Woolf named Edwardian, whose avalanches of furnishing threatened to crush the richness and freshness out of perception itself" (16)—despite the fact that he is echoing Cather's very language in her essay "The Novel Démeublé," where she complains that the novel has been "overfurnished" and wishes to "throw all the furniture out of the window" of fiction in order to "leave the scene bare for the play of emotions" (*OW* 35, 42).

4. Cather mentions Mrs. Boas in letters to Mrs. Charlotte Stanfield on 12 June 1921, 10 June 1922, and 16 Oct. 1926, Alderman Lib., Univ. of Virginia.

5. In enumerating domestic objects used or enjoyed by Cather, I am drawing on the following letters: to her mother, 26 Nov. [1921], Texas Woman's Univ. (TWU); to Carrie Miner Sherwood, 27 Dec. [1921] (WCPM); to Carrie Miner Sherwood, 13 March 1918, WCPM; to Blanche Knopf, undated but received in the Knopf office 28 Dec. 1928, Harry Ransom Humanities Research Center,

Univ. of Texas (HRC); to Blanche Knopf 10 July [1931], HRC; to Lydia, Pauline, and Mrs. Lambrecht, 19 Jan. [1935], WCPM; to Annie Pavelka, 19 May 1936, WCPM; to Irene Miner Weisz, 26 Dec. 1942, Newberry Lib.; to Carrie Miner Sherwood, 20 Jan. 1945, WCPM; to Irene Miner Weisz, [16 March 1925], Newberry; to Irene Miner Weisz, postmarked 12 Feb. 1923, Newberry; to Carrie Miner Sherwood, 18 Sept. 1943, WCPM.

6. Letter to Mary Virginia Auld, 21 Feb. [1920?], copy at Love Lib., Univ. of Nebraska; to Blanche Knopf, 27 Dec. [1921?], HRC; to Mary Virginia (Mrs. Charles F.) Cather, 26 Nov. [1921], TWU; to Zoë Akins, 18 Jan. 1937, Huntington Lib.

7. Letter to Witter Bynner, 7 June 1905, Houghton Lib., Harvard Univ.

8. Letter to Ferris Greenslet, 20 June [1920?], Houghton Lib., Harvard; letter to Elizabeth Shepley Sergeant, 13 Nov. [1916?], Pierpont Morgan Lib.

9. Letter to Zoë Akins, Feb. 1943, Huntington.

10. Letter to Zoë Akins, 5 Jan. 1945, Huntington.

11. Letters to Carrie Miner Sherwood, Sunday [11 Dec. 1932?], WCPM; Blanche Knopf, 10 July 1931, HRC; Irene Miner Weisz, postmarked 29 Oct. 1932, Newberry; Irene Miner Weisz, 26 Dec. [1942], Newberry.

12. Letters to Carrie Miner Sherwood, [11 Dec. 1932?], WCPM; to Blanche Knopf, 10 July [1931], HRC; to Irene Miner Weisz, 29 Oct. 1932, 26 Dec. 1942, and 4 Feb. 1922, Newberry.

13. Letter to Mrs. George P. Cather, 23 Feb. 1913, private collection of Mary Weddle, copy located at Love Lib., Univ. of Nebraska, in the papers of Bernice Slote; to Zoë Akins, 15 Jan. 1931, Huntington; to Blanche Knopf, 26 Dec. 1931, HRC; to Irene Miner Weisz, 11 Jan. 1926 and 16 March 1925, Newberry.

14. Letter to Cather from Ferris Greenslet, 22 Jan. 1917, Houghton Lib., Harvard; from Cather to Greenslet, 18 Nov. 1917, 11 July 1918, and 10 June 1940, Houghton.

15. Letter to Zoë Akins, [21 Nov. 1922], Huntington.

16. Steven Trout's recent book on Cather's participation in a "culture of commemoration" after the First World War, *Memorial Fictions,* is an important addition to that critical conversation.

1

Willa Cather

A Life with Quilts

Ann Romines

The American artist Georgia O'Keeffe, born in 1887, remembered that her first visual memory, at the age of "eight or nine months," featured a star-patterned patchwork quilt. Recalling even the smallest details of the fabrics in that quilt, O'Keeffe wrote, "This was all new to me—the brightness of light and pillows and a quilt" (O'Keeffe unpaged).

Willa Cather, born in her grandmother Rachel Seibert Boak's Virginia house fourteen years earlier, might have had similar early memories. For we know that quilts were a part of Cather's material environment from the first to the last years of her life. Her mother often told a favorite story of Willa's strong attachment to her cradle where she slept until she was three or four years old (Lewis 9), and it is likely that that cradle was made comfortable by hand-stitched quilts. Soon the little girl was observing quilt makers at work at her parents' home, Willow Shade: "When the old women came from Timber Ridge to make quilts, Willa Cather would creep under the quilting frames and sit there listening to their talk. . . . Many of these stories Willa Cather remembered all her life" (Lewis 10–11). By the time she was five, the child was piecing quilt blocks herself, as she sat in the kitchen with her grandmother Boak and "Aunt Till," who had been her great-grandparents' slave—again under the "spell" of the old women's tales (*Sapphira* 287–88). From this early age and on, throughout her life, Cather seems to have associated quilts with old women and their stories.

Such an early education in quilt making was entirely typical for a rural girl of Willa Cather's generation. Her companion, Edith Lewis, reported that Cather "took great pride in making those quilts. She did the piecing, and the old women quilted them with lamb's-wool from the lambs on the place." Also involved in this process was Marjorie Anderson, the Cathers' young servant woman who later accompanied them to Nebraska; she "helped [Willa] to select calico for the quilts she was set to piece" (11–12). So from the beginning Cather—like so many other women born in the nineteenth century—thought of quilts both as a mark of individual accomplishment *and* as a collaborative process in which other women helped her make aesthetic choices and complete her work, as when the "old women" did the more demanding tasks of preparing the wool batting and quilting the tops that Willa pieced.

Significantly, Cather got her early quilting lessons, as far as we can tell, from *older* women, who had received their own domestic educations before 1850, or from women (like Marjorie Anderson) who were significantly below the Cathers in social class.[1] In the early 1880s, however, when young Willa was sewing plain geometric patchwork, meant for practical use, the quilting fashion was beginning to change. In 1882 *Harper's Bazaar* announced the advent of the crazy quilt: "We have quite discarded in our modern quilts the regular geometric design once so popular. . . . Now we are very daring. We go boldly on without any apparent design at all" (quoted in Kirakofe 146). The most fashionable crazy quilts, elaborate improvisations, were made from perishable silks that could not be washed and were embellished with intricate silk embroidery, as well as occasional beading, lace, and fringe. They were intended for parlor ornamentation, not for warmth and use. Such creations epitomized "fancy work," such as Willa Cather professed to despise when, at the age of fourteen, she wrote in a Red Cloud friend's album that her "idea of real misery" was "Doing Fancy work" (Bennett, *World* 113). Just about that time, *Godey's Ladies' Book* proclaimed (somewhat prematurely) the end of the crazy quilt fashion, dismissing "'crazy' patchwork" as "the most childish, and unsatisfactory of all work done with the needle" (quoted in Kirakofe 149).

Throughout Willa Cather's life in the nineteenth- and twentieth-century United States, quilt fashions continued to change, proliferate, and recur, often tied to economic, political, and aesthetic changes, including the fluctuating status of women. Often quilts and their construction, preservation, and display became material links to earlier generations of sewing women. Although we have no current records of quilts that may have traveled with the Cather family from Virginia to Nebraska when they emigrated in 1883, it seems almost certain that such portable household essentials would have made the trip, as they did with so many westward emigrants. The picture of the Templeton household in "Old Mrs. Harris," similarly transplanted from the South and probably Cather's most complete fictional portrait of her family of origin, includes heavy (presumably wool-stuffed?) "old home-made quilts" (80) brought from their Southern home. One Cather family textile heirloom, almost certainly from Virginia, that did survive in Red Cloud is a woven coverlet, which family members recall seeing in use in Willa Cather's parents' Nebraska household (Romines, interview). And the letters that flew back and forth between the women and girls of Willa Cather's family, from Virginia to Nebraska and back, often mention homemade textile products, including rugs, clothing, and quilts.

The earliest of Willa Cather's female relatives to set up housekeeping in Nebraska, her favorite aunt Franc Cather, soon began to produce quilts there; she wrote in 1876 to her sister-in-law back in Virginia that she was "piecing a quilt; but get along very slowly—quilted one the first of the winter." Whether the women of Willa Cather's own household also made quilts after their move to Nebraska, a few years later, is not known. But we do know that soon after the Cathers' arrival young Willa began to visit neighbors who would become lifelong friends. In her most famous comments on her early Nebraska years, Cather recalled that (as in Virginia) she loved to listen to these women telling stories as they went about their domestic work (Bohlke 10–11). Some of these neighboring families—such as the Lambrechts and the Sadilek-Pavelkas—were active quilt makers, and young Willa probably saw them working on their quilts.[2]

So far as we know, Willa Cather herself did not remain a practicing quilter or practitioner of other needlework in her adult life. From her fiction, letters, and other texts (including some exemplary quilts), however, it becomes clear that she continued to respond to quilts and to the quilt culture of her times throughout her life. For example, a World War I–era Red Cross fundraising quilt, made and preserved in Red Cloud, is embroidered with Cather's name, among other local names.[3] (Customarily, on such quilts, names were embroidered in exchange for a financial contribution to the Red Cross.) And an indication of Cather's eye for quilt makers' techniques is also suggested by a gift she purchased for her mother on one of her European trips, probably in the 1920s. She chose Egyptian wall hangings (typically made for the tourist trade), which feature traditional Egyptian figures and motifs, executed in careful layered appliqué similar to the work on traditional mid-nineteenth-century American "display" quilts made by members of the Cather family. According to her niece, Willa Cather meant for these appliqué works to be displayed prominently in her mother's bedroom, above the bed.[4]

The most specific images of quilts in Cather's fiction occur in *One of Ours* (1922) and are connected with Mahailey, a character who has intimate ties to Cather's private life and her early quilting experience. According to Lewis, Mahailey is Cather's "most complete portrait" of Marjorie Anderson, the Cather family servant (11). Mahailey comes from a poor Blue Ridge family, just as Marjorie Anderson came from a large, poor family on Timber Ridge. Marjorie's mother was Mary Ann Marple Anderson, one of the old women who came to Willow Shade to quilt and to nurse young Willa in her childhood illnesses; Cather remembered her fondly as one of the great storytellers and influences of her life.[5] In *One of Ours,* Mahailey is the proud owner of three explicitly designated quilts.

> The only possessions Mahailey brought with her [from Virginia] when she came to live with the Wheelers [in Nebraska] were a feather bed and three patchwork quilts, interlined with wool off the backs of Virginia sheep, washed and carded by hand. The quilts had been made by her old mother, and given to her for a marriage portion. The patchwork on each was done in a different design; one was the popular "log-cabin" pattern, another the "laurel-leaf," the third the "blazing star." This quilt Mahailey thought too good for use.(85)

This is a very astute description, with an awareness of local and chronological quilting styles. The wool batting ties these quilts to a relatively cold region (Frederick County, Cather's birthplace, is Virginia's northernmost county), where sheep were plentiful, as they were at Willow Shade,[6] and to the descriptions of quilts that Cather herself pieced. Mahailey, who is an "old woman" at the end of World War I and remembers the Civil War, would likely have been born in the 1850s; her mother might have made the quilts for her "marriage portion" in the 1850s or 1860s (Virginia mountain women typically married very early). The "Log Cabin," which has many variations, was one of the most popular patchwork patterns of the nineteenth century. "Most experts agree that it emerged sometime during or immediately after the Civil War. *Log Cabin* quilts were immensely popular during the last quarter of the 19th century" (Kirakofe 152). So this would have been a very likely pattern for Mahailey's mother (or Mary Ann Anderson) to piece for her young daughter, and one that Willa Cather, growing up in the last quarter of the nineteeth century, would probably have known.

The "Laurel Leaf" is a less-familiar pattern—but one that would have had special appeal for Cather and for other residents of rural Frederick County, where mountain laurel grew abundantly. *Sapphira* is explicit about the beauties of the laurel blossom and leaf, describing "the wayward wild laurel which in June covered the wooded slopes of our mountains with drifts of rose and peach and flesh colour. And in winter . . . the laurel thickets spread green and brilliant through the frosty woods" (171–72). Two intricate appliqué patterns, both requiring fine cutting and stitching, celebrate the laurel. The "Mountain Laurel" pattern has been dated as early as 1820 by Hall and Kretsinger (108); and a similar "Laurel Leaves" quilt is dated 1865 by Safford and Bishop (158).[7] Especially in the 1850s and 1860s, appliqué was a common quilt-making technique among Frederick County's most skilled quilt makers: the three surviving quilts from that period known to be associated with Willa Cather's family all employ appliqué. So local and family associations would have made the "Laurel Leaf" another likely and credible choice for her.

Finally, the "Blazing Star," a large, intricate, pieced star pattern (of which there are several versions), reflects the nineteenth-century enthusiasm for star quilts, which women often executed as their "masterpiece" quilts (as did Cather's aunt, Sidney Gore). Such special quilts were indeed considered "too fine" for everyday use. A 1930s exhibit of Frederick County quilts (probably at the 1934 bicentennial celebration of the Hopewell Friends Quaker Meeting) included a number of intricate star quilts, which appear to be nineteeth-century "masterpiece" quilts that have been carefully preserved.

From the precise description of Mahailey's quilts, we know that Willa Cather was well versed in local and national nineteenth-century quilt culture and history. Given the closeness of this character to a person that Cather knew intimately and loved from her own birth until Anderson's death in 1924, it seems quite possible that the quilts described here—or quilts very like them—did indeed belong to Marjorie Anderson and were a part of the Cather household and of Cather's memories of home, both in Virginia and in Nebraska.

We also know that quilts continued to be a part of Cather's constructions of home when she had moved far from Virginia and Red Cloud. About 1932, when "the cloud of the depression rested very darkly" on parts of New York City, Cather's old friend Elizabeth Sergeant visited her in the new, "spacious" apartment that Cather and Lewis had taken on Park Avenue. Cather found her new home "comfortable and convenient," she told Sergeant, who was full of enthusiasm for her friend's new Nebraska book, *Obscure Destinies.* However, Sergeant's (left-leaning) disapproval of such luxurious surroundings for an artist is palpable in her account of the visit. The only feature of the apartment that she seems to approve is Cather's private bedroom.

> She led me from the sizable hall down a little corridor to her bedroom, where my coat was soon laid out on a calico patchwork counterpane, surely of Red Cloud make. This little room seemed bright and inviting and individual, and I hoped she wrote there—for how could Willa, so connected with primeval nature, write in the luxurious sheltered cave of the connecting main rooms. (250–51)

This account is interesting and important for two reasons. First, it reminds us of much that quilts had come to signify in the Depression 1930s when a revival of quilting and renewed interest in quilts were flourishing. Sergeant read the quilt on Cather's bed as a signifier of comfort, cheer, and stereotypically enduring small town ("Red Cloud") values.[8] In her view, this quilt (the only object mentioned in the room besides an unspecified bed) created an atmosphere where the rural Nebraska characters of *Obscure Destinies* would be welcome, although Sergeant feared those personages would be unwelcome and perhaps even banished by the "snobbery" that prevailed in the lobby of Cather's apartment building, "with its repressed attendants in uniform" (251). Second, Sergeant's account corroborates that, after a difficult period when Cather and Lewis had had to put their belongings into storage and live in a hotel, this quilt (and perhaps others?) was among the cherished possessions that had made the cut in the new apartment, where much of the previous furniture had been banished for "new tables and chairs, more formal than those in Bank Street," their previous home in Greenwich Village (252). The quilt is displayed prominently in an intimate, "individual" space. Sergeant assumes that it is "of Red Cloud make"—but it could also have been one of the Virginia quilts that Cather pieced as a young child. Those quilts are described by Lewis, the companion of Cather's New York life, and obviously she is familiar with them; the description is specific (12).

Whatever the provenance of the quilt that Sergeant saw in New York, we know that it was joined in 1935 by a new Nebraska quilt. That year, Willa Cather received a gift from old Webster County friends and neighbors. Mrs. C. F. Lambrecht and her daughters, Lydia and Pauline, made her a quilt in a style that was very popular at the moment, with blocks embroidered with realistic representations of American flowers. (Embroidered "state flower" quilts were popular in the 1930s and 1940s.) Cather's letter of thanks to her friends reflects her real pleasure in their gift, and the next year she wrote again to let them know that this treasured quilt had traveled with her from New York City to her house at Grand Manan, New Brunswick, where she was spending her summer vacation (*Calendar* #1249 and #1321). The flower quilt was with Willa Cather, then, and on her mind, just around the time that she was beginning work on her last published novel, *Sapphira and the Slave Girl.*

Thus it appears that, by her choice, quilts remained a quiet but constant presence in Cather's environment throughout her life. Nowhere are these links to quilt culture more clearly, subtly apparent than in the last novel, *Sapphira.* Except for its unprecedented autobiographical epilogue, which introduces us to the figure of young Willa Cather, stitching her patchwork, *Sapphira* is set in 1856 and 1857, around the village of Back Creek Valley, in Frederick County, Virginia. During those years, almost all of Cather's grandparents and great-grandparents, as well as other relatives, were living active adult lives in that community, and several of them served as partial models for the novel's characters. Also, this was a period of extraordinary activity and invention for American quilt makers, and we know that many of Cather's ancestors and relatives, as well as family friends and neighbors, participated in that tradition. Fortunately, at least three (and perhaps more, as yet unknown to scholars) family quilts from those years survive. Their survival demonstrates their value to the family members who preserved them. All three feature inscriptions, and one has been further embellished in recent decades by slips of paper, pinned on by a recent owner, with biographical information about some of the persons whose names or initials are inked or embroidered on the quilt. All this attests to a family tradition that quilts should be carefully read. As valued family possessions that were preserved, and quite possibly displayed, in the nearby homes of relatives, these quilts would probably have been seen—and certainly heard of—by young Willa Cather during her Virginia childhood years.

What do these quilts tell us? First, look at the Robinson-Cather quilt (fig. 1). It is a large album quilt with thirty-six pattern blocks, each inscribed or embroidered with the name or initials of its maker or (presumably) a member of her family. Two blocks are embroidered with a date, 1848, which suggests that the quilt was made around the middle of the nineteenth century. The background is white, and the prevailing colors are the red, green, and yellow cotton calicoes that were typical of that period. Five blocks are done in patchwork patterns, although only one is simple enough that a beginning needleworker, such as young Willa, might have attempted it. The others are appliqué blocks, many of which give their makers ample opportunity to showcase a repertoire of sewing skills: delicate cutting, difficult curved seams, tiny pieces, trapunto stuffing, fine stitches, discriminating choice and arrangement of fabrics. The names and initials are inked and embroidered in a variety of hands, some quite sophisticated, and at least two were applied with an elegant stencil—one for a man's name—indicating access to specialized equipment. Obviously, the squares were made individually, then assembled and quilted—by a group of women? or by a single woman? The quilting pattern is simple—straight lines and small squares—but evenly executed in small, expert stitches. If a group of women did the quilting, they were experienced and expert quilters.

Fig. 1. The Robinson-Cather quilt. This mid-nineteenth-century album quilt (dated 1848) was a collaborative project made by women who lived in or near the community of Back Creek Valley, Virginia, Willa Cather's birthplace. The quilt makers included several Cather relatives.

This quilt is the work of a sizable community of women with some variation in tastes and skills, able to collaborate on a complex project. The blocks allude to more than one current quilt style. Some, relatively simple blocks executed in a single fabric, evoke the serviceable utility quilt, while the most elaborate, appliqué blocks employing intricate designs and techniques, suggest the well-known album quilts being made and sold in the nearest city, Baltimore—quilts that would have been, in the 1840s and 1850s, the height of sophistication.

I have been working to read this quilt since I first encountered it: in 1997,[9] when Kit Robinson brought it to a Cather family gathering in Winchester to display to Cather scholars; the quilt (now known as the Robinson-Cather quilt) had been preserved by the family of her late husband, Congressman Kenneth Robinson. Mrs. Robinson (who died in 2002) had pinned the tiny biographical notes to the quilt, enabling me to discover that two first cousins of Willa Cather's grandfather William Cather, sisters Mary Caroline and Hannah Cather, had married brothers, Andrew A. and David Robinson. A third sister, Susan Gilkerson Cather, was seventeen and unmarried at the time the quilt was made; she was living with her widowed mother, Elizabeth Glaize Cather (1788–1873), and they collaborated on one of the quilt's most elaborate blocks, which mother and daughter both signed (see fig. 2). The red, green, and yellow calicoes that Elizabeth and Susan Cather used are identical to those in an adjacent block with a faded inked signature, "A E [or C] Cather." Who is *this* Cather? If we read the initials as A. C. Cather, it's tempting to speculate (but only to speculate!) that this is Willa Cather's grandmother (Emily) *A*nne *C*aroline (Smith) Cather, who apparently seldom, if ever, used her first name, Emily. Then, tracking Susan and Elizabeth Cather's palette of calicoes one block farther, we find the yellow fabric again, stitched into flowers that are almost identical in construction to Susan and Elizabeth's flowers, in yet another block signed "Cather"—this time with two illegible first initials. The repeated fabrics, motifs, and names send signals of kinship and collaboration and exchange across the varied field of the quilt, among sisters, mother, daughters, and other relatives. As if to remind us that such multiple codes are at work, the quilt features two identical blocks, delicate cutout wreaths with small stars in the block corners. The fabrics are identical, too—except that their colors are reversed in the two blocks, so that one has a red wreath and green stars and the other the opposite. These blocks were made by sisters, Ruth (Jackson) Jones and Sidney Jackson, and are appliquéd in indistinguishable tiny buttonhole stitches. Simultaneously, they signal similarity and difference.

Many of the faded inscriptions on this quilt are unreadable now. For its makers—and for Willa Cather, if she happened to see it during her

Fig. 2. This elaborate appliqué block from the Robinson-Cather quilt is signed by two members of the Cather family, Elizabeth Glaize Cather and her daughter, Susan Gilkerson Cather.

Virginia years, 1873–1883—there would have been much more to read. The three unusual lacy cutout blocks, for example, are typical of blocks seen on other local quilts and seem to tie this quilt to a local tradition.[10] The several Robinson names on the quilt link it to Frederick County Quaker tradition, for the Robinson family (and the Cathers who married into it) belonged to the Hopewell Friends, one of the oldest Quaker congregations in the area. The Hopewell Friends, like other Virginia Quakers, had a strong abolitionist tradition, and the one man whose name can now be identified on the quilt, Andrew A. Robinson (who married a Cather), spent the Civil War years in a Union prison camp in Indiana, as a Quaker conscientious objector (Kerns). Although no members of Willa Cather's immediate family were Quakers, the Cathers shared antislavery convictions with local Quakers. (This local Quaker community figures in *Sapphira*, helping with the arrangements for Nancy's escape.) Cather's great-great-grandfather and great-grandparents, along with many other relatives, such as the Robinsons, were buried in Gainesboro Cemetery, originally a Quaker burying ground. Indeed, that cemetery almost seems to replicate the Cather-Robinson quilt, with the same names of family, neighbors, and friends inscribed in adjacent plots.

When young Willa Cather perhaps saw this quilt, heard the stories related to it, and visited the family graveyard (as we know she did) where the names and stories recurred, she was already accruing the materials from which *Sapphira* was built. The "Back Creek" where her novel is set is a community known intimately over a span of several generations and yet evoked selectively, with spaces of absence as effective as the white field that sets off the quilt's patterned blocks. It is also a community that manages to function despite profound differences, such as those dramatized in the Civil War and among the quilt makers' (and Cather's own) families. Cather sketches such a community in her epilogue: "Mr. Whitford's son enlisted in the Northern army, as his father's son might be expected to do. His nearest neighbour, Mr. Jeffers, had a son in Ashby's [Confederate] cavalry. The fathers remained friends, worked their bordering fields, and talked to each other across the rail fence as they had always done" (275). Here the image of neighboring fields and fences, with signals of both similarity and difference sent across borders, evokes the similar field of the album quilt.

Nevertheless, one of the striking absences in Cather's novel is of exactly the sort of close female community of kinship and connection that the Robinson-Cather quilt seems to document. Although the antislavery Mrs. Bywaters (modeled on Cather's paternal great-aunt) and the slave owner Sapphira Colbert (modeled on her maternal great-grandmother) may greet each other with civility and cooperate on some civic matters (such as the post office), it is unimaginable that they might join with other women to create an album quilt. Both are relatively isolated, with few or no female peers—as is the novel's other major white female character, Rachel Blake, based on Cather's maternal grandmother, Rachel Boak. Sapphira, as plantation mistress, supervises a hierarchy in which slaves and white women of a lower class execute domestic work such as carpet making, sewing, and quilting. Mrs. Bywaters and Rachel share antislavery sentiments, but, as financially pressed widows who are heads of their households, they have constant responsibilities that seem to preclude the intimacies of a quilting community—let alone one that would permit a thirty-six block album collaboration! In this book, any specific mention of the comforts a quilt might offer is reserved for the slave characters; both Till and her daughter Nancy find warmth and solace in quilts wrapped around their shoulders. (In fact, Till's quilt is "wool-stuffed" [69], again specifically echoing the wool batting of the quilts made at Willow Shade.) Yet the novel is unable to give us any access to the female slave community in which those quilts must have been produced.

According to Ricky Clark, "*women made friendship or album quilts to reify community.* By making them women transformed personal relationships into visible, tangible form" (77)—a readable text, like the Robinson-Cather quilt. The absence of such texts, in quilted or other forms, in a novel that is set in a region and a period known to have produced many such quilts, suggests something seriously awry in the community constellation in which the novel is set, one with a slaveholding plantation at its center. And the novel's slave quilt makers are known only by the products of their labor: the wool-stuffed quilts. Their quilting community cannot be reified or even acknowledged by this text, given the limited access (and/or vision?) of its white female narrator.

The other two mid-nineteenth-century quilts known to be associated with Willa Cather's family were made by her grandfather Cather's sister, great-aunt Sidney Sophia Cather Gore (1828–1906), the model for Mrs. Bywaters. These are quilts executed at a high and individual level of skill and ambition; they are the "masterpiece" creations of a consummate needlewoman that were probably meant to become heirlooms, as indeed they have. (In 1990 the quilts remained in the possession of Sidney Gore's descendants, who immigrated to Oklahoma in 1910.) According to a quilt historian, "Mrs. Gore was an accomplished artist, even by the high standards of southern needlework tradition" (*Oklahoma Heritage Quilts* 17). The earlier of the two quilts (see fig. 3) is dated 1849. Sidney Cather had married Mahlon Gore, a Back Creek Valley storekeeper, in November 1847, and set up housekeeping in a small house on

Fig. 3. Pieced and appliquéd quilt, signed and dated 1849 by Willa Cather's great-aunt, Sidney Sophia Cather Gore. Back Creek Valley, Virginia.

Timber Ridge. The quilt's four large, identical eight-pointed stars are pieced of calicoes in blue, red, yellow, and green. They are interspersed with appliqué urns of flowers (somewhat resembling one of the Robinson-Cather album blocks) and flowering vines, surrounded by a border of pieced diamonds, and each corner is embellished with a pieced flower and appliqué leaves. In the exact center of this exactly square quilt, surrounded by another border, is one of the lacy cutout appliqué wreaths that recur on the Robinson-Cather quilt and on other local quilts of the time. The quilt is signed and dated in immaculately legible cross-stitch: "Sidney Sophia Gore 1849."[11] In this quilt (which seems to be almost exactly contemporary with the Robinson-Cather album quilt), young

Fig. 4. Mosaic patchwork quilt with appliqué borders. Made by Sidney Sophia Cather Gore for her son, Perry Cather Gore, 1854. Back Creek Valley, Virginia.

Sidney Gore established her fluency in the local and national quilt vocabulary of her time and created a unique and durable work of art.

Five years later, she worked in the red-green-white palette of the period and in perennially popular mosaic patchwork, which forms twenty large figures in the center of her second quilt (see fig. 4). Then (having a little trouble with her corners) she added two ambitious appliqué borders, first flowering vines and then swags. The outer corners are finished with appliqué flowers and the other two with appliqué wreaths, whose blank centers leave space for these inscriptions to the oldest of her three sons:

> A wish for Perry: Oh! Had I but the magic power to rule thy destiny, I'd have thee know no sad'ning hour, No pang of misery. I'd have thee ever free from sin, As pure in heart as now. No darkened shadow e'er should fling its image o'er thy brow. Sidney.

and in the opposite corner,

> Presented to Perry Cather Gore by his mother 1854.
> Remember thy creator in the days of thy youth.
> (*Oklahoma Heritage Quilts* 18)

Both Sidney Gore's quilts are elegant exercises in poise and control. These effects are augmented by her inscriptions on the second quilt. In the seven years since her marriage she had undergone a conversion experience and left her parents' Presbyterian church, in which she had been reared, for an evangelical Baptist congregation (the Hebron Baptist Church, which is portrayed as Mr. Fairhead's Baptist congregation in *Sapphira*), to which she would be deeply committed for the rest of her long life. She had become a mother. And, as an antislavery woman with a growing interest in national affairs, she was increasingly and anxiously aware of the controversies over slavery that would erupt in the coming Civil War. Her verses express an anguished desire for control that she knows she cannot achieve: she longs to protect her child from change, sadness, darkness, sin, and anything that might alter the "purity" of his childhood. Here she identifies herself not as the confidently self-possessed "Sidney Sophia Gore," as she signed her earlier quilt, but as "Sidney," "his mother." It is Perry's full name that she inscribes, not her own. And she ends with a Biblical admonition that her child "Remember thy creator." The quilt and its inscriptions imply an ambitious, omnicompetent woman who chafes at the inevitable limits of her own powers. And the survival of both these quilts among Sidney Gore's descendants, in pristine condition, suggests the enduring force of her admonition to preserve and to remember—to remember the creator of the quilts.

Willa Cather apparently loved and admired her Aunt Sidney Gore. When she returned to Virginia in 1896 for her first visit after her family's move to Nebraska, she stayed with this aunt. And Sidney's youngest son, James Howard Gore, who became a distinguished professor and public figure, was one of Cather's favorite cousins, to whom she remained connected for the rest of his life. After Sidney Gore's husband died in 1861, leaving her nearly destitute, she built an exemplary public life for herself (and her sons): she worked as a teacher and as postmistress, took an active interest in national affairs, was an activist for local church and community affairs, and established a successful health resort, "Valley Home." In 1890 Back Creek Valley was renamed "Gore" in honor of her achievements, making her name a public landmark that still remains on the Virginia map. However, Cather family letters also suggest some family joking about "Aunt Sidney" and her inevitable public presence, joking of which the attentive young Willa Cather was probably aware.[12]

In these three mid-nineteenth-century quilts stitched by Willa Cather's relatives, we can see two kinds of texts. One—the album—is primarily a community text. The other, as exemplified by Sidney Gore's two surviving quilts, is a self-possessed statement of an individual will, although it may draw deeply from a current vocabulary of quilting conventions. Quilts of both these kinds were probably the first woman-authored art that young Willa Cather saw.

Sapphira is marked by the priorities expressed by both these kinds of quilts. Because it features characters based on women she knew (or knew of) intimately, it performs one of the functions of an album quilt. It preserves fragments of their stories and their relations—even portions of the actual women's names: Till, Nancy, Rachel. Also, in album quilts the work of individual quilt makers is subsumed in a community text, taking its place in a whole that is not dominated by any single individual's contributions. When *Sapphira* was complete, Cather described her novel in much this way, as a communal text, to her old friend and critic Viola Roseboro'. She said that the book could scarcely be called fiction; so much of it was built from family and local Virginia stories that it was difficult for her to know where her own contributions began (WC to Viola Roseboro', 9 Nov. 1940). When *Sapphira* was published, it launched a correspondence between Cather and a number of readers who also had Virginia links to the local and family stories stitched into the novel. This correspondence apparently gave Cather considerable satisfaction, for she replied at some length to several of the letter writers and saved their letters, as was not her usual habit. Recurring subjects of these letters were the prototypes for women characters, such as Cather's grandmother, great-grandmother, Aunt Sidney Gore, "Aunt Till," Nancy, and Mary Ann Anderson (prototype for the character of Mrs. Ringer). As Ricky Clark suggests, album quilts acknowledge community by giving "tangible form" to women's relationships, and the letters confirm that *Sapphira* performed a similar function.

At the same time, Cather exerted her usual controlling interest in every detail of her completed text; she even chided her friend Dorothy Canfield Fisher for slightly misquoting her title and thus losing the effect of the doubled r's in *Sapphira* and *Girl* (WC to DCF, 14 Oct. 1940). The tension between the will of the controlling artist and the collaborative aesthetic of the album text, which must have been felt by many nineteenth-century quilters such as Sidney Gore and her contemporaries, is also echoed in Cather's attitude toward her own Virginia text. And many of the novel's female characters explore issues related to such tensions. *Sapphira*, of course, is a chilling portrait of a slave-owning woman whose power is grounded in her attempts at absolute control of everyone on her plantation. Her cruel machinations drive her young slave, Nancy, to despair, near-suicide, and flight, as she tries to evade the rape Sapphira has arranged for her. Yet the novel occasionally permits a positive view of Sapphira's habits of control; when her granddaughters are mortally ill, it is she who immediately summons "her" first-rate doctor, instead of the inept local one (something that her daughter and husband have not thought to do), sending for him with her swift slave messenger. As a result, one of the children (Mary, based on Willa Cather's mother) survives. Still, Sapphira's habits and methods of control are a—if not *the*—central problem of the novel.

On the other hand, Sapphira's daughter Rachel is largely seen within a community context that recalls the imbrications of the album quilt—

she attends the local church and sends her children to the local school, travels about the neighborhood as a nurse, offers supportive advice to Nancy, and calls on local resources when her daughters are ill. Nevertheless, when Rachel becomes aware of her mother's persecution of Nancy, she determines to follow the dictates of her own will and conscience with a decisive and powerful intervention, as she arranges for Nancy's escape from slavery to Canada. Yet, although she has inwardly opposed slavery since childhood, Rachel cannot feel certain about the rightness of her defiance of Sapphira's rule (and property rights). " 'It's hard for a body to know what to do, sometimes,' she murmured to herself. . . . 'Maybe I ought to have thought and waited' " (247). Such uncertainty is common among the novel's women (although somewhat dispelled by the fairy tale–like epilogue), and, as I have shown, it has clear analogues in the nineteenth-century quilt culture that Willa Cather knew.

Sapphira is also a text suffused by nostalgia, particularly in the epilogue, where Cather deals with her own early childhood memories. During the writing of the novel, Cather suffered crushing personal losses and was also distraught over the coming war in Europe, where many of her friends lived. Working on the novel was a respite from these contemporary troubles, she wrote to friends; the early memories eased and steadied her. Yet she obviously worked to keep her nostalgia from falling into sentimentality, through the novel's rigorous structure and restrained style.

In fact, Cather's 1935 letter of thanks to the Lambrechts, who had made her state flower quilt, suggests that the aesthetic issues that concerned her as an artist were also at play in her appreciation of quilts. She tells her friends that she recognized many of the flowers they embroidered (which were probably based on the purchased patterns for this quilt that were widely available) and specifies three favorites: lilies of the valley, peonies, and crocuses. Cather, a student of botany, obviously valued specificity and accuracy in renderings of the natural world, particularly plants; she included Latin botanical names for many of the remembered Virginia plants that she mentioned in *Sapphira*. Then she goes on to say that she "almost likes the solid squares better, because of the quilting" (*Calendar* #1249). This is a typical response for a seasoned connoisseur of quilts, who is likely to know that tiny, even quilting stitches require more skill and experience than either piecing or outline embroidery. It is also typical of Cather's own démeublé aesthetic, which valued (in *Sapphira* as in most of her other novels) blankness, absence, and "the thing not named."

In this essay, I hope I have shown three things. First, that quilts were a constant presence in Willa Cather's life. Second, that she was aware of the constantly changing language that quilt culture offered to American women during the nineteeth and twentieth centuries and that she alluded to that language, and to some of the major issues that quilt culture raised for women, in her fiction, particularly *Sapphira.* And finally, that she saw in quilts some of the aesthetic concerns that animated her own writing life. Recognizing Cather's links to quilt culture, we can see yet another way that she participated in the popular culture of her times and shared some of the most persistent traditions practiced by her family, her rural neighbors, and generations of quilt-making American women.

Notes

1. Perhaps significantly, Willa Cather's mother, Mary Virginia Boak Cather (1850–1931), is not associated with quilting or needlework in any of Cather's comments about her, or in her most extensive portrait in Cather's fiction, as Victoria Templeton in "Old Mrs. Harris."

2. One of the Pavelka quilts is pictured in Crews and Naugle.

3. The Red Cross quilt is the property of the Willa Cather Pioneer Memorial and Educational Foundation and the Nebraska State Historical Society, and it is currently on display in the Willa Cather Childhood Home in Red Cloud.

4. The appliqué hangings were given to Charlene Hoschauer, current co-owner of the Cathers' final home in Red Cloud, by Willa Cather's niece, Helen Cather Southwick, who relayed the history of these Cather family heirlooms (Interview with Charlene Hoschauer).

5. Lewis recounts Cather's vivid memories of Mary Ann Anderson: she was "the best of the story-tellers. She knew the family histories of all the countryside, and all the dramatic events that had become legends among the country people. Her talk was full of fire and wit, rich in the native idiom" (10–11). Cather also wrote fondly of her memories of Mary Ann and Marjorie Anderson in two letters to Rose Ackroyd, Mary Ann Anderson's granddaughter,

after the publication of *Sapphira* (WC to Mrs. Ackroyd, 16 May 1941 and 27 Dec. 1941).

6. Wool batting was relatively unusual, especially in the South; cotton batting was the norm. When wool was used, it was usually the batting for heavy utility quilts, made primarily for warmth, not for elaborately patterned quilts like those owned by Mahailey.

7. John March reports that "the older women in the area of Virginia where Willa Cather was a child know of no such pattern [as "laurel-leaf"], but believe she was referring to the 'Mountain Laurel' pattern" (422–23). However, March does not note that this is an appliqué pattern.

8. Sergeant's comments on Cather's quilt suggest that she shared a common attitude, which valued quilts as signifiers of earlier times that were valued for their simplicity. One quilt historian observes that, from the mid-nineteenth century onward, quilt culture was marked by a "note of nostalgia that would develop by the end of the century into a sustained lament for the passing of the pre-industrial way of life" (Ferrero, Hedges, and Silber 34). That lament was also a recurring note in Cather's fiction, and it may help to explain her own continuing attachment to quilts.

9. Two texts that I have found especially useful in my attempts at reading the Robinson-Cather quilt are historian Laurel Thatcher Ulrich's *The Age of Homespun: Objects and Stories in the Creation of an American Myth,* which is built around a series of richly historicized readings of textile objects produced by women, and quilt historian Linda Otto Lipsett's *Pieced from Ellen's Quilt: Ellen Spaulding Reed's Letters and Story,* an intensive reading of an album quilt.

10. One of Frederick County's best-known surviving quilts, known as the Hollingsworth quilt because it descended in that family, closely resembles the Robinson-Cather quilt: again thirty-six largely appliqué blocks, a similar palette, and the same recurring lacy cutout blocks. Robinson and Hollingsworth names occur on both quilts, and the quilting is similar. The Hollingsworth quilt inscriptions include two dates, 1858 and 1859. The two quilts' similarities suggest a strong local quilting tradition, perhaps linked to the Hopewell Friends ("Description of Property").

11. This signature seems even more of a self-assertion when one learns that Sidney Gore was partially self-named; the middle name "Sophia," which she included on this quilt, was "self-chosen" (Gore 1).

12. For example, Willa Cather's grandmother, Caroline Smith Cather, wrote to her daughter Jennie Cather Ayre, probably in 1873: "It is very cold and windy

for the commencement of the fair. I have not seen anyone go yet this morning but Aunt Sidney [Gore] and Perry [her son]. your aunty is on the committee of arrangements and I guess she thinks it is verry importent that she should be there." Caroline Cather to Mrs. John G. Ayre, 7 Oct. 1873 (?), Nebraska State Historical Society.

2

To Entertain, To Educate, To Elevate

Cather and the Commodification of Manners at the *Home Monthly*

Jennifer L. Bradley

In June of 1896 at the age of twenty-two, Willa Cather left Nebraska for Pittsburg (as it was then spelled) to begin her first full-time job in journalism. The publishers of the *Home Monthly* magazine, where she took a position as managing editor, wanted an editor who could step in and make things happen, and Cather was just the woman. As editor of her college literary magazine, she had gained practical experience with all facets of the publishing process, from writing and editing to proofing and typesetting. According to Bernice Slote, she "not only could take over a project or write most of a magazine, but it was her nature to do so" (12). This was exactly what the *Home Monthly* publishers Axtell and Orr wanted, and in Peter Bensen's judgment, in "Willa Cather at *Home Monthly*," it was the promise that she would indeed "run the whole works" that "lured Cather to Pittsburgh," where she was anxious to prove herself to her publishers and the people back home (229).

It is not clear what Cather's actual title was, but biographers confirm that she assumed most of the responsibilities for the magazine immediately upon her arrival in Pittsburg.[1] According to Cather biographer James Woodress, Axtell took his family on a trip West shortly after Cather's arrival in Pittsburg (114), leaving her totally responsible for getting out the first two issues, and E. K. Brown asserts she was soon "managing editor in everything but name" (80). In addition to planning the two issues and tutoring the inexperienced foreman in the composing room on layout, it was Cather's job to read and select manuscripts, correspond with contributors, and often to write much of the magazine's content herself. If not in title, then in responsibilities, Cather seems to have been operating as managing editor of the *Home Monthly* from June 1896 until sometime in July 1897. As such she was clearly responsible for setting the tone of the publication, within the limits of the publisher's editorial policy and their desire for profit. My purpose here is, with this degree of authority in mind, to examine the contents of the issues Cather produced in order to see to what extent she carried out the commercial and editorial goals of her employers and to what extent she called these into question when they conflicted with her own ideas.

The way to making a profit lay through advertising. But Cather also needed to satisfy the desires of her readers, and thus it was imperative that she familiarize herself with their demographics and interests. The middle-class Pittsburg women who read the *Home Monthly* were interested in a variety of topics, including family, fashion, housekeeping, travel, and celebrities. Most importantly, they were interested in social propriety and etiquette. They wanted to know how to behave to ensure social success. Cather had to learn to blend her readers' desire for instruction on social propriety, home, and family with her advertisers' desire to sell products. These two goals—both of which entailed the commodification of manners—sometimes worked at cross-purposes, and both were often at odds with her own literary ideals.

When Cather and the *Home Monthly* entered the magazine market in 1896, the industry was in a period of tremendous growth. The number of magazines in circulation rose from 700 in 1865 to more than 4,400 in 1890. By 1904 there were 2,835 monthlies alone with circulation rising from 18 million in 1890 to 64 million in 1905 (Tebbel 124; Mott 5; Casson 8–9; Presbrey 488). Other women's magazines like *The Woman's Home Companion, Good Housekeeping, The Delineator,* and the model for the *Home Monthly,* the *Ladies' Home Journal,* had done the experimenting and perfected the techniques of mass circulation, including "an effective strategy of low price, advertiser underwriting, and targeting of female customers" (Zuckerman 25). Cather had firmly established successful models upon which to base her editorial decision making.

The *Home Monthly* was a twenty-four-page quarto containing feature articles on travel and famous citizens, short stories, limited poetry, editorials, and monthly service department columns on fashion, child rearing, and dining. Portraying itself as fulfilling a need not yet met in the current regional market, the magazine announced an editorial policy based on gentility:

> It has seemed to the projectors of this enterprise that there is no publication in all the region in question reasonably well adapted to fill a niche in all its better class of homes, metropolitan, suburban, and rural. . . . It is hoped to accomplish this end by a careful utilization of rare facilities enjoyed for years past in the study of American home life and its needs, and prompt and unhesitating action right in line with such further discoveries as may be made.
>
> THE HOME MONTHLY is not ambitious of becoming a dignified review, nor is it to be used only as a vehicle for the dissemination of fashion gossip and culinary recipes. It is equally certain that it shall not be made a mere purveyor of sensational and unwholesome fiction. . . . Nothing need be said further than that these pages will be kept pure and clean in tone, and that all plans for THE HOME MONTHLY center in the aim to entertain, to educate, to elevate. ("The Home Monthly," August 1896, 12)

The policy stated here reflects a belief in what Arthur M. Schlesinger calls "the cult of elegance." At the end of the nineteenth and into the start of the twentieth century, many Americans were no longer "content to strive for the comforts rather than the luxuries of life." Those who "scaled the [social] heights" indulged in "greater pretentiousness and conspicuous consumption" (Schlesinger 27–29). Readers of the *Home Monthly* wanted to know what they needed to do to elevate themselves and their families to the status of living in one of the "better class of homes."

By broadly defining the "better class of homes" as coming from metropolitan, suburban, and rural settings, the *Home Monthly* editorial policy implies a widely embracing idea of who is eligible to enter the ranks of the social elite and implies that its readers will learn how. The emphasis on a "pure and clean" tone points to the publishers' desire to instruct readers in morality as well as propriety. Part of that instruction will come through articles describing the current fashion and entertaining trends, and part of it will come from articles focused on "the study of

American home life and its needs." According to historian Mary Ellen Zuckerman, readers wanted "concrete information that could assist them in their job of overseeing the household" (4). This desire was variously satisfied in all categories of the magazine's contents, including advertising, where the proposal to enlighten women about how to run their homes as among the "better class of homes" translates into evoking a desire for products for the home. Women had become the primary consumers of the household in what was rapidly becoming a consumer economy. By highlighting the role of homemaker for women, the *Home Monthly* was also highlighting women's role as a consumer and positioning itself among other "magazine experts" who "helped the perplexed housewife in the new job of consumption" (Zuckerman 35). As Ellen Gruber Garvey puts it in *The Adman in the Parlor: Magazines and the Gendering of Consumer Culture, 1880s to 1910s,* magazines became "texts embedded within the world of commerce and the world of their readers" (4). Women's magazines capitalized on their readers' sense of disequilibrium and stepped in to serve as resources providing crucial information on how to behave, what to wear, and what material possessions to acquire to reflect appropriate social standing. The shift to a consumer culture, in fact, called for an entirely new way of behaving in the world.[2] Women's magazines, with their strong dependence on advertising revenue, helped producers, retailers, and advertisers in the education of the female consumer.

Soon after her arrival in Pittsburg, Cather expressed her frustration over the editorial policy of the *Home Monthly,* calling it "namby pamby," but she sought to follow it as best she could (Woodress 114). And so with Axtell's quick departure she began the work of constructing a women's magazine, actually writing most of the material herself, though "without byline or under a pseudonym" (Slote 306).[3] She was directly responsible for providing women both direct and indirect cues on proper etiquette, within a design created to train her readers as consumers of products necessary to create a "perfect home."

By examining in detail the different elements at work in the magazine—advertising run in the magazine's pages, editorials and feature articles, fiction, and service departments—and identifying Cather's central role in decision making in all of these elements, we can see the internal tension and contradiction of the magazine's message, as well as Cather's own conflict. While the magazine professed to want to help women become wise, informed decision makers through the education provided within its pages, essentially the *Home Monthly* encouraged passivity and dependence in its readers. It is impossible to know whether Cather was completely aware of the mixed messages the magazine was sending its readers, but it does seem certain that she was aware of endorsing a very traditional role for women and that that was an endorsement with which she was not completely comfortable, for she found subtle ways to call into question the role she was also helping to construct.

In order to succeed in her new position, Cather, as managing editor, was willing to participate in the manipulation of her readers, but Cather, the artist, simply would not create the dependent, consumer-driven heroines or the type of fiction that usually appeared in the women's magazines of the time.

Advertising

Advertising was the foundation of the women's magazine industry at the turn of the century. Income from advertisers allowed publishers to lower their price to the ten-cents mark and even below, and the resulting increase in subscriptions increased the demand for advertising space. Advertising served both as the background for the magazine's contents and as an integral part of its message to readers. Many innovations in advertising were just coming into use, including placement of advertising amidst editorial material, increasingly sophisticated design featuring illustrations, and the use of specific persuasive strategies within the text of the ads. The advertising in the *Home Monthly*, unlike that of the more successful national magazines that relied on corporate advertisers, consisted almost exclusively of local advertising, but within the locally designed and prepared ads the new approaches to advertising are still apparent.

Whereas consumers had formerly depended on small specialty stores, stores that focused on one particular line of items and offered only a limited display of items for sale, the turn of the century brought a new retail experience—the department store. Department stores offered every variety of merchandise all in one location and all on display for shoppers to observe, touch, and desire. Among the *Home Monthly*'s biggest advertisers were two such stores in Pittsburg, Joseph Horne & Company and Boggs and Buhl. We can see in the Horne ad of November 1896 an emphasis on creating a consumer haven to which shoppers would be drawn: "The finest store building in America. Six great floors . . . devoted exclusively to high class retailing. Strangers in the city as well as all Pittsburghers and Alleghenians are cordially invited to make our store their general rendezvous for meeting friends, or for passing the time in quiet rest. . . . ALL ARE WELCOME" (back cover). The ad suggests the social nature of the department stores, an image encouraged by the stores themselves.

In addition to traditional appeals to quality and quantity, several new approaches were tested by advertisers in the *Home Monthly*, including the appeal of something new or a product using some advanced technology, the use of slogans, and the appeal of brand names. One other advertising strategy that appeared in limited use was fear. Some over-the-counter medications played on the consumer's fear of disease and especially a mother's fear of infant mortality. For example, Vapo-Cresolene claimed it "prevents the spread of contagious diseases by acting as a powerful disinfectant, harmless to the youngest child" (Aug. 1896, 19). Insurance ads also used fear to sell their products. They asked men, "Where will your wife get her first dollar after you're gone?" and suggested that it was a man's "sacred duty" to "relieve your widow and orphans of worry and embarrassment" by making sure they would be well taken care of with a substantial insurance policy (Equitable, Aug. 1896, inside back cover; Equitable, Nov. 1896, inside cover; Equitable, May 1897, back cover). Given their placement in a women's magazine, however, these ads were actually a warning to women to insist that their husbands obtain life insurance.

All of these innovations in advertising strategy were used to persuade consumers to buy products—specifically female consumers, and specifically products that both enhanced their role as homemaker and allowed them access to the material possessions of the upper class. Ads addressed to women offered various new products that would make their role as homemaker easier. Products like the Triumph Stove, Ezy Raisin Seeder, Flashskin Polishing Cloth and Goodwin Washer were touted as time- and labor-saving devices for the housewife. A variety of medicines and other cures were offered to women in the role as mother, including cures for whooping cough, croup, asthma, sour stomach, and bedwetting. All of these ads provided women with the products necessary to create a home that ensured safety and comfort for their families. For example, McElveen's Furniture Polish was the product for "[e]very woman in the United States whose pride and ambition is in the keeping of a perfect home" (Aug. 1896, 15). Advertisers not only provided access to the products necessary to achieve the ideal home, but in many ways were constructing the standards of a social ideal.

Ads dealing with the ideal home, or at least with the illusion of the ideal home, were surrounded by ads for products that would help a woman distinguish herself in society and secure her status as a lady. Angora kittens were "very stylish" and "[e]very lady is interested in anything new in china, cut glass, lamps, bric-a-brac, etc." (Nov. 1896, 15; T. G. Evans & Co., Oct. 1896, 24). There were advertisements for diamonds, "fine shoes" and "fine gloves," "stylish" hats, pianos, and carriages. One ad advised that a "lady is known by the stationery she uses"; one asserted that "[y]ou *need* a new dinner, tea, or after dinner set"; and another suggested to "young married ladies" that they could avoid "disappointments and discouragements with home cooking if they ordered cakes from our home cooking department" (Jos. Eichbaum & Co., Sept. 1896, 22; T. G. Evans & Co., Sept. 1896, inside front cover, emphasis added; Geo. K. Stevensonn & Co. Grocers, April 1897, 23). If a woman really wanted to impress her dinner guests, she could use Kuhn catering service, whose ads boasted it was the "leading society caterer," providing the "finest wares" and "finest service in this part of the state" and offering "the only correct tables for Dominos, Whist playing, and also a smaller table for Eucher" (April 1897, 23; Jan. 1897, 19; Feb. 1897, 23). In other words, if you had enough money, lack of experience with domestic skills and/or unfamiliarity with the correct rules of social etiquette was not a concern. A woman could simply purchase the appearance of social sophistication.

Illusion also played a role with respect to women working outside the home. While the editorial material in the *Home Monthly* repeatedly insisted upon the importance of a woman's focusing on her responsibilities as wife and mother and often disparaged those who chose to work outside the home, the advertisers were a little more progressive in their thinking. In addition to announcing post-secondary education that might lead to a career, the *Home Monthly*'s advertisers offered women opportunities for earning extra money by selling a variety of products from their homes—money that could then be spent on the wares being featured in the magazine. Many ads—such as those for Sun Rise Yeast, Egyptian Drug Company, Best Tea, Beveridge's Automatic Cooker, American Supply House, and Garfield Pepsin Gum—not only advertised products but also called for agents to sell these products. In a particularly detailed example, the Iron City Dish Washer company ad included a testimonial from a woman who made "$1,640 clear money in 87 days and attended to my household duties besides" (Oct. 1896, 24). These ads were clearly directed at housewives who were eager to earn discretionary cash that they could use to obtain the trappings of moneyed society. Women could achieve the illusion of membership in society through the prescribed material possessions even if they could not achieve the life of leisure required of a true lady.

Perhaps the biggest advertiser for female workers was the *Home Monthly* itself. While there were no ads for subscription work in the August, September, and October 1896 issues, in the eight remaining issues on which Cather served as managing editor there were fourteen ads for subscription work, offering everything from cash to premiums, including pianos, buggies, bicycles, sewing machines, watches, china, cameras, and vacations in Atlantic City, as incentives for collecting subscriptions. That is, the *Home Monthly* offered women who did subscription work access to the goods they desired in two ways, both in premiums representing the possessions of the leisure class and in cash to purchase additional possessions. Like some of the advertisers mentioned earlier, the *Home Monthly* also emphasized that work could be done "without seriously interfering with their home . . . duties" (Jan. 1897, inside back cover). So while the magazine espoused a philosophy based on the angel in the house, where women found complete satisfaction in their role as wife and mother, it also recognized the potential for women to sell magazine subscriptions to other women and was unwilling to forego that income to maintain its philosophy.

Bombarded with all of these ads designed to stimulate desire, women were left to try to decipher exactly what the ads meant and how to respond to them. Advertisers endowed products with seemingly endless benefits and layers of association and connotation, and women had to learn how to "read through the enticements and to assess the 'authenticity' of claims by 'interested advertisers and shopkeepers'" (Leach 148). Some women would have been able to acquire the skill of reading the ads critically, but others must have fallen prey to the desire they created. Providing goods for the family and providing love for the family became intertwined, and women looked to women's magazines to help them determine the best way to provide both.

Articles, Editorials, and Service Departments

Within the reading field constructed by advertising, the *Home Monthly* offered informational nonfiction and advice in a variety of categories or "departments"—all of which fell under Cather's responsibility. The most direct advice and information was given in service departments that focused primarily on women's roles as homemaker and mother and their desire to rise socially. As Zuckerman points out, "rapid industrialization and urbanization made United States women more uncertain about their 'proper role,' and hence more dependent on [women's magazines] for guidance" (37). Columns like "Things Good to Eat," "Health Topics," "For the Young Folks," and even "Books Old and New" address the needs of a woman as she runs her home and cares for her family, helping her do everything from prepare healthy and original meals for her family and care for chest colds and hiccups to entertain her children and select appropriate reading material. Questions on child rearing were especially emphasized in these service department columns, particularly in "Mothers and the Nursery" and "The Quiet Observer," two of the regularly featured service department columns.

The "Quiet Observer" was Erasmus Wilson, from whom Cather purchased a series of articles that focused on rearing children properly, with special attention to gender-appropriate behavior. In one of his early articles Wilson traces the inherent difference he sees between boys and girls back to the time when people lived in caves, when, according to Wilson, inherent gender differences could be seen in children's response to the carcass of an animal brought home by the father for food: "The first impulse of the toddling boy, naked, unshorn, and unwashed, was to take a club and hit the dead animal on the head; but his sister wanted to see its eyes, stroke its fur and pet it. His disposition was to kill, her's to protect; his to destroy, her's to preserve; his to hurt, her's to soothe. It was ever thus" ("A Boy and a Girl" Sept. 1896, 13; spelling retained from the original). Despite these natural dispositions, Wilson argues that a child is "little more than a piece of animate clay" that parents are to mold as best they can. While these columns suggest gendered behavior is inherent, apparently what qualifies as gender-appropriate behavior bears constant repeating.

Wilson's advice for the molding process and possible solutions to the problems parents might encounter includes keeping young girls from becoming tomboys by encouraging their "natural inclination for bright colors, ribbons, and bangles" ("A Boy and a Girl" Oct. 1896, 15). Or a father might discourage his daughter's use of coarse language and slang this way:

> Tell her how those coarse, unnecessary expressions sweep the delicate bloom from her lips, take the sweetness from her kisses and the pureness from her expression. . . . that hereafter simple girlish traits, refined manners and sweetness of disposition, with a tendency towards womanliness, will determine her place in the hearts of her friends, and in the esteem of all good people. ("And Now It Is Our Girl" 11)

According to Wilson, a child's manners are of grave concern to parents as they determine future social acceptability and thus future success. Like etiquette manuals published at the same time, Wilson defines success based on gender. He focuses on the ways a boy's behavior will determine his ability to reach his full potential and the ways a girl's behavior will determine her acceptability to others, especially possible suitors.

Wilson's advice to parents is an example of how women's magazines "both reflected gender roles in American society and helped construct and reinforce them" (Zuckerman xii). David Reed, in *The Popular Magazine in Britain and the United States,* calls the articles in women's magazines "as much prescriptive as descriptive" (72). While Wilson's advice on developing gender-appropriate behavior might be considered at least somewhat subtle in that it takes the form of an illustration or fictional scenario, other service departments in the *Home Monthly* used more overt and prescriptive means of constructing socially acceptable behavior.

"Mothers and the Nursery," a service department column written by

Mrs. J. E. Scott, is filled with very specific and practical suggestions on topics such as children's clothing, care of children's teeth, number of hours of sleep required for children, and bathing instructions. In one column Scott encourages parents to include children in social occasions because of "the politeness, the polish, and ease of manner that [children] get from the association with older people in society" and argues that this interaction results in "that natural, easy, dignified manner that we all admire so much in others and often try so hard, but unsuccessfully, to imitate" ("An Element of Success" 18). Like Wilson, Scott ties proper etiquette to future success; parents must teach their children about socially acceptable ways of behaving if they hope to ensure they will grow into successful adults.

Scott's helpful pieces of advice read as friendly and educational, as if an older sister, mother, or grandmother were offering nonjudgmental advice to the reader. Occasionally, however, her friendly column takes on a more prescriptive edge and her advice reads more like social law, as is the case when she addresses women working outside the home.

> To properly look after the physical, mental and moral welfare of the children in the home—and there is no home in the truest sense of the word where there are no children—requires more intelligence and ability than making a stump speech or writing a novel. . . . Countless thousands of children die every year because those who take care of them either don't understand or neglect their duties. ("Needed Knowledge" 18)

Scott not only asserts that motherhood and domesticity are the only real choice for a responsible woman, but she also argues that those women who do not have children are unworthy and warns that those who do not devote their entire attention to their children—that is, who work outside the home—may be punished with the death of their children. Scott's construction of etiquette is not only prescriptive, it's threatening.

The longest service department column in all of the issues produced during Cather's time at the *Home Monthly* was "Fashionland." The question "What should I wear?" was of such importance, in fact, that this column may have been "written and illustrated expressly for the *Home Monthly*" by Cather under the pseudonym Mildred Beardslee.[4] Columns like this deal less with a woman's role within the home and more with how women can succeed socially, and one of the keys to social success is appropriate attire.

According to William Leach in *Land of Desire*, fashion's intent "was to make women (and to a lesser degree men) feel special, to give them opportunities for playacting, and to lift them into a world of luxury or pseudo-luxury, beyond work, drudgery, bills, and the humdrum every-day," but its effect was often to "stir up restlessness and anxiety, especially in a society where class lines were blurred or denied, where men and women fought for the same status and wealth, and where people feared being left out or scorned because they could not keep up with others and could not afford the same things other people had" (91–92). Simultaneously, the fashion industry demanded constant change. Fashion columns in magazines urged people to buy, wear, dispose of, and buy again. "Since the specialness of any single fashion tended to go stale or vanish quickly as many consumers struggled to buy it, merchants had to supply the market at a feverish rate to maintain the fiction of glamour or uniqueness" (Leach 92). Merchants counted on the constant turnover in fashion to generate a constant demand for new clothing. To heighten the desire for new fashion, the industry, with the aid of women's magazines, created an emphasis on the change in seasons to indicate a changing fashion season and artificially create a time line for the acquisition of new clothes.

In "Fashionland" Cather documents trends in fashion through detailed descriptions, illustrations, and sewing directions, with the overall aim of helping women prioritize their fashion needs and expenditures in order to get the most social impact for their money. After all, as the column says, "to be prettily and modishly dressed is every woman's ambition who cares for her appearance at all, and yet how to accomplish it within one's means is quite another story, as Kipling says" (Oct. 1896, 21). With all the ready-made clothing available, it was becoming much easier for a woman to dress fashionably. As Cather argues, "To be badly dressed in these days makes one at once a most impossible person; and all because apparel never was so cheap" (Jan. 1897, 18). Her column is often filled with detailed descriptions and illustrations of outfits worn by famous women and observations about current trends in clothing design. By pointing to the clothing of wealthy women as her examples, Cather appeals to women's sense of competition: "One is never at one's best when conscious of looking the dowdy; on the contrary one is at one's best when she is perfectly sure of being quite as modestly and becomingly gowned as any woman in the room" (Dec. 1896, 15). That is, women need to match their clothing to that worn by other women and, if possible, emulate that worn by the famous women featured in the column. Not coincidentally, ads for Joseph Horne & Company, the *Home Monthly*'s biggest advertiser, always appear on the same page as the "Fashionland" column and feature the very items highlighted in that month's column. The *Home Monthly* helps women identify the clothing they need to move up the social ladder while simultaneously providing access to that clothing through its advertising. Yet a degree of discomfort with this emphasis may be indicated by the apologetic tone of the columnist's (possibly Cather's own) insistence, "However trivial the matter of dress may seem, it makes or mars many a woman's happiness, and is a far more important factor in life than would seem possible on the face of it" (Dec. 1896, 15).

In editorials and feature articles the *Home Monthly* took a somewhat less direct approach to influencing its readers' lives. Each issue contained a full page of editorial material, usually consisting of multiple unsigned short pieces. Although Cather probably did not officially possess the title of editor, it appears that she was as involved in the creation of these pages as she was with the rest of the magazine. Slote identifies six pieces on the editorial page as Cather's during the twelve months she was managing editor and asserts that Cather was probably "responsible for much of the rest of the content on the twelve editorial pages during her tenure" (308). Confirming Slote's suspicions, biographers and critics have identified fourteen editorials as Cather's, and new identifications continue.[5]

Women's magazines, as well as other magazines and newspapers of the time, covered the activities and lifestyles of the upper class because

> while members of the middle class could not emulate Mrs. Vanderbilt's ball or afford to give a $10,000 dinner party at Delmonico's, they enviously followed . . . the society columns, and since some of the mounting national wealth spilled over into their own pockets, they were better able than their class had ever been before to copy many of the ways of the smart set. (Schlesinger 30)

The *Home Monthly* likewise capitalized on its readers' desire to learn about the upper class by including not only feature articles but also editorials designed both to help strengthen the moral character of the rising middle class (by suggesting the connection between upper class success and moral fortitude) and to show readers the lifestyle they needed to emulate, a lifestyle centered on the acquisition of material goods.

Coverage of social and political events in the editorial pages, and especially comments on famous people and glittering social events, provided occasions for Cather to write set pieces for readers who sought to emulate the manners of the rich and powerful. While highlighting the advantages and freedom money and social class can provide, the editorials also emphasized the need for a strong moral code to match the outward appearance of social propriety. In "Consuelo, the Duchess of Marlborough," for example, the duchess's "successful and brilliant" party frames a larger discussion of accusations that she, a Vanderbilt, has married for the title. The editorial argues that because the duchess has proven herself to be "conservative and modest and free from snobbery" since obtaining the royal designation, perhaps the American public should be more generous in their response to the marriage (12). Editorials like these give readers hope that if they work hard and act properly they can earn a title, perhaps simply the title of lady, but only if their manners and morals appropriately reflect their title. At the same time, they outline the material possessions and luxuries one should acquire in order to hold the title. In this way, the *Home Monthly* and Cather intertwine morals and material possessions and blur the distinction between the two.

In addition to focusing on the activities of the upper class, the *Home Monthly* editorials also served to encourage a traditional view of gender-appropriate behavior, focused on a woman's role within the home. Woman, as "angel of the house," is the "moral regenerator" and focus of family life.

> Closeted within the sanctuary, this angel could nurture purity and dependence; she could retain her asexuality and child-like simplicity. Her cheery prettiness and lady-like accomplishments would make her a dutiful companion. Her innocence and helplessness would touch the heart of the most wayward. Her self-sacrifice and deference would assist the

> needy. Her example and soft reproach would be an enduring moral guide. (Loeb 19)

While trumpeting the role of woman as homemaker, the *Home Monthly* portrayed women who take on roles outside the home as living unfulfilling and lonely lives. Female reformers, in particular, are shown to neglect their responsibilities to family and home in pursuit of social causes that are often unsuccessful and exhausting. "The Way of the Reformer Is Hard" according to a May 1897 editorial describing the suffering of both Anna Dickinson and Phoebe Cousins for their part in the abolitionist and suffrage movements (12). The editorial points to "these two broken-down women, both of them ill, miserable, old before their time" as a "restraining example" for "the feverish, discontented young women of the country" and pronounces the "half contemptuous notoriety they have gained" to be scarce compensation for "what they have lost." It implies that the two women have lost their health and their minds in their work as reform advocates. The trend in the *Home Monthly*'s editorials is to portray women who agitate for reform or who live the lifestyle of the "new woman" as doomed to unhappiness—this in spite of the fact that Cather herself would be shown as a New Woman in a *Pittsburg Press* drawing of 18 March 1897 (Bohlke xxxii and Stout 48).

The editorial pages of the *Home Monthly* define for women their proper sphere in life. They are not meant to be reformers or engage in any other behavior that takes them away from their primary focus—the home. Besides whatever commitment its publishers may have felt to such principles, the magazine also wants women to be actively engaged in their role as homemakers because as homemakers they serve as consumers, buying the products advertised in its pages as necessary for the perfect home. The magazine further defines the necessary products and creates a demand and allure for them by including editorials that feature the glamorous lifestyles of the upper class. Female readers received a strong message from the pages of the *Home Monthly*'s editorials: It is your moral responsibility to behave like a proper wife, mother, and homemaker *and* to provide your family with as many of the material possessions as possible to indicate a rise from the perfect middle class home to the perfect upper class home.

Like the editorials, feature articles reinforce a woman's role as angel of the house. Longer articles on topics like the unpublished verse of Whittier, the methods used in instructing the deaf, the chrysanthemum ("the queen of autumn"), and the legends surrounding the three kings pertain to woman's role as educated teacher of her children, caretaker of the home and grounds, and religious instructor and role model. Articles on "the art of housekeeping" and home decorating further reinforce a woman's role within the home. According to Jennifer Scanlon, in *Inarticulate Longings: "The Ladies' Home Journal," Gender, and the Promise of Consumer Culture,* "the home was considered the 'natural' consumer unit, the housewife the 'natural' consumer" (13). As such, it was in the *Home Monthly's* best interest to keep women in the home where they could serve their natural role and remain the target audience for the magazine's advertisers.

Cather contributed two feature articles that reinforced traditional roles for women. The first was her September 1896 feature on the two potential first ladies, Mrs. McKinley and Mrs. William Jennings Bryan. In "Two Women the World Is Watching" Cather examines each woman's strengths and her relationship with her husband. She describes Mrs. McKinley as "gracious and charming" and observes that during her twenty-five years of marriage, her "life and interests have been those of her husband, as, in one way or another, actively or passively, every woman's must be" (4). Mrs. Bryan, she suggests, is an example of "the 'New Woman' type at its best"; she is interested in being an intellectual equal and helper for her husband, and she studied law and was admitted to the bar "in order to be better able to help him" (5). A very intelligent woman, Mrs. Bryan lacks, however, Mrs. McKinley's social grace: Cather laments that "society in Washington would be rather dull with Mrs. Bryan at its head, for she has neither taste nor aptitude for it" (5). In contrast, whether "at receptions, dinners, or theater parties," Mrs. McKinley "is always the woman who directs the wit and mirth of the occasions" (4). Both women are shown to be great assets to their husbands, but in comparing the two Cather favors the woman who is both a good wife and a good socialite.[6]

The second of these feature articles was "Nursing as a Profession for Women," aimed toward those women forced to work to support themselves during their premarriage years. Here, despite reviewing the long history of the profession and the rigors of the training, Cather never refers to nursing as a rewarding profession or even one from which a woman can gain a sense of satisfaction. But she does show it as a profession in which a woman with a strong constitution and personality and an honest work ethic can excel—that is, "if she has not married some susceptible physician in the mean time" (4). Of course, marriage is the ultimate goal for any woman, and one for which she should be happy to give up her profession.

It seems contradictory that a woman working to support herself would advocate marriage as the only acceptable option for women. The *Home Monthly,* however, is full of such contradictions and complications, as were most women's magazines. For example, the picture of women constructed by the longer three- to five-page feature articles is complicated by the shorter one- to two-page feature articles also included in the magazine. While the longer feature articles focus on the angel in the house, the shorter articles appeal to the angel as she tries to climb the social ladder by featuring detailed descriptions of the lifestyles, homes, and social events of the people of the upper class. The contradictions of the longer and shorter feature articles work together both to reinforce women's place within the home and to evoke consumer desire to be like the rich and privileged. Contradictions are natural when a magazine's primary goals are at cross-purposes: promoting traditional women's values and encouraging full participation in a consumer society. Scanlon's conclusions about the *Ladies' Home Journal* hold true for the *Home Monthly* as well:

> It was not an easy task to promote a simple life for women while at the same time promoting the primacy of consumer goods and material desires, nor was it easy to praise women's growing independence from onerous household tasks at the same time that one pleaded with women to limit the boundaries of that independence. . . . Finally, the notion of choice, central to the magazine's message and to the ideology of the larger consumer culture, was often illusory, as the magazine promoted fairly limited roles for women and often ignored or dismissed many of the choices real women faced. (4)

Cather's articles sought to promote the ideology expressed in her publishers' editorial policy, but the very nature of the business of the magazine forced her to present a more complicated picture.

A prime example of this complication comes in Cather's presentation of the bicycle. The safety bicycle, known as the Rover and looking very much like our modern day version with two wheels of equal size, was introduced in 1885. Two years later, with the introduction of rubber tires, people had a safe, comfortable mode of transportation that was easy to ride and relatively inexpensive to purchase (Hall, *Guide*). The new-found freedom the bicycle offered women was enhanced when manufacturers produced a drop-frame model made especially for and marketed to women. Commonly referred to as a "wheel," the bicycle became immensely popular, and its popularity can be seen in the pages of the *Home Monthly.*

In the twelve issues published during Cather's time as managing editor, nine different articles on cycling appeared. Starting with an August 1896 article by Will S. Power that declares cycling to be no longer a fad but a sport that is here to stay, the articles' topics include bicycle racing, popular cycling routes in and around Pittsburg, using cycling as a cure for stomach problems, bicycle touring, and bicycle shows. Many of these articles comment directly on women and cycling. For example, one suggests that a woman who is "dissatisfied with her sallow, muddy complexion which is caused by an inactive life and poor digestion can get rid of it by using a wheel" (Rowe Nov. 1896, 23). Yet the magazine clearly believes women need to be reminded of the need for moderation in cycling. In "Cycle Notes for Women" (Aug. 1896) Cather warns girls not to overdo and not to ride to the point of exhaustion.

Some of these conflicting messages come from the contested nature of the bicycle itself. The bicycle brought new freedom to American women through increased mobility. But while many celebrated these new opportunities, the wheel was also the victim of conservative attacks. Both the defense of and attacks on the bicycle took a medicalized form: "Pro-bicyclers asserted that bicycling would strengthen women's bodies—and thereby make them more fit for motherhood," while "anti-bicyclers claimed that riding would ruin women's sexual health by promoting masturbation, and would compromise gender definition as well" (Garvey 106). According to an article published in the *Brooklyn Medi-*

cal Journal in 1897, for example, "the bicycle teaches masturbation in women and girls" (page 84). These concerns were echoed in other medical journals, which usually pointed to the seat or saddle of the bicycle as the danger. Especially dangerous was "scorching"—riding bent over the handlebars, the posture adopted by those cycling for speed. But Dr. W. E. Fitch (1899) warned that even if the "saddle is properly adjusted for slow riding" the bicycle can still pose a threat, for "in an unusual effort at speed or hill climbing, the body is thrown forward, causing the clothing to press against the clitoris, thereby eliciting and arousing feelings hitherto unknown and unrealized by the young maiden" (155–56). Fitch's reference to the proper adjustment of the saddle may also indicate concern that some young women intentionally adjusted the angle of their seat to increase the friction and thus the masturbatory pleasure.

In order to counteract these concerns and still promote the bicycle to their advertisers' satisfaction, women's magazines featured articles on selecting the correct bicycle, seat adjustment, and riding position. In an August 1896 article in the *Home Monthly* entitled "Cycling for Health and Pleasure" the reader is advised that the first step after purchasing a bicycle is to "see that it is properly adjusted; that is, that the saddle and handlebars are at the proper height and angle" (Power 13). The article goes on to describe the proper method of sitting on the bicycle and uses three illustrations, including one entitled "Scorcher's Position," to suggest the appropriate and the inappropriate posture for proper riding. In the following month's issue an article on bicycle racing consistently refers to the racer as "he," yet still warns that riders sometimes improperly adjust their seats "entirely too high, too far back," and "tilted upward in front" (F. N. O. 17). According to Garvey, while this scorching position might be merely criticized in male riders, "for women, fast riding was condemned; deviations from upright decorous and graceful riding were more serious, and a woman's bicycle posture could be a significant measure of her propriety and sexual innocence" (115).

Cather herself was guilty of some of the riding behaviors critics warned against. In addition to riding her bicycle back and forth to work every day, she liked to relieve stress by taking her wheel out and racing the electric street cars (Bennett, "Pittsburgh" 65–66). Yet in the *Home Monthly* she needed to abide by her publishers' conservative views, so she instead negotiated the difference by providing instruction to women on the proper use of bicycles to help them take advantage of the freedom of the bicycle while still abiding by the proper rules of behavior.

Fiction

Like the other elements of the magazine, fiction in the *Home Monthly* tries to define for women their proper place as wives and mothers within the home. Stories instruct young women on choosing the proper mate and portray marriage as the ultimate and fulfilling goal. At the same time, the magazine's fiction addresses some of the dissatisfaction women experience in marriage, while always emphasizing the need for women to accommodate themselves to their husbands and children in order to avoid potential conflict. Though giving voice to women's dissatisfaction, the *Home Monthly* continually emphasized the rewards of traditional gender roles and endorsed proper etiquette despite social challenges. Yet within this prescribed message Cather still found a way to complicate the definition of proper gender roles and allude to the possibility of additional choices for women.

The contested nature of the bicycle as explored in editorial material and articles also found further exploration and reconstruction in fiction. Women's magazines at the turn of the century incorporated bicycles into their short fiction in an attempt to "reframe [the bicycle's] apparent social risks as benefits," featuring them in courtship plots as a means of turning critics' fears of newfound mobility and independence into newfound opportunities to meet appropriate young men (Garvey 107). In such stories the bicycle usually serves the purpose of introducing two young people of the same social class, often with similar social connections. By featuring it in a courtship plot, magazine fiction could recast the bicycle not as a means of female independence that would lead to the breakdown of the family but as a way of uniting middle-class couples, turning the bicycle from a solitary means of transportation to a community-building and specifically a union-building device (Garvey 125).

Cather uses the bicycle as courtship device in her short story "Tommy, the Unsentimental" (Aug. 1896). Theodosia, also known as Tommy, an independent Western woman with an excellent business sense developed while working in her father's bank, repeatedly helps her would-be fiancé, Easterner Jay Ellington Harper, by bicycling over "to straighten out the young man's business for him" (6). Harper reciprocates with attention and implied interest, but it is clear that he is disturbed because Tommy does not conform to the feminine and domestic ideal he expects. In the climactic scene Tommy rides to Harper's rescue by wheeling over to provide him with the cash he needs to stave off a run on his bank. Virgil Albertini in his article "Willa Cather and the Bicycle" calls Tommy's ride "heroic" and observes that "a lesser physical specimen could not have done it" (18). Albertini asserts that despite the twenty-five miles of rugged terrain, Tommy's "strength, stamina, amazing resources, and physical ability and her trusty bicycle overc[o]me the odds" (18–19). Yet Tommy's heroism is called into question by her Eastern friend Miss Jessica, who has attempted to accompany Tommy on her mission but instead has been left halfway through the trip exhausted and "all bunched up on the side of the road like a little white rabbit" (7). As she watches Tommy race off to save Harper, it occurs to her that Tommy "was not only very unkind, but that she sat very badly on her wheel and looked aggressively masculine and professional when she bent her shoulders and pumped like that" (7). Tommy's bent shoulders and pumping suggest a very masculine approach to riding, perhaps even scorching. Miss Jessica, the Eastern representation of proper femininity, looks upon this behavior with scorn.

Tommy offers an alternate interpretation of the situation. As she rides away, she reflects on the message she is to relay to Harper from Miss Jessica—that she would do anything to save him: "Poor Jess, anything but the one thing he needs. Well, your kind have the best of it generally, but in the little affairs of this sort my kind come out rather strongly. We're rather better at them than at dancing. It's only fair, one side shouldn't have all" (7). Tommy is separating women into two kinds: Jessica's kind and her own. Garvey suggests the two kinds are Easterner and Westerner and that Tommy's eventual insistence that Harper "marry [Jessica] and be done with it" acknowledges the kindred spirit of the two Easterners and the incompatibility of the East and the West (7). But Tommy is not the typical woman, even in the West. She is in fact a favorite among her father's friends, who enjoy her company because she is "just one of them" (6). She plays pool and cards and prepares professional-quality cocktails. She is not interested in any of the young men in town because they are "practical and sensible," and she knows even fewer of the women because there were none "who were in any sense interesting, or interested in anything but babies and salads" (6). That is, they are women like Jessica. Such women understand the rules of etiquette, know they can accomplish what they want to within those rules, and therefore embrace them fully and use them as a means for judging others, particularly other women. Women like Tommy also understand the rules of etiquette, but know they cannot live according to them, and therefore choose to live according to their own rules.

Yet Tommy realizes she is making a sacrifice in choosing to live outside the rules for proper female etiquette. She cannot find a partner. The men from town are uninteresting and "thoroughly of her own kind," and the man she is interested in is too conventional to really appreciate her, a flaw she sees as keeping him from really being a man. In fact, at the end of the story Tommy condemns all men as "awful idiots" and complains that they "never think of anything beyond their dinner" (7). Despite her criticism, Tommy's final lament, "But O, how we do like 'em!" suggests that she continues to hope the "right man," one who will appreciate her special characteristics, will still come along (7).

In Cather's bicycle romance, the traditional happy ending demanded by the genre and by the *Home Monthly* editorial policy is fulfilled with the marriage of two young people, Harper and Miss Jessica. Readers learn that although the heroine saves the day with her bicycle, she realizes that if she is going to choose to live outside the rules of proper behavior she will be forced to sacrifice her chance at romance. On the surface Cather reinforces the idea of the natural role of women as wives and mothers when she ends her story with Tommy's reflection that despite their idiotic nature women still love men; women are meant to be in marital relationships with men. Yet Cather's message, upon closer reading, is more complicated. While "Tommy, the Unsentimental" may be read as a cautionary tale warning female readers about the consequences of choosing an unconventional lifestyle, it is clear that Cather approves of Tommy's choice. Tommy is still the hero of the story, and Cather presents her as a woman to admire. In this way Cather complicates the *Home Monthly*'s message about the proper role of women and suggests that those women willing to sacrifice relationships with men can find new independence.

"Tommy, the Unsentimental" also complicates the *Home Monthly*'s message about the acceptability of the growing material culture, and in a way that demonstrates Garvey's distinction between Easterners and Westerners. Easterners are more susceptible to the allure of material possessions and in fact seem defined by them. Harper has been sent West by his father after a failed college career marked by spending "too much money" (6). While his new setting has made it "simply impossible to live . . . prodigally," the white carnations Harper has "sent down from Hastings twice a week as regularly as the mail" to wear in his button hole indicate his continued commitment to material excess (6). Likewise, Miss Jessica's "violet perfumes" and "sunshade" mark her as distinctly Eastern, and her toilet ritual leaves Tommy feeling "baffled" (6). Tommy is fond of both characters, but the narrator calls Harper a "foolish man" and Jessica a "dainty, white, languid bit of a thing" (6). The West is no place for such dedication to material possessions. So while Cather promotes the magazine's attention to commercialization by endorsing bicycle sales, she also subtly calls into question material extravagance.

Other short fiction by Cather published in the *Home Monthly* embraces a traditional approach to female roles and appropriate female behavior while continuing her commentary on the consumer culture. In "The Count of Crow's Nest" (Sept. and Oct. 1896), which uses characters of nobility in the tradition of sentimental fiction, the materialistic daughter of the Count is exposed for breaking the rules and being driven by money instead of a sense of social responsibility or grace and is therefore punished. The role of mother is celebrated in "The Burglar's Christmas" (Dec. 1896) as a mother catches her son robbing her home and instantly forgives him of all wrongdoing, despite the fact that he had left home many years earlier and was forced into a life of crime. The son's "shabby" poverty is set against the parental "new house," which is marked by "richly dressed" guests, servants, and "fashionable occupants" (9). In accepting his mother's forgiveness, the son comes to realize that his mother loves him as no other woman can and through this realization accepts God's presence in the world. Thus, Cather connects a mother's love for her child with God's love for his children and thereby elevates and celebrates the maternal role.

In what appears to be her most conventional story published in the

Home Monthly, "A Resurrection" (Apr. 1897), Cather again turns to the romance, this time with a heroine who is rewarded for her proper behavior. Margie, the town's schoolmistress, who lives at home caring for her invalid mother, is well past her prime marrying age. In her youth she was in love with Martin Dempster, a successful river man, but when Dempster goes to the city to make his fortune he is seduced by a young French woman and jilts Margie to marry her. Dempster's new wife quickly depletes all his savings with her extravagant living, and she eventually drowns as a result of her foolishness, leaving Dempster with an infant son. He quietly returns home and turns his son over to Margie to raise. Eventually Dempster rebuilds his life, but when he approaches her with the news that he is leaving town and wants to take his son, Margie is terrified of losing the child, who has come to be the only happiness in her life. She insists that "a woman must have something" and the little boy is her something to love (5). Martin later appears at her house and reveals that he is still in love with her and wants the three of them to be together and start a new life. Margie at first believes she is too old, but Martin eventually convinces her that she still has all the passion of her youth.

The theme indicated by the title of the story, "A Resurrection," suggesting that Margie is reborn through her marriage to Martin, was a fitting one for the Easter issue. Margie's manners, according to Cather's details, have remained intact during her time of distress. She has remained a lady, exhibiting proper behavior and grace despite the humiliation of Martin's abandonment. She sets an example for her students by continuing to teach and care for her mother despite her heartbreak, refuses to display her anguish in public, accepts the responsibility for rearing Martin's son with generosity and grace despite Martin's poor behavior, and then continues to dress in appropriate fashion for the sake of the child even when hopes of dressing to attract a husband have ended. Cather creates a character deserving of a second chance, deserving because she continues to act properly despite every obstacle and social insult, and the reward for her behavior is marriage.

It is a marriage that will not only erase her former humiliation, but will also raise Margie back to the level of financial comfort she enjoyed as a youth. Margie had been from one of the prominent families in Brownville, but the family fortunes had been lost, and she has been forced to work to support a very frugal lifestyle for her herself and her mother. Marriage with Martin means moving to Kansas City and being recast in a more appropriate role. For Margie is truly one of those women "who were made to ride in carriages and wear jewels and grace first nights at the opera, who, through some unaccountable blunder in stage management in this little comedie humaine, have the wrong parts assigned them, and cook for farm hands, or teach a country school" (4).

This happy ending, however, has come at the price of many years of self-sacrifice and pain. When read focusing on the conflict instead of the resolution, Cather's story is about a woman who has lived a life of resignation and humiliation. According to Scanlon, female protagonists in the fiction found in women's magazines often have to struggle with men, children, gender roles, and themselves before arriving at the prescribed "happy ending." "And although the stories generally deliver those happy endings, readers may be as moved by the women's struggles and the paths not taken as they are by the happiest of endings. In this way, the fiction invites subversive as well as prescriptive readings" (141). Cather's story calls for just such a subversive reading. Instead of rebirth through marriage, Margie's resurrection might rather be her determination to finally assert herself and demand respect. She will no longer let Martin dictate her circumstances. She will keep the child, despite Martin's biological claim. But Cather's embedded message of self-assertion is muted when Martin declares his love for Margie. While she must provide a happy ending, Cather's text also invites readers to reflect on Margie's sacrifice and final decision to assert her will. Once again Cather finds a subtle way to complicate the *Home Monthly*'s portrayal of the proper role for women. While reinforcing the benefits of the domestic life, Cather's fiction found ways to acknowledge women's complaints, dissatisfactions, and sacrifices.

Editorials, feature articles, fiction, service departments, and advertising all worked together in the *Home Monthly* to create in its readers the need for the magazine. Like other women's magazines of the time, it used a "simple, direct, persuasive style akin to everyday speech" to "cut through the reader's barriers of resistance and 'impose' an idea" (Fox 49). According to Richard Wightman Fox and T. J. Jackson Lears this editorial strategy turned the literary style of earlier magazines into a "pitch" in magazines at the turn of the century, a salesmen's technique designed to get readers to lower their defenses. By this means, editors attempted to convey the magazine's authority and expertise. Using a direct, powerful prose style "was the first step in the managerial 'naturalization' of content; it was done by conveying the glow of conviction" (Fox 49).

By setting itself up as the authority, the *Home Monthly* attempted to convince its readers they needed the insight and advice it offered. If a magazine could evoke such a need, it ensured its survival in the competitive magazine industry. As Edward Bok, editor of the *Ladies' Home Journal*, stated, a magazine succeeded when it ceased to be "an inanimate printed thing" and became "a vital need in the personal lives of its readers" (179, 292–93). Yet by making readers feel dependent on the magazine, the *Home Monthly* was counteracting its overt attempts to help women become independent consumers who could make important acquisition decisions for the family.

In editorials and feature articles readers were given a glimpse inside the world of the elite and thereby encouraged to emulate the behavior described; through these columns the *Home Monthly* worked to evoke a desire in readers for a better lifestyle and the material possessions that accompanied it. By continually emphasizing its inside information, the magazine asserted it could provide readers information not available elsewhere. Many articles, for example, featured bylines claiming an article was written exclusively for the *Home Monthly*. By describing social events and other activities of the famous and elite, it made its readers feel they were getting a special glimpse inside another world, giving them a sense of belonging, of being inside the circle of social activity. Yet at the same time, the readers' reliance on the magazine for such information confirmed their outsider status. Despite the magazine's attempt to convince readers they could climb the social ladder by simply following its advice, the effect was that other people experienced the real world and readers were outsiders looking in. They were continually reminded of the complexity of the world of the elite and taught to rely on the advice of the magazine's experts to negotiate the challenges imposed. "Instead of promoting participation, the magazines elevated 'seeing'; instead of encouraging readers' criticism, the editors interpreted for them—told them simply to 'stay informed'" (Fox 61). The *Home*

Monthly thus created in its readers a sense of anxiety, dependency, and voyeurism.

Cather complicated the mixed message even more in her fiction. The magazine worked to create an image of women as "angel of the house." Women were to put family above all else and turn their attention to consumerism to fulfill the needs of their family. Yet Cather's fiction featured strong heroines like Tommy, who rescues her would-be husband and then hands him off to another woman, and Margie, who starts out as self-sacrificing but eventually awakens to her own independence and sexual passion. To be sure, all of these comments are couched within what appear to be typical female-directed stories, so the readers may have been only partially aware of their subversive nature.

Women turned to magazines like the *Home Monthly* for advice and guidance on how to behave according to the standards set by society. They wanted to help move their families up the social ladder by creating the illusion of the ideal family and home, and they relied on women's magazines to provide both the definition of the ideal and the means for achieving it. Like most women's magazines, the *Home Monthly* provided its readers with unclear messages and perhaps added to the social anxiety they were already experiencing. By trying to create dependent and passive readers who relied on the magazine for guidance in every facet of home life, it encouraged women to be overly concerned with social appearances, especially those related to material possessions. Cather was determined to succeed in her position at the *Home Monthly* and was willing to adapt the style and content of her writing to match the magazine's editorial policy, but her inner conflict about the magazine translated into fiction that called that policy into question. This, coupled with the magazine's already contradictory message to women about their independence as consumers yet their dependence on the magazine and advertising, sent a baffling message to readers. They were enticed and taught to be dissatisfied; were offered an insider's view of society and yet always remained outside observers; were offered the instruction necessary to climb the social ladder but could never consider their instruction complete. Cather was able to participate in the construction of manners, but because of the editorial policy of the *Home Monthly* and the need to generate profits, she was unable to construct them in a satisfying manner.

Notes

1. Biographers vary somewhat in their identification of the work Cather undertook. Bennett writes that Cather "took a proffered job as editor of the 'Home Monthly'" (*World* 35), but she also refers to the position as "the managing editorship" of the magazine (*World* 190 and "Pittsburgh" 65). Phyllis Robinson and Janis Stout both refer to Cather as "editor," as does Slote (76, 50, 4). Others refer to Cather only as "managing editor," including Bensen in "Willa Cather at *Home Monthly*," who claims it was her "original title" (232). Other biographers, however, call the titles editor and managing editor into question. Lewis recalls Axtell's offering Cather a position as "one of its editors" (40), and E. K. Brown suggests Axtell's offer was for "a position in the editorial office" (73). Woodress and L. Brent Bohlke assert that Cather was originally hired to be "assistant editor" to Axtell (114,1). Byrne and Snyder argue that while Cather "may never formally have held that title on the magazine, the 1897 Pittsburgh city directory does list 'managing editor' as her title or occupation" (2). A letter dated 27 July 1896 (WCPM) indicates that Cather may indeed not have started out with the title of either editor or managing editor; she complains to Ellen Gere that the *Home Monthly* is really quite dull in content but boasts that she is practically the managing editor, an assertion suggesting it was a title she did not hold at the time.

2. In his groundbreaking *People of Plenty*, David Potter explains the transformation involved in a shift to a consumer culture: "In a society of abundance, the productive capacity can supply new kinds of goods faster than society in the mass learns to crave these goods or to regard them as necessities. If this new capacity is to be used, the imperative must fall upon consumption, and the society must be adjusted to a new set of drives and values in which consumption is paramount" (173). It was during this period of adjustment that women's magazines flourished.

3. As a result of a limited reserve of materials, Cather often published under pseudonyms to give the magazine the illusion of being comprised of articles from numerous contributors, a publishing practice common at the time. In addition, all of the editorials and many of the shorter features appear unsigned. To further complicate identification, the magazine does not contain a list of editors. "Axtell, Orr & Co." is listed as the publisher, but nowhere in the magazine are editors identified by name or position.

4. Bensen identifies Cather as Beardslee based on another article published

under that name entitled "Whittier's Unpublished Verse." He is, however, the only critic to identify this as one of Cather's many pseudonyms. Tim Bintrim argues that it is highly unlikely Cather is Beardslee, since the illustrations accompanying the column are attributed to Beardslee in the byline and Cather did not possess great artistic skill.

5. JoAnna Lathrop's *Willa Cather: A Checklist of Her Published Writings* identifies the fourteen editorials mentioned; her book compiles the excavation work of other scholars into one accessible source.

6. Bensen interprets this article differently, asserting that "Mrs. McKinley suffered by comparison" (235).

3

"That Kitchen with the Shining Windows"

Willa Cather's "Neighbour Rosicky" and the *Woman's Home Companion*

Park Bucker

Most readers first experience "Neighbour Rosicky" in literary anthologies or story collections. Appearing in such a form in a classroom setting, the popular novella can be read as Willa Cather's attack on 1920s materialism, with Rosicky and his family opting for the simple and noble pleasures of the land over petty profit and city wages. Cather presents the accumulation of monetary wealth as completely contradictory to both earthly and spiritual happiness. The story's framing character, Doctor Burleigh, reflects: "[P]eople as generous and warm-hearted and affectionate as the Rosickys never got ahead much; maybe you couldn't enjoy your life and put it in the bank too" (NRa 15).[1] Rosicky's wife, Mary, uses the identical financial image when she refuses to sell the farm's premium dairy products to a creamery agent, arguing, "I'd rather put some colour into my children's faces than put money into the bank" (25).

These references and other examples lead many critics to place this story firmly in the pastoral tradition. David Daiches dismisses the story as more appealing to "conventional taste" than her "more original work," arguing that "its earthiness almost neutralizes the incipient sentimentality, and the relation of the action to its context in agricultural life gives the story an elemental quality" (158). Describing all the stories in *Obscure Destinies,* Maxwell Geismar notes that "they center around an idyllic agrarian existence, however, they also present glimpses of a sort of industrial inferno" (202). In her seeming rejection of American consumption and urbanity, Cather preaches a return to the soil: rural life with its dependence on and integration with Nature is essential for a harmonious family life.

Yet Cather's contemporary readers first encountered the novella in the commercially charged context of the *Woman's Home Companion* (serialized in the April and May issues of 1930). In the 1920s and 1930s this mass-circulation magazine filled its pages with advertisements urging its female readers to consume national food brands and purchase modern kitchen conveniences. The periodical echoed its advertisers in its editorial content. In "You Get Only What You Pay For," an unsigned editorial from October 1930, the magazine argued that conspicuous consumption was both indispensable and inevitable: "Modern life has so many complications that a woman would hardly get through her day unless she took advantage of modern simplifications such as trade-marks, price standards and advertising. Women have no time to become experts in all the things they have to buy" (4). Yet the nostalgic tone of "Neighbour Rosicky" (published in *Woman's Home Companion* as "Neighbor Rosicky")[2] alludes to a better, simpler time when women could be true pioneers and "experts in all things."

Both Cather's story and the *Companion* present the kitchen as a physical site of family happiness, stability, and morality. Cather uses the word "kitchen" seventeen times in the story, more than any other room or building, including "barn" (eight times) and "farm" (thirteen times). (See appendix to this essay for partial concordance.) She describes the Rosicky kitchen as "warm" (NRa 9) and bright with "lamplight" (41). At the end of section IV—and the end of the story's first installment in the *Companion*—Rosicky focuses on his farmhouse as he crosses the fields at night: "That kitchen with the shining windows was dear to him" (41). Although the "sleeping fields" and "noble darkness" are "dearer" to Rosicky, the warmth of the kitchen amid the "frosty stars" serves as a churchlike beacon for him. The kitchen provides Rosicky with his favorite spot, "Father's corner" between the bench and the bountiful "window full of plants" where he keeps his Bohemian newspapers and tailoring supplies (26). Cather contrasts this homey corner of refuge with the wretched corner Rosicky inhabited during his apprenticeship as a tailor in London. At the end of the story Doctor Burleigh considers how Rosicky no longer resides "on the hill where the red lamplight shone" but rather in a corner graveyard (70). The story concentrates the many abstract virtues of rural life into the concrete propriety of the kitchen—the customary province of women. When examined in its original magazine publication, "Neighbor Rosicky" reveals not a blanket rejection of all things materialistic, but rather a focused endorsement of a material culture based on domestic skills, hospitality, and other traditional feminine arts.

Like many of her contemporaries, Cather published short stories in popular magazines to supplement her income while writing novels. Besides her old employer *McClure's*, her fiction appeared in almost all of the major periodicals of the period, including the *Century, Collier's, Cosmopolitan, McCall's, Saturday Evening Post, Scribner's Magazine,* and the *Smart Set.* But after winning the Pulitzer Prize in 1923, Cather relied less on earnings from periodical appearances, and essentially retired from professional short-story writing. Between World War I and 1932, when her last published story appeared in the *Ladies' Home Journal,* Cather placed only nine short stories in magazines. Of those nine, three—"Uncle Valentine" (1925), "Neighbor Rosicky" (1930), and "Two Friends" (1932)—appeared in the *Woman's Home Companion,* and the last two draw on the author's Nebraska experiences. The *Companion* also serialized Cather's Nebraska-based novel *Lucy Gayheart* in 1935. The magazine was edited by a friend of Cather's, Gertrude Battles Lane, arguably the most powerful female magazine editor of the 1920s and 1930s. Lane personally solicited fiction from Cather. Her papers at the Library of Congress include a letter dated 28 February 1933 from Cather wishing that she had a story for Lane but saying she had been idle since moving into a new apartment in November. Cather reports that she had been in the middle of composing a long story and promises to have it sent to the magazine when she finishes it. In 1936 Cather sent "The Old Beauty" to Lane. The editor wanted to publish the story even though she did not consider it among the author's best work, but because of Lane's reservation about it, Cather asked that the story be returned and not appear in the *Companion.* The author did not publish another short story in her lifetime.

Under Lane's leadership, the *Woman's Home Companion* became one of the leading mass-market magazines—or "slicks"—published between the world wars. In 1930 the periodical had a circulation of 2.5 million, making it the most popular magazine aimed exclusively at women. As suggested by its title, the periodical targeted middle-class homemakers, both urban and rural. Through both its articles and its advertisements it emphasized domesticity by catering to mothers, cooks, and housewives. Less than 10 percent of its 209 advertisements in the April 1930 issue feature beauty or glamour products, but are dominated instead by food products. But the magazine was much more than a homemaker's handbook of recipes and helpful household hints. Through editorials, Lane championed family-oriented social causes, such as the need for child labor laws and European disarmament. In connection with Cather's work, the magazine regularly celebrated the farm wife as possessing "heroic courage" and being the only truly successful "career woman." By her contributions to the family business, the farm wife is the only "professional" woman able to "reconcile a home and career . . . through a desire to give back [her income] into the family treasury rather than to win laurels for herself" (Ward and Glover).

Most literary critics have disparaged the "slicks" of this period as offering substandard, escapist fiction of little artistic merit. To be sure, the popular magazines did publish a large amount of inferior fiction, but their market demanded a large volume. The *Woman's Home Companion* and others published six to eight stories (or novel installments) per month to as wide an audience as possible. Weeklies like the *Saturday Evening Post* produced four times that amount. Rather than decry the amount of dreck popular magazines published, critics might find it remarkable instead how much fiction of high aesthetic value one can find among their slick pages. The *Companion*, like many other popular magazines, published many significant writers, giving them in some cases their largest readerships to date. According to circulation records, in 1930 2.5 million readers of the *Woman's Home Companion* had access to Cather's novella. Besides Cather, the *Woman's Home Companion* regularly published Sherwood Anderson, F. Scott Fitzgerald, DuBose Heyward, Booth Tarkington, and Edith Wharton. Edna Ferber was a particular favorite; the magazine serialized several of her novels. And as "Neighbor Rosicky" demonstrates, the fiction in the *Companion* was not the cast-off hackwork of otherwise good writers.[3]

For the April 1930 issue the *Companion* packaged "Neighbor Rosicky" well. Cather's name was featured prominently on the cover, and the story was placed first in the issue with two large, well-rendered illustrations by Maurice L. Bower. The editors must have known they had something good. Hayden Carruthers wrote each issue's "postscript" in which he provided color commentary on the issue's content. In regard to this issue's lead story he wrote: "A good story, Neighbor Rosicky, by Willa Cather, who has a habit of writing that kind; and the second part is coming in May" (204). He also queried the author on how to pronounce Rosicky: "Miss Cather writes: 'Just as it is spelled, Roz-ic-ky, with the accent on the first syllable.' But how about the sound of the *o;* does the first syllable rhyme with *was* or *froze*? Let's assume it's the former!"

A collation of "Neighbor Rosicky" in the *Woman's Home Companion* and its first book appearance in *Obscure Destinies* (1932), as "Neighbour Rosicky," reveals few changes made to conform with the conservative "family-oriented" editorial policy employed by most of the slicks. (See the Scholarly Edition of *Obscure Destinies.*) Such few as there are, however, are significant.

Unlike such contemporaries as Ernest Hemingway, Cather did not struggle with her editors over vulgar words or coarse subject matter. One exception is the story's reference to alcohol consumption absent from the 1930 magazine version. When Doctor Burleigh visits the Rosicky farm after staying up all night with a neighboring patient, Rosicky "smiled his twinkling smile, put some more coal on the fire, and went into his own room to pour the Doctor a little drink in a medicine glass" (NRa 10). In the *Companion,* Rosicky "smiled his twinkling smile and put some more coal on the fire" (NRb 8). Since the story was being published during Prohibition, the magazine's editors were likely averse to depicting Rosicky committing a crime.

The immigrant Rosickys also appear less foreign in the pages of the *Companion* than in *Obscure Destinies,* partly because the magazine employed standard American spelling. This alteration may appear a superficial change but becomes significant in the case of "neighbor" as the word serves as a title for the story. An intentional British spelling sets off the word "neighbour" as an honorific title for Rosicky the character. Like "Young Goodman Brown," or "Citizen Kane," a seemingly innocuous descriptor like "neighbor" takes on ennobling connotations when emphasized as the title "Neighbour Rosicky."

Mary Rosicky's magazine kitchen is also more generically American than the book version. A comparison of Mary serving her husband lunch illustrates not only Cather's revision process, certainly independent of magazine concerns, but also how she—or her editors—crafted the story for a popular audience.

> *Woman's Home Companion*
> Mary took the twisted cake covered with poppy seeds out of the oven, lightly broke it up with her hands and sat down opposite him. (NRb 9)

> *Obscure Destinies*
> Mary took out of the oven a pan of kolache stuffed with apricots, examined them anxiously to see whether they had got too dry, put them beside his plate, and then sat down opposite him. (NRa 20)

The magazine's "twisted cake" becomes exotic "kolache" that have a danger of becoming "too dry." Cather also amplifies Mary's role in the *Obscure Destinies* version of the passage, rendering her as a dutiful wife-hostess, anxious that her baked goods turn out well.

Ironically, "Neighbour Rosicky" employs product placement, while the "Neighbor Rosicky" of the advertisement-laden *Woman's Home Companion* does not. In the book version, Cather refers to the Rosickys' car as a Ford (7, 33). In the magazine the family drives merely a car. The advertiser index for the April and May issues, in which Cather's story appears, lists only one automobile manufacturer: the Ford Motor Company.

The story's first published critic was a reader, "C.M.V." from Michigan, whose letter to the editor was published in August. She (assuming the writer of the letter was female) describes the story as being

> so pleasantly different from the general run of short stories you have been publishing lately that I have taken fresh courage and have decided to renew my subscription once more if you will promise some more on this order instead of so many of those tiresome, senseless, meaningless yarns we have had the last few months. Perhaps they are more modern and up-to-date, but honestly, I'm not so very old either, that I can't see anything new and modern. . . . please let's not get too far away from good wholesome old-fashioned stories of good honest warm-hearted people,

Fig. 5. Maurice L. Bower's lead illustration for the second installment of "Neighbor Rosicky" (*Woman's Home Companion,* May 1930) emphasizes the magazine's domestic focus.

> stories our children can read without getting all fussed up over false ideals. (130)

What are the "wholesome, old-fashioned" attributes of the story that resonated so much with this reader? In the kitchen-dominated pages of the *Woman's Home Companion,* these virtues are greatly associated with the character of Mary Rosicky. According to the magazine's own standards, she is the ideal homemaker: hardworking, knowledgeable, unassuming, hospitable, bountiful both in body and spirit, and perfectly in sync with her husband. Her kitchen windows shine both literally and figuratively. The story's second installment opens with an illustration of Mary kneeling, placing a pie on the oven, while looking up adoringly at her husband (see fig. 5). The lead illustration for the story's first installment depicts a similar scene of domesticity: Polly—as a Mary-in-training—clearing a supper table while Rosicky looks on

Fig. 6. Rosicky's daughter-in-law Polly performs the duties of a farm wife in the novella's first illustration (April 1930).

from behind (see fig. 6). As Doctor Burleigh notes, Mary was an uncommon woman who "felt physical pleasure" at the sight of good fortune for those she loved. With Mary's first appearance, Cather places great emphasis on the character as a perfect hostess and housekeeper. She moves automatically in the kitchen when the doctor unexpectedly appears, directing her daughter to set another place. Yet Mary is not ostentatious in her hospitality. Cather explains that some country housekeepers would have tried to show off for the doctor, or follow some artificial decorum "to spread a white cloth over the oilcloth, to change the thick cups and plates for their best china, and the wooden handled knives for plated ones" (10). But not Mary. Her good manners are instinctual. By sharing the family's intimate, everyday objects with the doctor, she automatically places the guest at ease.

Despite her humility, Mary does pride herself on her primary duty, providing food, and by extension, sustenance and life. Even on the nights that she bore each of her six children, she never let any doctor get "away from this house without breakfast" (NRa 13). She dreams of sending food out to the doctor's hoped-for wife. Like the pages of the *Woman's Home Companion,* Cather fills her story with food imagery. Characters savor apple and coffee cakes, candy, and kolaches stuffed with apricots. She mentions coffee—Rosicky's favorite drink—eleven times. Meals, both in the story and in the magazine, merit special attention. The word "breakfast" or "breakfasts" occurs seventeen times, "dinner" four, and "supper" thirteen. The word "food" occurs only once (20).

Cather also casts Mary as a rejuvenating figure, as she dispenses an old wife's kitchen wisdom to Doctor Burleigh on how to keep a youthful appearance: "I don't like to see a young man getting grey. I'll tell you something, Ed; you make some strong black tea and keep it handy in a bowl, and every morning just brush it into your hair, an' it'll keep the grey from showin' much. That's the way I do" (NRa 14). Mary could serve as the allegorical figure of bounty with her near supernatural ability to make things grow. Throughout the winter she is uncannily able to keep her geraniums in bloom; this Earth Mother named Mary has a "Jerusalem" cherry tree ready for Christmas "full of berries" (42).

The story's major conflict derives from Rosicky's doubt that his daughter-in-law Polly, a modern American "town girl," will be able to live up to Mary's "old fashioned" ideal and become a good farm wife to his son Rudolph. Otherwise the couple will have to abandon the family homestead and be condemned as "wage-slaves" of the city. The reader is first introduced to the 1920s "modern woman" not through Polly, but rather through Pearl, the dry-goods clerk who waits on Rosicky in the first part of the story. Pearl serves as a thematic precursor for Polly; they have a similarity in names, professions (Polly had been a clerk before her marriage), and dress. Both women sport the modern fashions of bobbed hair and painted eyebrows. Cather presents Pearl as a stylish but ultimately unsavory example of the Jazz Age's "flaming youth," a girl "fussed up over false ideals." While Rosicky buys "candy fur de women" Pearl tartly retorts, "As usual. I never did see a man buy so much candy for his wife. First thing you know, she'll be getting too fat" (NRa 16). When he explains that he doesn't care for the current style of "trim women," she calls him "Mr. Bo-Hunk," sniffs, and snobbily elevates "her India-ink strokes" (17).

Each month the *Woman's Home Companion* ran a beauty column by

Hazel Rawson Cades titled "Good Looks" in which it offered advice on proper dress and makeup techniques. By the late 1920s it was no longer opposed to all "bobbed" or short hair as many publications were when the style first began a decade earlier. But in September 1928 the magazine advised, "If your hair is bobbed, no matter what your age, never let the barber cut it off in the back in a harsh, artificial line, straight, curved or pointed. And don't let him cut it too high or thin it too much at the lower edges. It's much better style to have the hair too long than too short, and too ragged than pruned too much" ("Long or Short, Everybody Likes Nice Hair" 87). The "Good Looks" column expressed a similar opinion on eyebrows, urging women in October 1928 not to "trim them too much"; brushed eyebrows "look much more natural than if you just paint them on" ("Look at Her Eyes" 119). In the magazine's "Neighbor Rosicky" Pearl's eyebrows are "shaved," a much harsher description than Cather's later revision of "plucked" made for *Obscure Destinies.* The *Companion* disparaged any look that made a woman look artificial, and thereby deceptive, making "Miss Pearl," in the magazine's opinion, a "fashion don't." She represents the deceitful, big-city ways of town girls, an attitude and philosophy that Polly Rosicky must reject.

In order to ensure a "happy ending" for the story—a near prerequisite for magazine fiction—Polly, whom Cather describes three times as an "American girl," must successfully adapt to farm life, thereby securing the next generation's happiness. Cather introduces Polly as wearing the same fashion uniform as her town counterparts: "She was a trim, slim little thing, with blue eyes and shingled yellow hair, and her eyebrows were reduced to a mere brush-stroke, like Miss Pearl's" (NRa 35). But the reader quickly realizes that she bears only a superficial resemblance to the caustic Pearl. Polly (with a much plainer name than the glamorous-sounding "Pearl") seems polite and hardworking, albeit overwhelmed with her new rural environment. She transforms into a good farm wife through the direct involvement and kindness of her father-in-law, Rosicky. Unlike the stereotype of a spare and stoic farmer, Rosicky insists that Polly and her husband Rudolph go into town for some simple luxuries of ice cream and a picture show. Rosicky's recollection of his harsh Dickensian London Christmas is told expressly in English for Polly's benefit. In his story Rosicky becomes a provider of food for his poor English landlady, a well-meaning but failed homemaker. Affected by his story, Polly resolves to be a hostess for New Year's Eve. Cather signals her positive change through the domestic acts of hospitality and propriety. Polly plans to provide supper for the entire family and promises her husband to "not let your mother help at all; make her company for once" (57).

Polly completes her evolution during Rosicky's heart attack, which she witnesses from her kitchen. Polly, first described as a "trim, slim little thing" (35), rushes to her father-in-law's side "with the swiftness of a slim greyhound" (63). Cather has translated the stylish, frivolous "slimness" to a strong and sleek natural one. During Rosicky's near-fatal attack Polly exhibits the calm demeanor and concern of a good nurse, another requirement for the ideal homemaker. Her metamorphosis becomes complete when Rosicky correctly guesses that she is pregnant. At first "she frowned with her funny streaks of eyebrows, and then smiled back at him" (65). The natural impulse of her smile breaks through the artificial—and deceitful—mask of her face paint. In a magazine filled with advertisements for baby food, articles on child rearing, and editorials fighting to lower the infant mortality rate, Polly secures the story's happy ending by proving fertile.

In other magazines of the period, the story of a successful young woman often depicted a naive and artless country girl who moves to the big city and succeeds through sophistication and glamour. But in the *Woman's Home Companion* Cather does the opposite. Polly evolves from a shallow and artificial "town girl" to a skillful, bountiful, and courageous rural woman. "Neighbor Rosicky" not only appeared in an instrument of material culture—a woman's magazine that targeted middle-class female consumers—but is also about material culture itself in its positive evaluation of the domestic and culinary arts. The story could serve as an editorial for the magazine in its presentation of these womanly skills as offering an emotional salvation for its characters. In his final moments Rosicky reflects on Polly's conversion: "He was thinking, indeed, about Polly, and how he might never have known what a tender heart she had if he hadn't got sick over there. Girls nowadays didn't wear their heart on their sleeve. But now he knew Polly would make a fine woman after the foolishness wore off. Either a woman had that sweetness at her heart or she hadn't. You couldn't always tell by the look of them; but if they had that, everything came out right in the end" (NRa 68–69). In this kitchen-based story filled with references to food and eating, Cather skillfully uses "sweetness," a gustatory or taste image, to describe the inner beauty and heroism of every good housekeeper.

Notes

1. Unless otherwise noted all page references for "Neighbour Rosicky" are from its first book appearance in *Obscure Destinies,* 1932; paperback reprint, Vintage Books, 1974.

2. Beginning in the early 1920s, Cather adopted the British spellings for such words as "colour," "splendour," "plough," and "grey"; she maintained this preference for the rest of her career.

3. Among the classic American short stories that first appeared in popular magazines are F. Scott Fitzgerald's "The Rich Boy" (*The Red Book Magazine,* Jan. and Feb. 1926) and "Babylon Revisited" (*The Saturday Evening Post,* 21 Feb. 1931); and Ernest Hemingway's "The Short Happy Life of Francis Macomber" (*Cosmopolitan,* Sept. 1936).

Appendix: Selected Thematic Concordance for "Neighbour Rosicky"

Each word under consideration is followed in parentheses by the number of times it appears in the story and is then shown in context for each appearance. Page and line number references are given for each extract, with the references based upon the story's publication in *Obscure Destinies* (New York: Knopf, 1932).

ACRES (2)
49.5: said. 'Ain't we got forty *acres*?' " 'We ain't got an ear,'
70.23: He thought of city cemeteries; *acres* of shrubbery and heavy stone,

ALFALFA (3)
46.17: days when we didn't have *alfalfa* yet,—I guess it
62.7: would root and "take the *alfalfa*." Rudolph said that was nonsense.
62.11: great store by that big *alfalfa* field. It was a feed

AMERICA (2)
29.7: and buy wood from South *America* and the East from the
43.1: the cousin had gone to *America*. Anton tramped the streets for

AMERICAN (3)
7.3: afraid Mary mightn't like an *American* daughter-in-law, but it seems to
34.22: so easy to stop. An *American* girl don't git used to
39.19: tick. Generally speaking, marrying an *American* girl was certainly a risk.

ANIMALS (2)
32.2: the earth and the farm *animals* and growing things which are
67.10: sure, in the way that *animals* are. Polly remembered that hour

APPETITE (1)
51.18: I always had a good *appetite,* like you all know, an'

APPLE-CAKE (1)
34.11: father took another piece of *apple-cake* and went on: "Maybe next

APRICOTS (1)
20.14: pan of kolache stuffed with *apricots,* examined them anxiously to see

BANK (3)
15.10: and put it into the *bank,* too.[section break] When Rosicky left
25.9: than put money into the *bank.*" The agent shrugged and turned
40.1: one was book-keeper in the *bank,* one taught music, and Polly

BARN (8)
5.20: and do chores about the *barn,* but you can't do anything
9.13: had come back from the *barn* and were washing up for
35.20: Mr. Rosicky. Rudolph's at the *barn,* I guess." She never called
61.12: and slip down to the *barn* and give his work-horses a
62.21: a work-team idle in his *barn,* Rosicky went over to his
63.7: the horses back to the *barn.* He got them into the
63.8: He got them into the *barn* and to their stalls, but
65.12: like dis. Down at de *barn* I say to myself, dat

BARNYARD (1)
19.4: The snow, falling over his *barnyard* and the graveyard, seemed to

BASEMENT (1)
43.10: repair shop in a Cheapside *basement,* underneath a cobbler. He didn't

BEASTS (1)
19.19: for vegetation and men and *beasts,* for the ground itself; a

BED (6)
53.18: heart. I set on my *bed* wid dat platter on my
55.19: an' lay down on my *bed,* an' I ain't waken up
63.24: of was lying on Polly's *bed,* and [page break] Polly bending over him
68.3: is he now?" "On the *bed.* He's asleep. I was terribly
68.7: home and put him to *bed,* though he protested that he
69.13: try to get to his *bed* if he could. He rose

BEDDING (1)
29.1: They bought [page break] good beds and *bedding* and had their pick of

BEDROOM (2)
38.8: an' dress yourself up." The *bedroom* door closed behind her, and
43.20: three rooms; a kitchen, a *bedroom,* where Lifschnitz and his wife

BEDS (1)
29.1: the loft. They bought [page break] good *beds* and bedding and had their

BEER (2)
27.19: and a little went for *beer,* a little for tobacco; a
28.4: after the performance they had *beer* and maybe some oysters somewhere.

BERRIES (1)
42.11: Jerusalem cherry trees, full of *berries.* It was the first year

BILLOWY (1)
70.16: The moonlight silvered the long, *billowy* grass that grew over the

BITE (1)
52.24: will eat chust one little *bite* of dat goose, so I

BITING (1)
42.4: no snow, but a bitter, *biting* wind that whistled and sang

BITTER (4)
42.3: cold; no snow, but a *bitter,* biting wind that whistled and
56.22: across the fields with the *bitter* wind at their backs, his
57.13: no rain. March was as *bitter* as February. On those days
61.7: a cent from anyone in *bitter* need,—never had to

BITTERLY (1)
57.11: badly for farmers. It was *bitterly* cold, and after the first

BLACK (4)
14.18: Ed; you make some strong *black* tea and keep it handy
64.4: kept the tea-kettle and the *black* pot going. She put these
64.10: out of his jaws, the *black* circles round his eyes disappeared,
70.18: few little evergreens stood out *black* in it, like shadows in

BLOOD (1)
23.13: looked firm and full of *blood.* His cheeks had a good

BLOOM (1)
42.10: a big red geranium in *bloom* for Christmas, and a row

BLOOMING (1)
14.1: geraniums to keep them *blooming* all winter, Mary? I never

BLOSSOMS (1)
30.7: Trinity churchyard put out its *blossoms,* he was tormented by a

BLUE (6)
20.7: oilcloth figured with clusters of *blue* grapes, a place was set,
23.1: his cup, [page break] he ran his *blue* handkerchief over his lips. When
35.15: trim, slim little thing, with *blue* eyes and shingled yellow hair,
61.17: The spring came warm, with *blue* skies,—but dry, dry
64.8: was drawn up stiff and *blue,* with the sweat pouring off
70.19: pool. The sky was very *blue* and soft, the stars rather

BLUE-GREEN (1)
62.18: in fields of that strong *blue-green* colour. One morning, when

BOUGHT (3)
17.14: not so productive. When he *bought* his land, he hadn't the
28.25: corner of the loft. They *bought* [page break] good beds and bedding
55.18: asleep. I pile all I *bought* on de kitchen table, an'

BREAD (3)
14.15: a nice loaf of nut *bread,* if you only had one.
50.11: or a loaf of fresh *bread,* Polly seemed to regard them
51.24: us nothin' but a little *bread* an' [page break] drippin' for supper,

BREAKFAST (15)
8.17: had had such a good *breakfast* at Rosicky's, and that when
9.4: attended to, Burleigh refused any *breakfast* in that slovenly house, and
9.14: and were washing up for *breakfast.* The long table, covered with
11.7: Marshall till you eat some *breakfast.* My wife, she's terrible fur
12.16: able to get a decent *breakfast*! I don't know what's the
12.20: "if Doctor Ed had got *breakfast* there, we wouldn't have him
13.2: in the cold without his *breakfast.*" "I wish I'd been in
13.11: away from this house without *breakfast.* No doctor ever did. I'd
13.17: that!" "Father, did you get *breakfast* for the doctor when we
13.19: used to bring me my *breakfast,* too, mighty nice. I was
14.9: worried about you. Settin' at *breakfast,* I looked at you real
33.13: they were talking at the *breakfast* table about starting early that
55.24: She ain't stop fur no *breakfast;* she git de Christmas
68.10: dressed and sat down to *breakfast* with his family. He told
68.14: when he got home. After *breakfast* he sat down by his

BREAKFASTS (2)
13.6: heads. "I missed some good *breakfasts* by not being." The boys
19.21: long nights for sleep, leisurely *breakfasts,* peace by the fire. This

BRIGHT (3)
9.15: long table, covered with a *bright* oilcloth, was set out with

37.9: elbows, the old man's funny *bright* eyes, made Polly want to
41.19: but the sleeping fields and *bright* stars and the noble darkness

BROOMS (1)
41.14: a court full of old *brooms* and mops and ash-cans.

BROWN (8)
4.16: like a sick man. His *brown* face was creased but not
4.18: his lips, under his long *brown* moustache. His hair was thin
8.10: hold out such a warm *brown* hand when he said good-bye.
21.7: little rolls in his broad *brown* fingers. The thickened nail of
23.11: was burned a dark reddish *brown,* and there were deep creases
61.22: blew up in clouds of *brown* dust that hid the horses
66.19: holding his warm, broad, flexible *brown* hand. She had never seen
67.6: lump; it was a warm *brown* human hand, with some cleverness

BUSINESS (3)
20.21: the right language for transacting *business:* "Now what did Doctor Ed
27.12: time. He minded his own *business* and envied nobody's good fortune.
56.10: rich man, in de importing *business,* an' dey been travelling togedder.

BUY (10)
16.5: about every other week you *buy* ticking, Mr. Rosicky, and always
16.20: never did see a man *buy* so much candy for his
17.14: he hadn't the money to *buy* on High Prairie; so he
24.22: saving. They saw their neighbours *buy* more land and feed more
29.6: down to the docks and *buy* wood from South America and
32.19: save a little money to *buy* his liberty. When he was
39.1: hurried [page break] whisper: "You go an' *buy* dat girl some ice cream
53.20: dat poor woman save to *buy* dat goose, and how she
55.3: give me money enough to *buy* a goose!' "Dey laugh, of
55.14: open. I go dere an' *buy* a big goose an' some

CAKES (2)
55.6: give me hot coffee and *cakes,* an' make me tell all
55.15: an' potatoes and onions, an' *cakes* an' oranges fur de children,

CANDY (4)
16.19: nine, and put in some *candy* fur de women." "As usual.
16.21: a man buy so much *candy* for his wife. First thing
33.22: knife or a box of *candy* pleased the older ones as
39.2: girl some ice cream an' *candy* tonight, like you was courtin'.

CAR (15)
7.14: comes. In town in the *car*?" Doctor Burleigh rose. "No, I'm
9.6: was too deep for a *car*—eight miles to Anton
33.18: to let me have de *car* tonight. Maybe some of you
34.4: I want to take de *car* down to Rudolph's, and let
34.8: an' he can't afford no *car* yet." That settled it. The
34.14: Rudolph going to have the *car* every Saturday night?" Rosicky did
34.24: Rudolph can have the *car* every Saturday night [page break] till
35.11: That evening Rosicky drove the *car* the half-mile down to Rudolph's
36.6: tonight, an' I brought de *car* over fur you two to
38.10: anxious. He had seen the *car* and was sorry any of
38.17: warning finger. "I brought de *car* over fur you an' Polly
38.21: don't the boys want the *car*, Father?" "Not tonight dey don't."
62.20: gone to town in the *car*, leaving a work-team idle in
67.18: heard Rudolph coming in the *car*, she ran out to meet
70.6: the moonlight. He stopped his *car*, shut off the engine, and

CARROTS (1)
20.4: with her apron full of *carrots*. They went into the house

CARS (1)
7.17: Ford. I ain't much for *cars*, noway." "Well, it's a good

CATTLE (1)
71.10: in the cornfield, Rosicky's own *cattle* would be eating fodder as

CENT (1)
61.7: never had to take a *cent* from anyone in bitter need,

CHRISTMAS (12)
33.15: or so to see the *Christmas* things in the stores before

42.2: On the day before *Christmas* the weather set in very
42.10: red geranium in bloom for *Christmas,* and a row of Jerusalem
51.7: in London? I had one *Christmas* dere I ain't never forgot.
51.8: Times was awful bad before *Christmas;* de boss ain't got much
51.2: lawful fur me! "Day before *Christmas* was terrible foggy dat year,
52.3: us a good dinner on *Christmas* Day. After supper de boss
52.5: streets to listen to de *Christmas* singers. Dey sing old songs
54.4: her after I spoil de *Christmas.* So I put on my
55.25: no breakfast; she git de *Christmas* [page break] dinner ready dat
56.17: woman, and fur dat fine *Christmas* dinner you give us all.'
57.12: the first light snows before *Christmas* there was no snow at

CITIES (7)
31.3: was the trouble with big *cities;* they built you in from
37.20: reproach in it. "Dem big *cities* is all right fur de
59.24: like the treacherous people in *cities* who live by grinding or
60.5: of the world in big *cities.* Here, if you were sick,
71.1: anything in the living world. *Cities* of the dead, indeed; cities
71.2: Cities of the dead, indeed; *cities* of the forgotten, of the
71.14: do the work of great *cities* and had always longed for

CITY (8)
24.16: his skull. He was a *city* man, a gentle man, and
28.10: York the finest, richest, friendliest *city* in the world. Moreover, he
37.13: "You always lived in the *city* when you were young, didn't
51.10: bein' poor in a big *city* like London, I'll say! All
54.5: and go out into de *city.* I tell myself I better
59.14: off yours. But in the *city,* all the foulness and misery
60.12: likely to do in the *city.* If he'd had a mean
70.23: beautiful graveyard. He thought of *city* cemeteries; acres of shrubbery and

CITY-BRED (2)
22.6: or spoke roughly. He was *city-bred,* and she was country-bred; she
23.24: and he was gentle,—*city-bred,* [page break] as she always said.

CLEAN (7)
23.9: right. But his neck, always « *clean* » shaved except in the busiest

38.20: You go put on a « *clean* » shirt, quick!" "But don't the
39.9: young people came out, looking « *clean* » and a little stiff. Rosicky
44.15: of there, never get a « *clean* » shirt to his back again.
45.15: an' plenty water to keep « *clean.* » When you got them, you
48.12: in the water, he put « *clean* » clothes on you and a
48.13: clothes on you and a « *clean* » shirt on himself, an' by

CLOTHES (10)
26.11: a woman patching at his *clothes,* or at the boys'. He
26.24: nearly always hungry, when his *clothes* were [page break] dropping off him
29.11: convenience, and Rosicky kept their *clothes* in order. At night and
43.17: the customers called for their *clothes* themselves, and the coppers that
44.16: do, he wondered, when his *clothes* actually dropped to pieces and
47.17: windmill an' took off your *clothes* an' put you in. Them
47.19: took off all his own *clothes,* an' got in with you.
48.2: and you three with no *clothes* on. I was in the
48.6: father couldn't git to his *clothes;* they was all hangin' up
48.12: the water, he put clean *clothes* on you and a clean

COAL (3)
10.22: twinkling smile, put some more *coal* on the fire, and went
39.13: the kitchen. He put some *coal* in the stove and shut
64.3: She stopped only to throw *coal* into the stove, and she

COAT (2)
9.24: him off with his fur *coat* and hung it up, and
42.7: sat inside, making over a *coat* that Albert had outgrown into

COBBLER (1)
43.10: a Cheapside basement, underneath a *cobbler.* He didn't much need an

COFFEE (11)
5.14: me not to drink my *coffee* no more." "I wouldn't, in
5.17: separate a Bohemian from his *coffee* or his pipe. I've quit
9.10: welcome, and such good strong *coffee* with rich cream. No wonder
9.11: want to give up his *coffee*! He had driven in just
9.17: full of the smell of *coffee* and hot biscuit and sausage.

11.12: anything herself. She drank her *coffee* and sat taking in everything
20.13: in his chair, stirring his *coffee* in a big cup, Mary
20.19: wasn't going to have any *coffee*. She replied in English, as
22.20: hung up." Rosicky drank his *coffee* from time to time, while
55.6: restaurant and give me hot *coffee* and cakes, an' make me
68.11: He told Mary that his *coffee* tasted better than usual to

COFFEE-CAKE (2)
20.8: set, and he smelled hot *coffee-cake* of some kind. Anton never
50.10: When his mother sent over *coffee-cake* or prune tarts or a

COLOUR (7)
4.17: wrinkled, he had a ruddy *colour* in his smooth-shaven cheeks and
23.13: His cheeks had a good *colour*. On either side of his
25.8: milk. I'd rather put some *colour* into my children's faces than
62.18: fields of that strong blue-green *colour*. One morning, when Rudolph had
64.12: a little of his natural *colour* came back. When his daughter-in-law
66.14: music or an eye for *colour*. It was quiet, unobtrusive; it
67.3: quicksilver, flexible, muscular, about the *colour* of a pale cigar, with

COOK (2)
53.11: I had your mudder to *cook* fur me." "Go on and
53.21: she get some neighbour to *cook* it dat got more fire,

CORN (10)
5.23: of breath." "How about shelling *corn*?" "Of course not!" [page break] Rosicky
46.15: Fourth of July? All the *corn* an' the gardens. An' that
46.19: your father was out cultivatin' *corn*, and I was here in
49.2: on the gardens an' the *corn*. "'Corn,' he says, 'there ain't
49.3: the gardens an' the corn. "'*Corn*,' he says, 'there ain't no
49.3: he says, 'there ain't no *corn*.' "'What you talkin' about?" I
49.7: ain't got none. All the *corn* in this country was cooked
57.20: planted over again, planted in *corn*. It had happened before, but
61.20: to plant them over in *corn*. Rosicky would stand at the
62.9: were working so hard planting *corn*, their father felt he couldn't

CORNER (10)
26.6: This spot was called "Father's *corner,*" though it was not a
26.6: though it was not a *corner* at all. He had a
28.24: have a sleeping-room in one *corner* of the loft. They bought
44.2: wrap himself in. The other *corner* was rented to a wretched,
52.10: belly. "I went into my *corner* real quiet, and roll up
52.18: little wooden box in my *corner* fur a stool, 'cause I
53.22: she put it in my *corner* to keep it away from
53.24: hung up to shut my *corner* off, an' de children wasn't
54.2: she put it in my *corner* because she trust me more'n
61.21: would stand at the fence *corner* and watch them, and the

CORNERS (1)
43.23: slept, and a living-room. Two *corners* of this living-room were curtained

CORNFIELD (2)
18.6: snow was falling over the *cornfield* and the pasture and the
71.9: and over yonder, in the *cornfield,* Rosicky's own cattle would be

CORNSTALKS (2)
18.4: the rows of pale gold *cornstalks* stood out against the white
18.21: home. Over there across the *cornstalks* his own roof and windmill

CORN-SHELLER (1)
22.2: pitch hay or run de *corn-sheller.*" Mary wanted to jump up,

COUNTRY (15)
8.12: a poor boy in the *country* before he went away to
10.9: he belonged to her. Some *country* housekeepers would have stopped to
11.14: when he was a poor *country* boy, and was boastfully proud
17.8: a wonderfully rich stretch of *country,* the finest farms in the
19.15: graciously over so much open *country.* On his cap and shoulders,
31.18: parents had lived in the *country,* but they rented their farm
31.23: he was sent into the *country* to her parents. He stayed
32.9: desire to return to the *country* never left him. To work
35.5: is used to more than *country* girls. I lay awake nights,
45.11: be hard times in this *country.*" Rosicky filled his pipe. "You

49.8: All the corn in this *country* was cooked by three o'clock
57.15: the wind fairly punished the *country*, Rosicky sat by his window.
59.12: and rapacious woman. In the *country*, if you had a mean
59.22: sure, even in their own *country* town here. But they weren't
71.15: always longed for the open *country* and had got to it

COUNTRY-BRED (1)
22.6: was city-bred, and she was *country-bred;* she often said she wanted

CREAM (4)
9.10: good strong coffee with rich *cream.* No wonder the old chap
25.2: them to sell him their *cream,* he told them how much
25.4: neighbours, had made on their *cream* last year. "Yes," said Mary,
39.2: buy dat girl some ice *cream* an' candy tonight, like you

CROP (3)
39.6: him. There had been a *crop* failure all over the county.
49.10: mean you won't get no *crop* at all?' I asked him.
49.13: he'd worked so hard. "'No *crop* this year,' he says. 'That's

DINNER (4)
27.18: self-indulgent. He liked a good *dinner,* and a little went for
52.2: to give us a good *dinner* on Christmas Day. After supper
56.1: she git de Christmas [page break] *dinner* ready dat morning, and we
56.18: and fur dat fine Christmas *dinner* you give us all.' An'

DISHES (6)
9.15: oilcloth, was set out with *dishes* waiting for them, and the
35.14: dress, clearing away the supper *dishes.* She was a trim, slim
36.8: de picture show." Polly, carrying *dishes* to the sink, looked over
36.16: Polly, an' I'll wash de *dishes* an' leave everything nice fur
38.14: in a kitchen apron, carrying *dishes* to the sink. He flushed
39.11: his own time with the *dishes.* He scoured the pots and

DRANK (3)
11.12: to eat anything herself. She *drank* her coffee and sat taking

22.20: dere clo'es hung up." Rosicky *drank* his coffee from time to
30.8: away. That was why he *drank* too much; to get a

FARM (13)
5.19: you've got to cut out *farm* work. You can feed the
8.20: Marshall's,—a big rich *farm* where there was plenty of
8.22: a great deal of expensive *farm* machinery of the newest model,
24.18: he had married a rough *farm* girl, he had never touched
31.13: go out there as a *farm* hand; it was hardly possible
31.19: country, but they rented their *farm* and had a hard time
32.2: with the earth and the *farm* animals and growing things which
32.10: To work on another man's *farm* would be all he asked;
35.7: make Rudolph discontented with the *farm*." The boys put as good
40.13: that Rudy would quit the *farm* and take a factory job
58.18: to work hard on the *farm*, and probably they would never
60.11: they could do on the *farm* was better than the best
70.2: summer he started for the *farm*. His mind was on other

FARM-HOUSE (1)
9.8: place. He didn't know another *farm-house* where a man could get

FARM-IMPLEMENT (1)
15.13: office he went into the *farm-implement* store to light his pipe

FARMER (4)
4.10: it for you." The old *farmer* looked up at the Doctor
5.9: and frowned at the old *farmer*. "I think if I were
44.19: still early when the old *farmer* put aside his sewing and
66.23:—very strange in a *farmer*. Nearly all the farmers she

FARMER'S (1)
34.20: town girl to be a *farmer's* wife. I don't want no

FARMERS (2)
57.10: winter turned out badly for *farmers*. It was bitterly cold, and
66.23: a farmer. Nearly all the *farmers* she knew had huge lumps

FARMING (2)
31.12: papers, describing prosperous Czech *farming* communities in the West. He
45.21: Father, or I'll quit this *farming* gamble. I can always make

FARMS (2)
17.9: stretch of country, the finest *farms* in the county. He admired
17.18: enjoyed looking at these fine *farms,* as he enjoyed looking at

FOOD (1)
20.10: anyhow he didn't like the *food.* So Mary always had something

FORTUNE (3)
11.20: personal exultation in any good *fortune* that came to them. Burleigh
27.13: business and envied nobody's good *fortune.* He went to night school
32.23: Omaha delegates to try his *fortune* in another part of the

FREEDOM (1)
30.9: get a temporary illusion of *freedom* and wide horizons. Rosicky, the

GRASS (6)
18.9: all overgrown with long red *grass.* The fine snow, settling into
18.10: snow, settling into this red *grass* and upon the few little
18.16: lie down in the long *grass* and see the complete arch
30.5: knew something did. When the *grass* turned green in Park Place,
70.16: moonlight silvered the long, billowy *grass* that grew over the graves
71.4: this little square of long *grass* which the wind for ever

GRAVES (1)
70.17: grass that grew over the *graves* and hid the fence; the

GRAVEYARD (7)
17.21: miles, he came to the *graveyard,* which lay just at the
18.8: a nice dry snow. The *graveyard* had only a light wire
18.13: pretty. It was a nice *graveyard,* Rosicky reflected, sort of snug
19.4: over his barnyard and the *graveyard,* seemed to draw things together
19.6: all old neighbours in the *graveyard,* most of them friends; there

70.3: his road ran by the *graveyard* did he realize that Rosicky
70.22: this was really a beautiful *graveyard*. He thought of city cemeteries;

HAND (13)
8.10: out such a warm brown *hand* when he said good-bye. Doctor
23.3: with the back of his *hand*. Mary sat watching him intently,
31.13: out there as a farm *hand;* it was hardly possible that
37.16: turned round to him, her *hand* fell naturally into his, and
45.18: and shut his big right *hand,* and dropped it clenched upon
61.4: for repair work from the *hand* of a hungry child who
61.13: eat it out of his *hand* in their slobbery fashion. It
65.16: or somet'ing." Polly took his *hand*. He was looking at her
66.1: the first to know." [page break] His *hand* pressed hers. She noticed that
66.19: his warm, broad, flexible brown *hand*. She had never seen another
66.21: wasn't a kind of gypsy *hand,* it was so alive and
67.6: was a warm brown human *hand,* with some cleverness in it,
67.15: anything as from old Rosicky's *hand*. It brought her to herself;

HANDS (6)
21.15: from her temples with both *hands* as if she were a
28.20: of furniture left on his *hands*. One of the young workmen
46.2: pantry and was wiping her *hands* on the roller towel, thought
51.17: meet on me, an' my *hands* was chapped raw. But I
66.17: You felt it in his *hands,* too. After he dropped off
68.18: better than his, and her *hands* steadier. He lit his pipe

HEART (16)
3.3: Rosicky he had a bad *heart,* Rosicky protested. "So? No, I
3.4: "So? No, I guess my *heart* was always pretty good. I
4.3: to me for? It's your *heart* that makes you short of
5.6: no pills fur a bad *heart,* Doctor Ed. I guess the
6.2: brows. "I can't make my *heart* go no longer'n it wants
8.7: tales about some other man's *heart,* some old man who didn't
21.12: a little older, and my *heart* ain't so good like it
21.20: something the matter with your *heart*? Doctor Ed says so?" "Now
21.24: anything de matter wid my *heart,* only it ain't so young

53.17: but very bad in de *heart.* I set on my bed
56.23: wind at their backs, his *heart* leaped for joy when she
60.18: to anyone who touched his *heart.* What Rosicky really hoped for
65.6: impulsively. "It just broke my *heart* to see you suffer so,
68.24: have known what a tender *heart* she had if he hadn't
69.2: Girls nowadays didn't wear their *heart* on their sleeve. But now
69.5: had that sweetness at her *heart* or she hadn't. You couldn't

HOME (22)
4.8: You've got five boys at *home* to do it for you."
7.13: and you'd better be getting *home* before it comes. In town
12.4: (he was still living at *home* then), said: "The last time
12.9: about that when he come *home,* and I said it wasn't
18.20: And it was so near *home.* Over there across the cornstalks
20.1: drove on. [page break] When he reached *home,* John, the youngest boy, ran
20.11: for him when he got *home.* After he was settled in
28.13: what he called a happy *home* life. Very near the tailor
32.22: the tailor shop and went *home* with the Omaha delegates to
39.15: for them when they got *home* late at night. Then he
41.4: out his pipe and walked *home* across the fields. Ahead of
41.8: working on machines, all coming *home* tired and sullen to eat
43.15: you when you took work *home* to a customer. But most
52.8: t'ink maybe if I go *home,* I can sleep till morning
54.22: de Austrians, but like de *home* folks talk it. "I guess
55.17: could carry! When I git *home,* everybody is still asleep. I
56.13: passage when dey was goin' *home* soon on a boat. My
56.21: arm in arm, were running *home* across the fields with the
62.2: alfalfa-field that lay between the *home* place and Rudolph's came up
68.7: That afternoon they took Rosicky *home* and put him to bed,
68.13: Doctor Ed when he got *home.* After breakfast he sat down
69.21: few weeks after he got *home* he was hard driven. Every

HOMELIKE (1)
18.14: reflected, sort of snug and *homelike,* not cramped or mournful,—

HORSE (3)
9.23: One ran to put his *horse* away, another helped him off

13.23: boys were getting the Doctor's *horse*, he went to the window
47.16: father took you to the *horse* tank down by the windmill

HORSEHAIR (1)
43.25: Rosicky slept on an old *horsehair* [page break] sofa, with a feather

HORSES (7)
17.22: hay-land. There he stopped his *horses* and sat still on his
19.16: cap and shoulders, on the *horses'* backs and manes, light, delicate,
19.24: was coming, clucked to his *horses*, and drove on. [page break] When he
61.23: brown dust that hid the *horses* and the sulky plough and
62.22: his son's place, put the *horses* to the buggy-rake, and set
63.7: he had better get the *horses* back to the barn. He
71.7: they met that sky. The *horses* worked here in summer; the

HOUSE (18)
6.6: off it. Sit around the *house* and help Mary. If I
6.8: want to stay around the *house*." His patient chuckled. "It ain't
9.5: any breakfast in that slovenly *house*, and drove his buggy—
13.11: have got away from this *house* without breakfast. No doctor ever
13.24: the window to examine the *house* plants. "What do you do
14.2: Mary? I never pass this *house* that from the road I
16.12: lots of pillows at your *house*." "Sure. She makes quilts of
18.1: he could see [page break] his own *house*, crouching low, with the clump
20.5: carrots. They went into the *house* together. On the table, covered
22.15: like, an' stay round de *house* dis winter. I guess you
26.1: winter he stayed in the *house* in the afternoons and carpentered,
29.9: were as foolish about their *house* as a bridal pair. Zichec,
35.12: to Rudolph's new, bare little *house*. Polly was in a short-sleeved
45.22: roading, or at the packing *house*, and be sure of my
63.11: off. He started for the *house*, bending lower with every step.
63.20: We can get to the *house* all right." Somehow they did,
67.23: could hardly get to the *house*. He suffered so I was
68.6: and they went into the *house*. That afternoon they took Rosicky

HOUSEKEEPERS (1)
10.9: belonged to her. Some country *housekeepers* would have stopped to spread

HOUSEWIVES (1)

28.17: order, for the rich German *housewives* up-town. The top floor of

HOUSEWORK (1)

40.9: her sisters. She didn't dislike *housework,* but she disliked so much

HUNGER (1)

11.23: was like that. When his *hunger* was satisfied, he did, of

HUNGERED (1)

58.16: why it was he so *hungered* to feel sure they would

HUNGRY (10)

10.6: chickens, the calves, her big *hungry* boys. It was a rare
13.20: nice. I was always awful *hungry!*" Mary admitted with a guilty
26.24: when he was nearly always *hungry,* when his clothes were
28.7: him completely. He was never *hungry* or cold or dirty, and
44.12: of dripping to the two *hungry,* sad-eyed boys who lodged with
52.7: ways, till I got awful *hungry.* I t'ink maybe if I
53.9: don't want him to be *hungry!*" "Da's long ago, child. I
53.11: child. I ain't never been *hungry* since I had your mudder
53.23: keep it away from dem *hungry* children. Dey was a old
61.4: from the hand of a *hungry* child who let it go

JACKET (3)

8.2: plush cap and his corduroy *jacket* with a sheepskin collar, and
51.16: no overcoat, chust a short *jacket* I'd outgrowed so it wouldn't
61.11: put on his cap and *jacket* and slip down to the

JACKETS (1)

26.13: patched all the overalls and *jackets* and work shirts. Occasionally he

KITCHEN (17)

6.11: old man hanging round the *kitchen* too much. An' my wife,
9.16: for them, and the warm *kitchen* was full of the smell
36.22: on a nail behind the *kitchen* door. He slipped it over
37.2: room. "I washed up de *kitchen* many times for my wife,

38.14: saw his father in a *kitchen* apron, carrying dishes to the
39.12: the milk and swept the *kitchen.* He put some coal in
41.5: the lamplight shone from his *kitchen* windows. Suppose he were still
41.9: to eat supper in a *kitchen* that was a parlour also;
41.17: before he went inside. That *kitchen* with the shining windows was
42.6: going on in the Rosicky *kitchen* all day, and Rosicky sat
43.20: upstairs in three rooms; a *kitchen,* a bedroom, where Lifschnitz and
45.3: they sat round in the *kitchen,* and the younger boys were
46.20: I was here in the *kitchen* makin' plum preserves. We had
46.22: it's always hot in the *kitchen* when you're preservin', an' I
48.3: on. I was in the *kitchen* door, an' I had to
55.18: all I bought on de *kitchen* table, an' go in an'
55.21: she come out into her *kitchen.* My goodness, but she was

LAMPLIGHT (2)
41.5: fields. Ahead of him the *lamplight* shone from his kitchen windows.
70.5: the hill where the red *lamplight* shone, but here, in the

LAND (11)
7.2: out for himself, on rented *land.* "And how's Polly? I was
17.14: productive. When he bought his *land,* he hadn't the money to
17.16: they grumbled, that if their *land* hadn't some clay in it,
24.23: saw their neighbours buy more *land* and feed more stock than
31.15: that he could ever have *land* of his own. His people
31.20: family had ever owned any *land,*—that belonged to a
42.5: and sang over the flat *land* and lashed one's face like
57.18: in the ground. All that *land* would have to be ploughed
58.17: be here, working this very *land,* after he was gone. They
58.21: as staying here on the *land,* he wouldn't have to fear
59.13: you could keep off his *land* and make him keep off

LANDED (1)
27.5: He was twenty when he *landed* at Castle Garden in New

LANDLESS (1)
40.19: his son. To be a *landless* man was to be a

LIBERTY (2)

30.17: York was empty. Wall Street, *Liberty* Street, Broadway, all empty. So
32.19: little money to buy his *liberty.* When he was thirty-five, there

LIFE (19)

15.9: maybe you couldn't enjoy your *life* and put it into the
24.3: each other in trying times. *Life* had gone well with them
24.5: had the same ideas about *life.* They agreed, without discussion, as
24.11: thrown overboard in a hard *life* like theirs, and they had
24.13: It had been a hard *life,* and a soft life, too.
24.13: hard life, and a soft *life,* too. There wasn't anything brutal
24.21: accord not to hurry through *life,* not to be always skimping
26.18: mind run back over his *life.* He had a good deal
26.19: good deal to remember, really; *life* in three countries. The only
27.9: upon that part of his *life* as very happy. He became
28.5: somewhere. It was a fine *life;* for the first five years
28.13: he called a happy home *life.* Very near the tailor shop
30.24: buildings, without the stream of *life* pouring [page break] through them, were
31.21: to a different station of *life* altogether. Anton's mother died when
40.20: wage-earner, a slave, all your *life;* to have nothing, to be
58.14: find what he wanted in *life* for himself; now he was
59.16: neighbours was part of your *life.* The worst things he had
67.14: never learned so much about *life* from anything as from old
71.16: to it at last. Rosicky's *life* seemed to him complete and

LIGHT (9)

15.14: into the farm-implement store to *light* his pipe and put on
18.8: The graveyard had only a *light* wire fence about it and
19.17: the horses' backs and manes, *light,* delicate, mysterious it fell; and
29.3: The loft was low-pitched, but *light* and airy, full of windows,
44.22: gleam of sun, and the *light* failed at four o'clock. He
52.15: smell. Dere was a gas *light* in a ball across de
52.22: to de window where de *light* comes in, an' touch it
57.11: cold, and after the first *light* snows before Christmas there was
66.22: so alive and quick and *light* in its communications,—very

LONELY (1)
70.24: heavy stone, so arranged and *lonely* and [page break] unlike anything in the

LONESOME (2)
34.7: an' I'm afraid she's gettin' *lonesome,* an' he can't afford no
37.15: you? Don't you ever get *lonesome* out here?" As she turned

MARRIED (8)
6.24: oldest son, Rudolph, who had *married* in the spring, was getting
14.8: Ed. Why don't you git *married*? I'm worried about you. Settin'
14.12: they'd come faster if I *married.*" "Don't talk so. You'll ruin
16.16: wife. You know Polly, that *married* my Rudolph. How much my
23.18: and broader than when she *married* him; his back had grown
24.17: man, and though he had *married* a rough farm girl, he
35.22: She was sensitive about having *married* a foreigner. She never in
39.7: than once been sorry he'd *married* this year. In a few

MARRY (2)
39.20: a risk. A Czech should *marry* a Czech. It was lucky
40.15: ago, to get money to *marry* on. He had done very

MARRYING (1)
39.18: the clock tick. Generally speaking, *marrying* an American girl was certainly

MONEY (12)
17.14: his land, he hadn't the *money* to buy on High Prairie;
25.3: he told them how much *money* the Fasslers, their nearest neighbours,
25.9: my children's faces than put *money* into the bank." The agent
32.18: began to save a little *money* to buy his liberty. When
39.5: cash, but he took the *money* as if it hurt him.
40.15: two years ago, to get *money* to marry on. He had
42.20: down into London, with no *money* and no connexions except the
45.23: and be sure of my *money.*" "Maybe so," his father answered
51.14: an' you ain't got no *money,*—not a damn bit.

55.3: for God's sake give me *money* enough to buy a goose!'
61.3: time, had had to take *money* for repair work from the
61.5: so wistfully; because it was *money* due his boss. And now,

MUSIC (4)
29.17: They were both fond of *music* and went to the opera
40.2: in the bank, one taught *music,* and Polly and her younger
52.6: songs an' make very nice *music,* an' I run round after
66.13: was like an ear for *music* or an eye for colour.

MUSICAL (1)
40.4: All four of them were *musical,* had pretty voices, and sang

NEIGHBOUR (4)
3.2: When Doctor Burleigh told *neighbour* Rosicky he had a bad
9.3: handed over to the assisting *neighbour* woman, and the mother was
53.20: and how she get some *neighbour* to cook it dat got
59.12: if you had a mean *neighbour,* you could keep off his

NEIGHBOURS (10)
19.6: And they were all old *neighbours* in the graveyard, most of
24.22: and saving. They saw their *neighbours* buy more land and feed
25.3: money the Fasslers, their nearest *neighbours,* had made on their cream
33.19: can go in with de *neighbours.*" Their faces fell. They worked
47.22: to say how all the *neighbours* was goin' to meet at
49.17: father behaved, when all the *neighbours* was so discouraged they couldn't
49.20: as we was, an' our *neighbours* wasn't a bit better off
50.2: that, all the same, the *neighbours* had managed to get ahead
59.15: misery and brutality of your *neighbours* was part of your life.
71.8: worked here in summer; the *neighbours* passed on their way to

NOTHING (10)
19.7: of them friends; there was *nothing* to feel awkward or embarrassed
21.11: me off." "He don't say *nothing* much, only I'm a little
30.18: much stone and asphalt with *nothing* going on, so many empty
36.21: think of it." Rosicky said *nothing.* He found a bib apron
40.20: all your life; to have *nothing,* to be nothing. Rosicky thought

40.21: to have nothing, to be *nothing.* Rosicky thought he would come
46.10: Your father wouldn't never take *nothing* very hard, not even hard
71.5: the wind for ever stirred. *Nothing* but the sky overhead, and
71.11: fodder as winter came on. *Nothing* could be more un-deathlike
71.12: un-deathlike than this place; *nothing* could be more right for

OILCLOTH (3)
9.15: table, covered with a bright *oilcloth,* was set out with dishes
10.11: a white cloth over the *oilcloth,* to change the thick cups
20.60: n the table, covered with *oilcloth* figured with clusters of blue

OPERA (3)
27.20: He often stood through an *opera* on Saturday nights; he could
27.23: were the great days of *opera* in New York, and it
29.17: music and went to the *opera* together. Rosicky thought he wanted

ORCHARD (2)
18.2: low, with the clump of *orchard* behind and the windmill before,
48.16: have a picnic in the *orchard.* We'll eat our supper behind

PARLOUR (1)
41.10: a kitchen that was a *parlour* also; with another crowded, angry

PEOPLE (14)
11.16: success, always saying: "What do *people* go to Omaha for, to
11.18: right here?" If Mary liked *people* at all, she felt physical
12.18: what's the matter with such *people.*" "Why, Mother," said one of
15.7: ahead. Maybe, Doctor Burleigh reflected, *people* as generous and warm-hearted and
19.11: it,—only with certain *people* whom he didn't understand at
31.15: land of his own. His *people* had always been workmen; his
39.8: a few minutes the young *people* came out, looking clean and
54.17: an' I could see de *people* havin' parties inside. While I
55.1: right [page break] up to dem gay *people* an' begun to beg dem:
57.8: experienced and worldly than his *people.* [section break] The winter turned
59.7: do with dishonest and cruel *people.* They were the only things

59.21: London streets. There were mean *people* everywhere, to be sure, even
59.24: hardened, sharpened, like the treacherous *people* in cities who live by
66.12: a special gift for loving *people,* something that was like an

PIPE (8)
5.18: from his coffee or his *pipe.* I've quit trying. But the
15.14: farm-implement store to light his *pipe* and put on his glasses
39.16: sat down and had a *pipe* and listened to the clock
41.3: work. Rosicky shook out his *pipe* and walked home across the
45.12: this country." Rosicky filled his *pipe.* "You boys don't know what
50.21: story, Rosicky laid aside his *pipe.* "You boys like me to
68.18: hands steadier. He lit his *pipe* and took up John's overalls.
69.11: like yesterday. He put his *pipe* cautiously down on the window-sill

PLOUGH (1)
61.23: the horses and the sulky *plough* and the driver. It was

PLOUGHED (1)
57.19: land would have to be *ploughed* up and planted over again,

PLOUGHING (1)
61.19: a bone. The boys began *ploughing* up the wheat-fields to plant

POOR (13)
8.11: Doctor Burleigh had been a *poor* boy in the country before
11.14: him when he was a *poor* country boy, and was boastfully
12.24: But I'm sorry for that *poor* woman, how [page break] bad she'll feel
26.23: German tailor who was wretchedly *poor.* Those days, when he was
37.21: is terrible hard fur de *poor.*" "I don't know. Sometimes I
39.21: was the daughter of a *poor* widow woman; Rudolph was proud,
43.7: By chance he met a *poor* German tailor who had learned
44.10: multitudes of fleas, though the *poor* woman did the best she
49.19: we enjoyed ourselves that year, *poor* as we was, an' our
49.22: 'em grieved till they got *poor* digestions and couldn't relish what
51.10: ain't so much fun, bein' *poor* in a big city like
53.8: the neck beneath his ear. "*Poor* little Papa, I don't want

53.19: to me; how hard dat *poor* woman save to buy dat

PRAIRIE (3)
10.20: announcing him to the whole *prairie.* Rosicky hadn't said anything at
17.10: county. He admired this High *Prairie,* as it was called, and
17.15: money to buy on High *Prairie;* so he told his boys,

PRETTY (7)
3.5: guess my heart was always *pretty* good. I got a little
15.17: and stood about until the *pretty* girl with the plucked eyebrows,
18.12: and the headstones, looked very *pretty.* It was a nice graveyard,
36.10: with my work tonight, and *pretty* tired. Maybe Rudolph would like
40.4: of them were musical, had *pretty* voices, and sang in the
47.3: "'Nothin,'" he says, 'but it's *pretty* hot, an' I think I
63.6: time, and his breath was *pretty* short, so he thought he

RED (7)
13.8: mother because she flushed so *red,* but she stood her ground
14.4: She snapped off a dark *red* one, and a ruffled new
16.7: off the heavy bolt with *red* stripes. "You see, my wife
18.9: was all overgrown with long *red* grass. The fine snow, settling
18.10: fine snow, settling into this *red* grass and upon the few
42.9: John. Mary had a big *red* geranium in bloom for Christmas,
70.5: on the hill where the *red* lamplight shone, but here, in

ROOM (4)
10.23: and went into his own *room* to pour the Doctor a
22.18: a closet in de boys' *room* and make dem two little
37.1: the door [page break] of her own *room.* "I washed up de kitchen
37.12: at the door of her *room,* murmuring tearfully: "You always

ROOMS (1)
43.20: family lived upstairs in three *rooms;* a kitchen, a bedroom, where

SCHOOL (3)
8.12: he went away to medical *school;* he had known Rosicky almost

27.14: fortune. He went to night *school* and learned to read English.
36.2: her class in the high *school* in town, and their friendship

SCHOOLHOUSE (1)
47.23: goin' to meet at the *schoolhouse* that night, to pray for

SEA (3)
29.7: and the East from the *sea* captains. The young men were
29.15: on summer nights all the *sea* winds blew in. Zichec often
31.8: they ever were in the *sea.* On that very day he

SEASON (3)
17.5: the first snow of the *season,* and he was glad to
19.20: for the ground itself; a *season* of long nights for sleep,
29.5: lumber put up there to *season.* Old Loeffler used to go

SEASONS (1)
23.10: shaved except in the busiest *seasons,* was not loose or baggy.

SHIRT (6)
38.20: go put on a clean *shirt,* quick!" "But don't the boys
44.15: there, never get a clean *shirt* to his back again. What
44.23: to shave and change his *shirt* while the [page break] turkey was
48.13: on you and a clean *shirt* on himself, an' by that
60.17: one, he would give the *shirt* off his back to anyone
64.13: When his daughter-in-law buttoned his *shirt* over his chest at last,

SHIRTS (1)
26.14: overalls and jackets and work *shirts.* Occasionally he made over a

SHOP (7)
27.7: him work in a tailor *shop* in Vesey Street, down near
28.13: life. Very near the tailor *shop* was a small furniture-factory, where
32.22: and Rosicky left the tailor *shop* and went home with the
41.6: were still in a tailor *shop* on Vesey Street, with a
42.23: he went to the pastry *shop,* however, he [page break] found that the

43.9: tailor, Lifschnitz, kept a repair *shop* in a Cheapside basement, underneath
51.5: you know about dat tailor *shop* I worked in in London?

SHOPPING (1)
16.1: always prolonged [page break] his *shopping* by a little joking; the

SHOPS (1)
31.17: and grandfather had worked in *shops.* His mother's parents had lived

SHORT (8)
3.6: asthma, maybe. Just a awful *short* breath when I was pitchin'
4.3: your heart that makes you *short* of breath, I tell you.
5.22: the fields that makes you *short* of breath." "How about shelling
23.20: his arms and legs were *short.* He was fifteen years older
24.14: wasn't anything brutal in the *short,* broad-backed man with the
39.4: wid me." Rudolph was very *short* of cash, but he took
51.16: have no overcoat, chust a *short* jacket I'd outgrowed so it
63.6: and his breath was pretty *short,* so he thought he had

SICK (6)
4.15: did not look like a *sick* man. His brown face was
37.3: wife, when de babies was *sick* or somethin'. You go an'
60.5: cities. Here, if you were *sick,* you had Doctor Ed to
65.11: I hate it to be *sick* on you like dis. Down
67.20: Rudy, your father's been awful *sick!* He raked up those thistles
69.1: had if he hadn't got [page break] *sick* over there. Girls nowadays didn't

SKY (5)
18.17: the complete arch of the *sky* over him, hear the wagons
44.21: sewing and his recollections. The *sky* had been a dark grey,
70.19: shadows in a pool. The *sky* was very blue and soft,
71.5: ever stirred. Nothing but the *sky* overhead, and the many-coloured fields
71.7: on until they met that *sky.* The horses worked here in

SLIM (3)
16.24: ain't much fur all dem *slim* women like what de style

35.15: dishes. She was a trim, *slim* little thing, with blue eyes
63.16: with the swiftness of a *slim* greyhound. In a flash she

SMELL (5)
9.17: kitchen was full of the *smell* of coffee and hot biscuit
51.13: streets is full, an' you *smell* 'em all de time, an'
52.12: my head down, till I *smell* somet'ing good. Seem like it
52.14: noway. I can't understand dat *smell*. Dere was a gas light
52.22: in, an' touch it and *smell* it to find out, an'

SMELLED (1)
20.7: place was set, and he *smelled* hot coffee-cake of some kind.

SMILE (3)
7.10: His voice and his twinkly *smile* were an affectionate compliment to
10.22: he merely smiled his twinkling *smile*, put some more coal on
37.19: with his peculiar, knowing, indulgent *smile* without a shadow of reproach

SNOW (11)
9.6: drove his buggy—the *snow* was too deep for a
17.5: wagon, it was beginning to *snow*,—the first snow of
17.5: to snow,—the first *snow* of the season, and he
18.5: against the white field. The *snow* was falling over the cornfield
18.7: wind,—a nice dry *snow*. The graveyard had only a
18.10: long red grass. The fine *snow*, settling into this red grass
19.3: of his own hayfield. The *snow*, falling over his barnyard and
19.14: fine sight to see the *snow* falling so quietly and graciously
42.3: set in very cold; no *snow*, but a bitter, biting wind
45.6: sorry. They wanted a deep *snow* that would lie long and
57.12: before Christmas there was no *snow* at all,—and no

SNOWED (1)
45.5: sorry they were it hadn't *snowed*. Everybody was sorry. They wanted

SNOWFALL (1)
17.24: seat, looking about at the *snowfall*. Over yonder on the hill

SNOWS (1)
57.12: and after the first light *snows* before Christmas there was no

SNOWSTORM (1)
19.13: Well, it was a nice *snowstorm;* a fine sight to see

SOIL (1)
17.13: was some clay in the *soil* and it was not so

SPRING (3)
6.24: who had married in the *spring,* was getting on. [page break] Rudolph
29.21: get a little restless. When *spring* came round, he would begin
61.17: him chuckle with pleasure. The *spring* came warm, with blue skies,

STARS (3)
41.16: up at the frosty winter *stars* and draw a long breath
41.19: the sleeping fields and bright stars and the noble darkness were
70.20: very blue and soft, the *stars* rather faint because the moon

STOCK (4)
5.20: work. You can feed the *stock* and do chores about the
8.20: where there was plenty of *stock* and plenty of feed and
24.23: more land and feed more *stock* than they did, without discontent.
59.1: to have to sell your *stock* because you had no feed.

STOMACH (2)
22.10: It's your breathing and your *stomach* that's been wrong. I wouldn't
53.17: I felt better in de *stomach,* but very bad in de

STORY (4)
21.8: his right thumb told the *story* of his past. "Well, what
46.12: mind to tell you a *story* on him. Maybe you boys
50.20: When Mary had finished her *story,* Rosicky laid aside his pipe.
51.2: bothersome to tell a long *story* in English (he nearly always

SUMMER (5)
3.7: I was pitchin' hay last *summer,* dat's all." [page break] "Well now,

18.18: the wagons go by; in *summer* the mowing-machine rattled right
29.15: in the world, and on *summer* nights all the sea winds
70.1: moonlight night in early *summer* he started for the farm.
71.7: The horses worked here in *summer;* the neighbours passed on their

SUN (4)
30.15: in Park Place in the *sun.* The lower part of New
32.11: he asked; to see the *sun* rise and set and to
44.22: with not a gleam of *sun,* and the light failed at
48.21: wind got cooler as the *sun* was goin' down, and it

SUPPER (13)
35.14: gingham dress, clearing away the *supper* dishes. She was a trim,
38.12: family should come just then. *Supper* hadn't been a very pleasant
41.9: tired and sullen to eat *supper* in a kitchen that was
45.2: Polly were coming over for *supper.* After supper they sat round
45.3: coming over for supper. After *supper* they sat round in the
47.7: should git up a nice *supper* for us tonight. It's Fourth
48.14: time I'd begun to get *supper.* He says: 'It's too hot
48.16: the orchard. We'll eat our *supper* behind the mulberry hedge, under
48.18: trees.' "So he carried our *supper* down, an' a bottle of
52.1: little bread an' [page break] drippin' for *supper,* because she was savin' to
52.3: dinner on Christmas Day. After *supper* de boss say I can
56.24: his family come over for *supper* on [page break] New Year's Eve.
57.1: "Let's get up a nice *supper,* and not let your mother

TABLE (6)
9.14: up for breakfast. The long *table,* covered with a bright oilcloth,
11.2: from his end of the *table* and spoke to her in
20.5: the house together. On the *table,* covered with oilcloth figured with
33.13: were talking at the breakfast *table* about starting early that evening,
33.16: began. Rosicky looked down the *table.* "I hope you boys ain't
55.18: I bought on de kitchen *table,* an' go in an' lay

THIN (4)
4.19: brown moustache. His hair was *thin* and ragged around his ears,
15.19: was free. Those eyebrows, two *thin* India-ink strokes, amused him, because

16.9: goose-fedder pillows, an' de *thin* stuff don't hold in dem
23.7: Yes, his hair had got *thin,* and his high forehead had

THING (5)
5.7: Ed. I guess the only *thing* is fur me to git
5.18: quit trying. But the sure *thing* is you've got to cut
16.21: candy for his wife. First *thing* you know, she'll be getting
35.15: was a trim, slim little *thing,* with blue eyes and shingled
63.23: steer his course. The next *thing* he was conscious of was

THINGS (13)
10.15: to put out my good *things* for you if you was
12.11: for me to do them *things* up to the last, for
19.5: the graveyard, seemed to draw *things* together like. And they were
24.12: never disagreed as to the *things* that could go. It had
25.6: Fassler children! Pale, pinched little *things,* they look like skimmed milk.
32.2: the farm animals and growing *things* which are never made at
32.12: and set and to plant *things* and watch them grow. He
33.15: so to see the Christmas *things* in the stores before the
50.5: his father's way of doing *things.* He wished he knew what
59.8: people. They were the only *things* in his experience he had
59.16: of your life. The worst *things* he had come upon in
61.10: When he thought of these *things,* Rosicky would put on his
70.2: His mind was on other *things,* and not until his road

TOWN (17)
7.13: home before it comes. In *town* in the car?" Doctor Burleigh
17.7: it. He rattled out of *town* and along the highway through
20.9: kind. Anton never lunched in *town;* he thought that extravagant, and
25.14: Mary very soon got into *town* to see Doctor Ed, and
33.11: little Josephine, and went to *town* to the moving-picture show. One
34.1: and Mother are going to *town,*" Frank said, "maybe you could
34.6: show. She don't git into *town* enough, an' I'm afraid she's
34.19: It comes hard fur a *town* girl to be a farmer's
35.5: good you thought about that. *Town* girls is used to more
35.10: to their Saturday nights in *town.* That evening Rosicky drove the
36.2: in the high school in *town,* and their friendship began in

36.5: "My boys ain't goin' to *town* tonight, an' I brought de
37.5: look prettier'n any of dem *town* girls when you go in.
59.22: even in their own country *town* here. But they weren't tempered,
60.15: over on his brothers, then *town* would be the place for
62.20: when Rudolph had gone to *town* in the car, leaving a
71.9: passed on their way to *town;* and over yonder, in the

TREES (4)
42.11: a row of Jerusalem cherry *trees,* full of berries. It was
47.18: you in. Them two box-elder *trees* was little then, but they
48.17: mulberry hedge, under them linden *trees.*' "So he carried our supper
48.23: curled up on the linden *trees.* That made me think, an'

WIFE (11)
6.7: If I had a good *wife* like yours, I'd want to
6.11: kitchen too much. An' my *wife,* she's a awful hard worker
11.7: you eat some breakfast. My *wife,* she's terrible fur to ask
14.14: hotel. I could send your *wife* a nice loaf of nut
16.8: red stripes. "You see, my *wife* is always makin' goose-fedder
16.15: fedder quilt for my son's *wife.* You know Polly, that married
16.21: so much candy for his *wife.* First thing you know, she'll
34.20: girl to be a farmer's *wife.* I don't want no trouble
37.2: kitchen many times for my *wife,* when de babies was sick
43.21: bedroom, where Lifschnitz and his *wife* and five children slept, and
64.22: no use to scare my *wife.* It's nice and quiet here,

WIFE'S (1)
11.1: all seated, he watched his *wife's* face from his end of

WIND (9)
18.7: hay-land, steadily, with very little *wind,*—a nice dry snow.
42.4: snow, but a bitter, biting *wind* that whistled and sang over
46.14: we had that terrible hot *wind,* that burned everything up on
48.20: I can tell you. The *wind* got cooler as the sun
48.25: your father if that hot *wind* [page break] all day hadn't been terrible
56.22: the fields with the bitter *wind* at their backs, his heart
57.14: On those days when the *wind* fairly punished the country, Rosicky

58.9: the panes rattled and the *wind* blew in under the door,
71.4: of long grass which the *wind* for ever stirred. Nothing but

WINDOW (7)
13.23: horse, he went to the *window* to examine the house plants.
26.3: in the chair between the *window* full of plants and the
52.16: always shine in at my *window* a little. I got up
52.21: I carry it to de *window* where de light comes in,
57.15: country, Rosicky sat by his *window.* In the fall he and
58.8: start. Sitting beside his flowering *window* while the panes rattled and
68.14: he sat down by his *window* to do some patching and

WINDOW-SILL (1)
69.11: pipe cautiously down on the *window-sill* and bent over to ease

WINDOWS (9)
14.3: road I don't see your *windows* full of flowers." She snapped
29.3: light and airy, full of *windows,* and good-smelling by reason of
30.19: going on, so many empty *windows.* The emptiness was intense, like
41.5: lamplight shone from his kitchen *windows.* Suppose he were still in
41.12: and squeaking pulleys at the *windows* where dirty washings hung on
41.18: That kitchen with the shining *windows* was dear to him; but
51.11: London, I'll say! All de *windows* is full of good t'ings
51.20: dem pork pies in de *windows* was awful fur me! "Day
54.16: de ground floor, wid big *windows* all fixed up fine, an'

WINTER (10)
8.16: for Mrs. Rosicky. Only last *winter* he had had such a
14.1: to keep them blooming all *winter,* Mary? I never pass this
19.24: he merely told himself that *winter* was coming, clucked to his
22.15: stay round de house dis *winter.* I guess you got some
26.1: an old woman yet. [page break] That *winter* he stayed in the house
40.14: He had worked for a *winter* up there, two years ago,
41.16: look up at the frosty *winter* stars and draw a long
57.10: than his people. [section break] The *winter* turned out badly for farmers.
62.4: because during that open windy *winter* a great many Russian thistle
71.11: would be eating fodder as *winter* came on. Nothing could be

WOMAN (16)

7.6: a fine girl. Dat widder *woman* bring her daughters up very
8.23: and no comfort whatever. The *woman* had too many children and
9.3: over to the assisting neighbour *woman,* and the mother was properly
12.24: I'm sorry for that poor *woman,* how [page break] bad she'll feel the
21.23: did like to hear a *woman* talk soft. He didn't say
25.22: man, he wasn't an old *woman* yet. [page break] That winter he stayed
26.11: couldn't bear to see a *woman* patching at his clothes, or
39.21: daughter of a poor widow *woman;* Rudolph was proud, and if
44.10: of fleas, though the poor *woman* did the best she could.
53.19: me; how hard dat poor *woman* save to buy dat goose,
55.20: up till I hear dat *woman* scream when she come out
56.17: a good boy to my *woman,* and fur dat fine Christmas
59.11: of a scheming and rapacious *woman.* In the country, if you
61.8: at the face of a *woman* become like a wolf's from
69.3: Polly would make a fine *woman* after the foolishness wore off.
69.4: foolishness wore off. Either a *woman* had that sweetness at her

WOMAN'S (1)

12.12: was terrible strong, but that *woman's* weakly. And do you think

WOMEN (4)

11.22: them. Burleigh didn't know many *women* like that, but he knew
16.19: in some candy fur de *women.*" "As usual. I never did
16.24: much fur all dem slim *women* like what de style is
54.12: drunks all along; men, and *women* too. I chust move along

WORK (18)

4.7: and you can't do heavy *work* any more. You've got five
5.19: got to cut out farm *work.* You can feed the stock
8.24: many children and too much *work,* and she was [page break] no manager.
22.16: guess you got some carpenter *work* for me to do. I
26.14: the overalls and jackets and *work* shirts. Occasionally he made over
27.7: a protector who got him *work* in a tailor shop in
27.15: English. He often did over-time *work* and was well paid for
30.2: On Monday he plunged into *work* again. So he never had
32.10: country never left him. To *work* on another man's farm would

36.10: But I'm late with my *work* tonight, and pretty tired. Maybe
41.2: love and serious about his *work*. Rosicky shook out his pipe
43.15: given you when you took *work* home to a customer. But
47.4: an' I think I won't *work* no more today.' He stood
51.8: de boss ain't got much *work*, an' have it awful hard
55.9: my name and where I *work* down on paper, an' both
58.18: gone. They would have to *work* hard on the farm, and
61.3: to take money for repair *work* from the hand of a
71.14: had helped to do the *work* of great cities and had

WORKED (8)
4.5: years old, and you've always *worked* hard, and your heart's tired.
31.17: his father and grandfather had *worked* in shops. His mother's parents
33.20: neighbours." Their faces fell. They *worked* hard all week, and they
40.1: four sisters, and they [page break] all *worked;* one was book-keeper in the
40.14: job in Omaha. He had *worked* for a winter up there,
49.12: couldn't believe it, after he'd *worked* so hard. "'No crop this
51.6: about dat tailor shop I *worked* in in London? I had
71.7: met that sky. The horses *worked* here in summer; the neighbours

WORKER (1)
6.12: wife, she's a awful hard *worker* her own self." "That's it;

WORKING (6)
7.4: but it seems to be *working* out all right." "Yes, she's
26.22: spent in London, in Cheapside, *working* for a German tailor who
41.8: bunch of pale, narrow-chested sons *working* on machines, all coming home
42.22: who was supposed to be *working* at a confectioner's. When he
58.17: sure they would be here, *working* this very land, after he
62.9: was nonsense. The boys were *working* so hard planting corn, their

WORKMAN (1)
27.10: happy. He became a good *workman*, he was industrious, and his

WORKMEN (2)
28.21: hands. One of the young *workmen* he employed was a Czech,
31.16: His people had always been *workmen;* his father and grandfather had

WORLD (12)
28.11: richest, friendliest city in the *world.* Moreover, he had what he
29.14: the quietest place in the *world,* and on summer nights all
31.5: You lived in an unnatural *world,* like the fish in an
32.23: in another part of the *world.* [section break] Perhaps the fact
35.23: foreigner. She never in the *world* would have done it if
59.17: in his journey through the *world* were human,—depraved and
60.5: see one out of the *world* in big cities. Here, if
60.8: the kindest man in the *world,* buried you. It seemed to
60.20: they could get through the *world* without ever knowing much about
62.16: his childhood in the old *world.* When he was a little
66.8: feeling that nobody in the *world,* not her mother, not Rudolph,
71.1: unlike anything in the living *world.* Cities of the dead, indeed;

WORLDLY (1)
57.8: sisters were more experienced and *worldly* than his people.

4

Taking Liberties

Willa Cather and the 1934 Film Adaptation of *A Lost Lady*

Michael Schueth

In October 1934 Americans opened their newspapers to find a new movie playing downtown—*A Lost Lady,* starring Barbara Stanwyck and Frank Morgan, based on the novel by Willa Cather. The placement of Willa Cather's name next to Barbara Stanwyck's (which was usually featured sweeping across the page in most ads) marked a critical moment in Cather's career. While popular audiences were familiar with her name from her publication of stories and novels in mass-market magazines, this was a moment when her name and reputation were exploited by a medium appealing to a vast popular audience, and without her control. The film and, perhaps more importantly, its advertising survive as a showcase of how Hollywood transformed Cather's novel into an entirely different language of entertainment, for commercial purposes.

The cooptation of Cather by Hollywood reveals the shifting nature of professional writing in the 1920s and 1930s as literary agents and publishers found new profit-making markets for their writers. Few writers could resist the lure of Hollywood's big-money offers for rights to their work, and Cather was no exception. Further, the relationship between Hollywood and literary texts documents how both popular and classic literature were becoming more complex as material objects, exploitable in numerous ways. Film historian and critic Judith Mayne suggests that the massive Hollywood industry was part of the emergence of a new kind of public sphere, "one shaped by the institutions of consumerism," which often chose profit margins over art (1). The Hollywood adaptation of Cather's novel into a product appealing to a mass-market audience of moviegoers (mostly women) suggests much about American culture and its treatment of the artist as a consumable product. Unlike films based on novels by authors long dead, such as Charles Dickens or Jane Austen, living writers are in the midst of producing new work and therefore are continually developing their literary reputations. As we will see with the film adaptation of *A Lost Lady*, film adaptations and Hollywood publicity machines became a new force in the construction of a writer's reputation. Indeed, literary reputation became a complex site of competing images projected to the public by critics, writers themselves, publishers, and now Hollywood marketing departments.

In this essay I will pay special attention to the advertising of the 1934 film of *A Lost Lady*, since that was the primary means by which Warner Brothers used Cather's name as a selling device. The sheer breadth of the advertising—including newspaper ads, shop window displays, and radio promotions—gave Cather's name wide exposure to an audience that may only slightly have overlapped her readership. Central questions regarding the twentieth-century literary marketplace emerge when one considers the Hollywood packaging of Willa Cather's work and reputation: Who has control over a writer's reputation? How is the public informed about a writer? How much control can a writer have over her work?

In the second and third decades of the twentieth century, Hollywood movies consumed the attention of the American public. With rapid innovations in film technology, such as improved projectors and the division of films into reels, allowing for longer movies, leading filmmakers such as D. W. Griffith (*Birth of a Nation*) were able to tell more sophisticated stories. With such advancements, the film industry in the United States became a cultural juggernaut, reshaping concepts of amusement, entertainment, class systems, and narratives. Moreover, the film industry became big business. As Mayne suggests, after World War I Hollywood became "so dependent on the profit principle that the cinema at times seems to resemble a vulgar Marxist fantasy" (96). Indeed, Americans became so enamored with the cinema that by 1938 some 80 million tickets were sold every week; since the total U.S. population was only around 123 million, that number represents weekly moviegoing by 65 percent of the total population (Minnesota On-line Media Project).

With the boom in popularity of movies, and with growing profits, there was a corresponding increase in filmmakers' demand for subject matter. In the silent film era, filmmakers recognized that the lack of sound placed limitations on their ability to tell complex stories. Filming well-known works of literature became a standard choice for many filmmakers because it gave them a chance to work with story lines their audiences already knew. As producers realized, well-known works of literature also provided a built-in marketing benefit: readers who admired a book were drawn into seeing the filmed version, and the quality of the literary work translated into a perception that the film might also be good. *Uncle Tom's Cabin,* one of the first literary works put to film, was filmed more than ten times in the silent film era beginning in 1903 (Gifford 144). With the popularity of film adaptations of novels, Hollywood grew dependent on novelists. Virginia Woolf noted in 1926, "All the famous novels of the world, with their well known characters, and their famous scenes, only asked, it seemed, to be put on the films. The cinema fell upon its prey with immense rapacity, and to this moment largely subsists upon the body of its unfortunate victim" (Geduld 88).

By the late teens and twenties, and in an institutionalized way by the thirties, American authors were cashing in on Hollywood's interest. Edith Wharton, Dorothy Canfield Fisher, Theodore Dreiser, Ernest Hemingway, F. Scott Fitzgerald, and William Faulkner all participated in the lucrative windfall that came with selling their film rights to movie studios. Theodore Dreiser, for example, was paid $150,000 in 1931 for the film rights to *An American Tragedy.* By 1934, four of Edith Wharton's major novels (*The Age of Innocence, The House of Mirth, The Children,* and *Glimpses of the Moon*) had all been adapted. Indeed, such writers as Hemingway, Faulkner, and Fitzgerald depended on Hollywood film projects to support their writing careers. Frank M. Laurence notes that while some of Hemingway's Hollywood films were embarrassing, they nevertheless "served to widen his name recognition even within the public that might never have read a word he wrote" (24–25). Because book sales rise in the wake of a major film production of a literary work, writers could make money both from the sale of copyright and from the resulting book sales even when the Hollywood movies were terrible.

Cather knew this from experience. She sold the rights to *A Lost Lady* twice, once in 1924, which led to the now-lost 1925 silent film starring Irene Rich, and again in December 1929, for $6,000, which ultimately led to the 1934 Warner Brothers film. She also sold rights to *The Song of the Lark* in 1932. Although she initially refused to do so, Ferris Greenslet, her editor at Houghton Mifflin, continued to press her to sell. He wrote to her persuasively, advising,

> Don't you really think that since neither of us would ever be compelled to see the picture if we didn't want to, and since of the millions of persons who would see it only a very small percentage would be admirers of your literary art, you might take the cash and let a little of the credit go, not forgetting that some of the millions of spectators might be inspired to become readers of all your books? (FG to WC, 26 February 1932).

When Cather finally agreed, her reason was not for the fee involved or the standard promises of books sales or new, avid readers. She wrote Greenslet that from her earlier experience with the 1925 filmed version of *A Lost Lady,* the rise in book sales was short-lived and the fan letters she received were from messy and illiterate people (WC to FG, 13 March 1932). Even so, despite her strong feelings about the matter, Cather agreed to sell the rights in order to guard her art against what she apparently believed was a greater risk. She exchanged her agreement to sell the rights to *The Song of the Lark* for a commitment by Houghton Mifflin never to ask her to sell the film rights to *My Ántonia.* Greenslet comforted her by writing that he was "more than ever convinced that there is not only a picture but a good picture in it, one that we need not necessarily be ashamed of" (FG to WC, 15 March 1932). *The Song of the Lark* never reached production, however, and Cather must have been relieved.

Greenslet's optimism that a "good film" would come out of *The Song of the Lark* was perhaps misplaced, given that film adaptations in the late 1920s and early 1930s were notoriously poor. As film historians Gerald Peary and Roger Shatzkin note, while Hollywood exploited works of "highbrow" literature, such works of art were often pushed into a "body of established conventions that tended toward melodrama" (6). Maureen Turim, discussing the adaptation of *Main Street* into Warner Brothers' 1936 film *I Married a Doctor,* says that the studio "hoped to attract old devotees of *Main Street,* while appealing to a different audience who identified with the film through its new title as a 'woman's film'" (207). In 1932, after his disappointment with the film adaptation of *An American Tragedy,* for which he was highly paid, Theodore Dreiser wrote that a "movie representative admitted that they would prefer . . . to buy the title [of the novel] only" (Geduld 207). Dreiser complains that in film the artist has been replaced by "a more or less purely commercial and so business-minded group" who exert "a material tyranny over a new and even beautiful art form" (Geduld 209).

Likewise, with the 1934 adaptation of *A Lost Lady,* the storyline was exploited for its romantic possibilities. On 21 February 1934 Gene Markey, coauthor of the screenplay, wrote a Warner Brothers interoffice memo detailing his interest in adapting *A Lost Lady* because it could be turned into a "picture of dignity and great dramatic power." In the midst of the Great Depression and of restrictive moral codes in the film industry, Markey noted, however, that "there is much to be done with it—the creation of a whole new beginning—and a whole new ending—to avoid the low-key depression feeling effect [*sic*] the last half of the novel." Indeed, the novel underwent a major rewriting in the screenplay. In briefly touching on the storyline of the film in order to indicate the scope of this rewriting, I will be quoting from a short plot summary made by Warner Brothers.

The movie begins with a completely new opening in which we see an engaged Marian at a lavish party at which her fiancé is suddenly shot to death by the jealous husband of a woman with whom he had "been carrying on a secret affair." "Shattered," Marian takes a rest cure in the mountains where she suffers a fall and is rescued by Daniel Forrester, "one of the country's leading corporation lawyers," who was also "ordered to the mountains" by physicians. Forrester falls in love with Marian, who begins to recover under his friendship, and eventually asks her to marry him. Marian accepts his proposal with an "understanding that honesty rather than love shall be the watchword between them." Niel Herbert takes only a minor role in the film as Forrester's junior partner, who "stirs no response in Marian." Frank Ellinger "drops by from the sky like a thunderbolt in his aeroplane" at the Forresters' new luxurious country estate, falls instantly in love with Marian, and the two carry on a secret love affair. When Forrester learns of his wife's betrayal, he suffers a heart attack. The script treatment goes on to explain that "through long months of hopeless illness, Marian nurses her husband . . . and learns, through a newspaper story, that Ellinger is about to marry a wealthy San Francisco girl." In the end, Marian and Forrester reunite as Marian realizes that "she loves this man who has been so devoted to her."

Judith Mayne suggests that in "adapting traditional novels as well as best-sellers, the classical Hollywood cinema promises that the reading experience will be recaptured in the movie theatre." Because of this, she contends, criticism on novel-film adaptations has long hinged on the "artistic superiority" of either the novel or the film and tends to "focus on authorship almost exclusively" (101–2). According to Mayne, novel-film criticism needs to account for the specific historical contexts informing film adaptations, reading those films under "the complexities engendered by a juncture of texts, viewers, and history" (105). Such a contextual reading of the *Lost Lady* film adaptation proves useful as a means to understand the massive changes Warner Brothers made to the storyline.

One of the significant and revealing aspects of the *Lost Lady* adaptation is the shift of the film's setting from a remote Nebraska "thirty or forty years ago, in one of those small grey towns along the Burlington railroad" (*LL* 7) to a contemporary upper-class, glitzy Chicago. As we have seen, Warner Brothers was nervous about the "depressing" and "low key" aspects of the novel, apparently because of the contemporary economic crisis of the Great Depression. For many Americans during the Depression, movies were a cultural daydream to escape from the drudgery of unemployment lines and soup kitchens. Moreover, the film erases Cather's complicated critique of modern materialism, especially in her characterization of Captain Forrester and Ellinger; it rewrites Forrester as a rich corporate lawyer who has money and security and Ellinger/Peters as a rich, bored playboy. As the movie industry embraced the bottom line in its own business practices, so too did the industry build propaganda into films to defend capitalist business practices. Cather's critique of "new materialism," as biographer James Woodress calls it (349), and her nostalgic look backward to the pioneer West populated "by dreamers, great-hearted adventurers" who loved the land

and protected it from exploitation (*LL* 102) were perhaps dangerous to Hollywood studios intent on exploitation themselves.

No matter how different the film was from Cather's novel, Warner Brothers' marketing of it used Cather's name to reinforce the "serious" dramatic power of the film. While her contract with Warner Brothers was specific in detailing publicity restrictions, including a clause stating that "no words shall be used which expressly or by inference convey the idea that the Owner [Cather] has written or supervised in any respect the dialogue or any other element of the motion picture," this did not stop Warner Brothers from exploiting her name. Memos from the studio's executives suggest that there was serious consideration of just how to work Cather's name into advertising text. In a 25 May 1934 memo, for example, Jim Seymour suggests,

> Inasmuch as we have taken some liberties with Willa Cather's prize-winning novel in modernizing it, I recommend the following form of main title credit
>
> A Lost Lady
> Screenplay by Gene Markey and Kathryn Scola
> Based on Willa Cather's novel/or/Based on the novel by Willa Cather.

Even while advising the use of Cather's name in the advertising text, though, Seymour is careful to suggest that "it would be a mistake to mention the novel and/or novelist's name on the first main title." By June, however, as indicated by another short memo, Warner Brothers executives wanted an even more direct connection between the movie and Cather's name. The new credit put forward in the memo reads, "Barbara Stanwyck in 'A Lost Lady' by Willa Cather."

Indeed, the final newspaper advertisements sent to theater companies suggest that Warner Brothers considered Cather's name a highly marketable commodity. Newspaper ads for the movie, ranging in size from one-inch-by-one-column size to full-page layouts, featured Cather's name in a range of styles. Examples vary from "Willa Cather's celebrated novel of a woman who tried to make marriage take the place of love comes to the screen in triumph" to "From the novel by Willa Cather, American's Greatest Woman Writer." The use of Cather's name highlights her literary celebrity and a faith on the part of Warner Brothers that her name was solid enough to sell movie tickets. Further, Cather's proclaimed stature as "America's Greatest Woman Writer" was used to market the film both to those who read and admired her work and to those unfamiliar with her work, especially, it seems, to a targeted audience of middle-class women who were fond of formulaic romance films.

In the same press book, Warner Brothers constructed a sophisticated advertising campaign that included "tear sheets" for newspaper advertising, pre-penned movie reviews, photos of Barbara Stanwyck and Frank Morgan and the other stars, and newly emerging merchandise tie-in campaigns for dress shops, milliners, pipe and tobacco stores, and even pet stores (since Forrester's character has a collie in several scenes). The press book opens with large block lettering, featuring the film's "Important Selling Values." Nestled between "star value" and "production value" is "story value," which reads, "the great American novel by Willa Cather, Pulitzer Prize winner, made into a great dramatic hit!" In large lettering underneath the selling points is the advice to managers to "Back 'Em Up with Big-Time Exploitation." Exploitation indeed. Above all, every aspect of Barbara Stanwyck—including her hair, clothing, and shoes—was featured as a product movie fans could buy at local shops.

Stanwyck's role as an emerging star was a guiding influence in the film's promotion. Warner Brothers was intent on making her a star of their studio, so all of the publicity revolved around her. For example, publicity calls Stanwyck a "dramatic genius" and says that the role of Marian Forrester is "made real" by her performance. As with Cather's name, the studio turned Stanwyck into a commodity. The "Stanwyck Swirl" for example, was, according to the press book, "a startling new hairdress introduced by Miss Barbara Stanwyck" which can "top off your chic appearance—at business, at the theatre, at home." Sarah Berry in her recent book *Screen Style: Fashion and Femininity in 1930s Hollywood* suggests that Hollywood actresses were often made into cults of personality who were not only put forward as "stars" but also as leading representatives of American womanhood and lifestyle (27). In this way, while stars were often featured as being glamorous and rich, they nevertheless functioned to give middle-class women an ideal lifestyle to emulate as they purchased similar, affordably priced clothing and accessories modeled in the movies. One pre-penned article for newspapers educated women on the dress styles shown in *A Lost Lady:* "It is the contention of Orry-Kelly, famous designer of gowns for all the Warner Bros.-First National stars, that an actress must sense dramatic effect in costume. Consequently, for 'A Lost Lady,' taken from best seller [*sic*] of Willa Cather, famous Pulitzer Prize winner, Barbara Stanwyck has the wardrobe that reflects every mood." Middle-class viewers were encouraged to emulate Stanwyck's style by consuming the goods identified with her.

Further, as consumers were sold Stanwyck's sophisticated style, they were simultaneously buying into Cather's reputation as "best seller," "Pulitzer Prize winner," and "great American writer." As such, Cather was also used to represent middle-class American taste. As Joan Acocella explains of Cather's reputation, "Throughout the thirties, even though her work was now becoming uneven, Cather was one of America's best-loved novelists. . . . Universities gave her honorary doctorates. *Time* put her on its cover. And the regular book reviewers—some of them excellent, but not leftist, not vanguard—generally praised her" (25). Cather's widespread success in the 1930s ensured that people knew her name, even among those who had never read her novels. With name recognition, she became a public personality, and her name in turn became a highly marketable commodity. Movie ads proclaimed Cather's credibility, her status as the "greatest," against the melodramatic elements of the film's storyline. Tag lines such as "Willa Cather's throbbing revelation of a woman's heart!" seem grounded in some artistic merit to potential moviegoers, and so going to see a formulaic romance film attains middle-class respectability because it was written by (as another ad exclaims) "the magic pen of America's greatest woman writer!"

Further, a host of promotional strategies were suggested in the press book, revealing how Warner Brothers was specifically marketing *A Lost Lady* to middle-class women. One promotion, simply referred to as the "Problem Contest," suggested that for a prize of free tickets to the film women could write to their newspaper editors a 100-word essay answering the following question: "If YOU were the heroine of 'A Lost Lady,' portrayed by Barbara Stanwyck which of the three men would YOU choose in your quest for complete happiness in life?" Another suggested a "Femme Frolic" because, as the promotion material suggests, "This picture is truly a woman's picture." Managers were told that they could "pep up" a "For Women Only" matinee "by having a psychologist down to give a short lecture on some of the situations in the film." Also, for "next to nothing," managers could buy still shots from key scenes accompanied by "punch lines," which amount to exclamatory lines from the film's script. For example, one still captures Barbara Stanwyck saying, "I know you saved my life—but don't try to save my soul!"

While Warner Brothers tried diligently to tie Cather's name into its promotions, critics responded by separating her name from the film. Critics such as the one for the *New York World-Telegram* realized that "most of the qualities which tore across the pages of Miss Cather's novel have flown out through the wide studio windows of Hollywood" (4 October 1934). The *New York Herald Tribune* reviewer, Richard Watts Jr., said that "even if the photoplay called 'A Lost Lady' didn't pretend to be an adaptation of Willa Cather's genuine American masterpiece, one of the finest novels ever written in this country, it would still be a highly unsatisfying motion picture." Film critics reviewing *A Lost Lady* understood that Cather had little, if any, control over the adaptation of her novel, and in their reviews they note a difference between Cather's authorship of the novel and the authorship of the film. The tension here between critics and their attack on the film adaptation reflects Cather's complicated position in her culture at the time. Middlebrow film critics wanted to save her reputation from "the lowest common denominator" and place her into a more respectable upper middle-class status, even while her name was widely known and celebrated.

While there is no known direct response by Cather to the 1934 film, Alfred Knopf, her publisher and close personal friend, states that "she used to say to me that if she had wanted to write a play or a motion picture she would have written a play or motion-picture script" (38). He further relates, "The experience [of the 1934 *Lost Lady* adaptation] was so disillusioning that she determined never to risk repetition. One day Benjamin H. Stern, our close friend and long-time lawyer, who also represented her for a number of years, told me in his office that he had an offer from Hollywood that ran into six figures. Ben's office was on the thirty-fifth floor of the French Building and I immediately told him that I would as soon jump out the window as mention this offer to Miss Cather. I added that I thought if he wished to retain her good will, that he should not mention it to her either. He didn't" (38). Other offers did come in, however. In 1936 Cather wrote to Zoë Akins that she did not approve of a dramatic adaptation of *A Lost Lady* written by Daniel Totheroh, noting that he didn't in the least understand Mrs. Forrester's character (15 Dec. 1936 Huntington). That same year Cather wrote to Helen Sprague that young contemporary writers were caught up with the idea of being a writer, attaining celebrity status, and getting into the movies. As far as Cather was concerned, this was a passing fad (8 March 1936). After the release of *A Lost Lady* she also rejected all offers for radio and phonograph renditions of her work, some of which could have been financially rewarding, claiming that the actors turned her work into sentimental nonsense (Cather to Woollcott, 8 Feb. 1935 Harvard). We can safely conclude that Cather disliked the film of *A Lost Lady* and all that went with it.

Toward the end of the 1930s, as Cather's health declined and as she suffered from the deaths of her brother Douglass and other loved ones, her attention turned to how she could protect her image after her death. While living, Cather could easily say no to radio and film productions, but after her death, who could possibly ensure that the integrity of her work remained undisturbed? The temporary answer lay in her will, where she placed a prohibition on stage productions, motion pictures, radio broadcasts, and other reproduction methods discovered thereafter. Although not perfect, such a stipulation ensured that for at least seventy-five years beyond her death, Cather could employ some artistic control over her art.

What emerges after the release of the Warner Brothers film *A Lost Lady* is Cather's retreat from the public spotlight. By the mid-1930s, as L. Brent Bohlke notes, Cather felt so "completely besieged by the movies, attorneys, investment representatives, and relatives" that she "finally resorted to having her telephone shut off during her working hours and having her secretary write formal letters in place of the personal responses she would rather have made" (xxv). In this protected, personal space, Cather turned to her work. Though out of the public spotlight, she maintained her literary presence through projects such as the Autograph Edition of her collected works and her controversial essay collection, *Not Under Forty*, both of which served as capstones to her career. In solidifying her aesthetics, especially through her essays in *Not Under Forty*, Cather brought to her public a way of reading her writing, a set of principles by which to judge her work.

Throughout Cather's career she showed a keen sense of attention to the most minute of details. Knopf relates that Cather interested herself in almost every aspect of her books' design, from the selection of the paper to the typeface to advertising copy (Knopf 14). With a loss of the artistic control central to Cather's artistic principles, the 1934 adaptation of *A Lost Lady* reveals how the film industry capitalized on her name and literary reputation, as well as how far she would go to protect her work, even when that meant losing what could have been substantial income. Cather's celebrity status was tiresome for her: while it provided the stability and comfort to write as she pleased, it vexed her to see her work and name misused and manipulated for material rather than artistic purposes.

Acknowledgments

All Warner Brothers memos and advertising discussed in this paper are part of the *Lost Lady* Film Collection donated to Archives and Special Collections at the University of Nebraska-Lincoln by Dan Ladely, director of the Mary Riepma Ross Film Theatre at the University of Nebraska-Lincoln. Without Mr. Ladely's kind donation of his research files to the archives, this paper would not have been possible.

Letters from Ferris Greenslet to Willa Cather (shelf mark bMS Am 1925 341) are quoted by permission of the Houghton Library, Harvard University, and Houghton Mifflin.

5

Object Lessons

Nature Education, Museum Science, and Ethnographic Tourism in *The Professor's House*

Anne Raine

Despite her well-documented fascination with objects, Willa Cather is best known as a writer of landscape. While Dreiser, James, and Wharton grappled with the flood of material objects that constitute the "hard facts" of urban modernity,[1] Cather's best-loved novels seem to sweep readers out into the open spaces of nature, evoking a more intimate relationship with the natural world than seems possible in the urbanized, industrialized twentieth century. For many, Cather's evocations of sublime natural spaces are especially compelling because they seem rooted in firsthand, biographical encounters with the land. However, it's important to note that Cather was also a tourist: not only a native of the Nebraska prairie, but also a consumer in a growing economy of nature education and tourism. In this essay, I read Cather's novel *The Professor's House* as an ambivalent response to the recognition that in the twentieth century, nature *is* material culture: not virgin territory, but a set of social discourses and practices, including images and advertisements, roads and railways, scientific documents and National Park Service policies, tourist facilities and museum exhibits.

In *The Song of the Lark* (1915), Cather incorporates her own visit to Walnut Canyon, Arizona, into the story of Thea Kronborg's artistic development. In *The Professor's House* (1925), she returns to the Southwest, and specifically to Mesa Verde National Park, to explore the broader cultural implications of that earlier experience of nature tourism. In the earlier novel, Thea's communion with nature is solitary and singular. In contrast, *The Professor's House* frames Tom Outland's similar experiences as part of a larger question that was also being addressed by conservationists and nature educators: the question of how to produce meaningful contact with nature for modern Americans who, unlike Cather's pioneer heroines, are not "tied to the soil" through intimate working knowledge of the land (*WCIP* 72). This novel struggles to reaffirm the utopian vision of nature as landscape that animates Cather's earlier work, but it also unsettles that earlier pastoral vision in three important ways. First, the "nature" that *The Professor's House* valorizes is not the familiar agrarian landscape of *O Pioneers!* (1913) or *My Ántonia* (1918), but the remote, exoticized, aestheticized space of the modern national park. Second, in its repressed fascination with material objects as metonymic representatives of nature, *The Professor's House* reveals its own origins in both the national park landscape *and* the urban "land of desire" constituted by the department store and its educational corollary, the natural history museum.[2] Finally, by focusing on anthropological rather than natural-historical objects, this troubled novel invites us to grapple with yet another important dimension of the early twentieth-century culture of nature: the complex and often troubling relationships among nature education and tourism, anthropology, modernist primitivism, and the politics of Indian removal that underlies the modernist project of wilderness preservation.

The Professor's House responds to a widespread anxiety in early twentieth-century American culture: the troubled recognition that industrialization, modern science, and the rise of urban consumer culture had fundamentally altered the relationship between human beings and nature. As Joseph Urgo has recently noted, Cather's work was powerfully informed by public debates about wilderness preservation and by the efforts of conservationists and nature writers to "[make] conservation a matter of public spirit and national policy" (Urgo, "National Parks" 46).[3] Cather shared with conservationists and nature educators a desire to bring modern Americans "more into sympathy with the natural world in which we dwell" (Bailey 27). She also shared their recognition that a modern culture of "nature-sympathy" could no longer be based on the shared experience of local nature that had characterized the agrarian past. Since more than half of all Americans now lived in urban areas, a common culture of nature had also to be constructed out of the urban experience, in which "nature" was not a coherent local landscape but rather the exotic, fragmented, fetishized product of a complex discursive economy of nature education and tourism. Accordingly, in *The Professor's House*, Cather experiments with a literary form inspired in part by the national park and the museum diorama. In so doing, she abandons the "earthy" heroines of her earlier novels—here represented only in effigy, in the mummified body of "Mother Eve"—to explore the imaginative possibilities offered by the more authoritatively modern figure of the male museum scientist.[4] Against the Professor's and her own suspicion of both professional science and urban consumer culture, Cather attempts to reimagine modern science as nature education[5] and to consider the possibility that material objects—here, the cliff-dweller artifacts Outland finds in the mesa—might be mobilized to produce authentic knowledge of nature for an increasingly urbanized American public. Rather than a simple rejection of the commodified landscape of modernity, this novel represents Cather's effort to imagine a modern relationship to nature that is reducible neither to mere consumption nor to a fantasy of return to an idealized pastoral or primitive past. Yet the novel remains ambivalent, fractured not only by the distance between the Blue Mesa and the cluttered, commodified urban environment but also by uncertainty about the power of nature education to resist capitalism's transformation of living nature—and of the Native American cultures often viewed as part of nature—into mere resources for consumption and profit.

By the time Cather visited Mesa Verde in 1915, a booming nature-tourist industry was transporting increasing numbers of Americans to see nature in the wild. Railroad companies promoted national parks (as well as ancient cliff dwellings and Pueblo Indian communities) as tourist destinations, building hotels and producing posters and souvenir guidebooks to encourage rail travel in the West. Beginning in 1916, the newly established National Park Service would supplement the railroads' production and promotion of "Nature" with improved facilities and services emphasizing "healthful recreation and education" rather than mere "amusement."[6] Mesa Verde had been incorporated into the growing system of national parks in 1906; by 1915 it offered automobile access, telephone lines, hot meals, comfortable accommodations, tourist brochures, tour guides, and an informal lecture series, and would soon add an on-site museum (see Harrell). Meanwhile, urban institutions like the American Museum of Natural History were bringing nature to the urban masses in the form of mounted specimens and artifacts. Through firsthand contact with material objects, museum educators argued, visitors could experience not nature's wide-open spaces but nature as still life: natural objects displaced and displayed, resonant metonyms for nature as a living whole (or, in the case of anthropological artifacts, metonyms for a more intimate relationship between human and nonhuman nature).[7] Like the national parks, the museum claimed to offer the modern public a knowledge of nature grounded in active firsthand investigation and to make authentic, progressive, rejuvenating contact with nature accessible to "the every-day man."[8]

Still life—the presentation of nature as an arrangement of material objects—was central to urban nature education because it literally made nature accessible. By bringing natural objects close enough for visitors to see and touch, the museum offered an experience of proximal intimacy with nature that, proponents claimed, enabled a more accurate and authentic form of knowledge than could be gained through the mediations of scientific data, printed words, or photographic images. However, that accessibility came at a price. As art historian Meyer Schapiro writes in an essay on Cézanne, the objects of still life are "no longer on their natural ground and might be replaced by artificial [ones]. Like the commodities in the windows of a shop they are a world of things, nature transposed or transformed for man" (45–46). And this transformation was especially troubling in the literalized still life of the natural history museum: scientists could bring nature to the museum only by killing the animals and removing them from their natural surroundings, severing the complex interrelationships of organisms and environment that it was the business of modern nature education to make plain. Integral elements of living environments were transformed into individual objects, displaced, decontextualized, and rearranged according to human desires, much like the commodities that circulated on the market and were displayed in the windows of department stores.[9]

Against this fetishization of material objects, museum scientists developed the educational technology of the diorama—also called the "life group" in anthropology and the "habitat group" in natural history—

which presented specimens within visual representations of their natural habitats. While still reminiscent of the department store display window, the diorama was designed not simply to showcase the objects, but to make visible each object's role within a particular network of ecological or cultural relationships—or both, since the theme of many anthropological "life groups" was "the relation of man to nature" (Jacknis, "Franz Boas" 100). The diorama thus embodies a conflict between two pedagogical imperatives: to make nature accessible to the urban public and to teach visitors that natural objects are only "natural" when they are part of the site-specific ecological (and in the case of anthropological specimens, socio-ecological) relationships that the diorama makes visible, but which the object's presence in the museum disrupts. That conflict between accessibility and socio-ecological integrity is central to Cather's novel as well, and informs the novel's uncertainty about what "kind of value [material] objects [can have] for [us]," and by extension, what kind of relationship the modern urban dweller can have to the natural world that these objects represent (*PH* 244).

Set in a Midwestern college town but with its heart in the rugged landscape of the Southwest, *The Professor's House* seems far removed from the distilled, "centripetal" space of the museum (Bryson 105). In fact, Cather went out of her way to distance her novel, and the national park that inspired it, from the museum's emphasis on material objects. In "The Novel Démeublé" (1922) she insists that "realism" does not depend on detailed description of material objects; criticizing naturalism's failure to transcend the soulless materialism of the laboratory and the marketplace, she urges writers to "throw all the furniture out of the window" and "leave the room as bare as the stage of a Greek theatre" (*OW* 37, 42). In a 1938 letter on *The Professor's House,* she goes even further: here, the ideal aesthetic space she had imagined as "one passion and four walls" is not just stripped of furniture, but turned inside out and dissolved into the unbounded expanses of nature (*OW* 43). The novel's structure, she explains, was inspired by Dutch paintings of domestic interiors containing "a square window, open, through which one saw the masts of ships, or a stretch of grey sea." In describing the paintings, Cather approvingly evokes still life's intimate realm of creaturely routines and domestic artifacts. But in *The Professor's House* what the letter initially describes as "living-rooms warmly furnished" and "kitchen[s] full of food and coppers" become houses "overcrowded and stuffy with new things" (*OW* 31).[10] As in seventeenth-century Dutch still life, these "new things"—spoils of what Godfrey St. Peter calls an "orgy of acquisition" reminiscent of "Napoleon looting the Italian palaces"—unsettle the proximal intimacy between human beings and the object-world, invoking the abstract spaces of commerce and embodying new forms of abundance incommensurate with domestic needs (*PH* 152–53; Bryson 96–104). Against this disturbing spectacle of acquisition and abundance, *The Professor's House* replaces the paintings' glimpse of grey sea (with "ships plying [its] waters" in another allusion to the Dutch commercial empire) with the image of the Blue Mesa. The novel's middle section, "Tom Outland's Story," seems not merely to "open the square window and let in the fresh air that blew off the mesa," but to sweep readers bodily out into the redemptive space of the Western landscape (*OW* 31).

In an essay published in the *Denver Times* describing her 1915 visit to Mesa Verde, Cather asserts that "The Mesa Verde is not, as many people think, an inconveniently situated museum," but rather a story, and a story rooted in a particular natural landscape. "It is the story of an early race, of the social and religious life of a people indigenous to that soil and its rocky splendors," Cather writes, "the human expression of that land of sharp contours, brutal contrasts, glorious color and blinding light" ("Mesa Verde" 333). Archaeologists like Gustav Nordenskiöld and Jesse Walter Fewkes might focus on excavating and cataloguing the objects buried in the mesa,[11] but *The Professor's House* insists that the meaning of Tom Outland's story does not lie in the artifacts Tom's diary so lovingly describes, but rather in the rugged landscape that Professor St. Peter calls "Outland's country" (270). Initially driven by the desire to make people "understand the kind of value those objects had had for [him]," Tom eventually decides that what matters is not the objects, but "the feeling of being *on the mesa*" (244, 239). By the end of the novel, St. Peter explicitly identifies Outland with "those sculptured peaks and impassable mountain passes— . . . those long, rugged, untamed vistas dear to the American heart [and] calling to all," suggesting that the "glittering idea" Tom Outland embodies is the sublime, patriotic image of American nature that was being promoted by, and materially embodied in, the expanding national park system (270, 110).

In privileging landscape over material objects, Cather transforms

Tom Outland from a pot hunter and amateur archaeologist into a kind of evangelist for national park tourism. *The Professor's House* shares with conservationists like Sierra Club founder John Muir a belief that "whole-souled exercise" in the national parks could restore physical and spiritual health to over-civilized modern Americans (Muir, *National Parks* 1). Like her characters Thea Kronborg and Tom Outland, Cather found the Southwest a compelling invitation to active bodily participation in the landscape of nature. As she later declared, "nobody could just 'sit and look' in such a place—the rock walls challenged one to climb" (qtd. in Sergeant 133). In "Tom Outland's Story," Cather shows how active, embodied investigation of the mesa—fording rivers, scrambling up cliffs, tasting the water and drinking in the air—can produce an intimacy with nature that approximates the working knowledge previous generations had gained through agricultural labor.[12] Like Cather's other alter egos, Thea Kronborg in *The Song of the Lark* and Jim Burden in *My Ántonia,* Tom finds profound happiness in being "dissolved into something complete and great," immersed not merely in the contemplation of a sublime vista but in the proximal knowledge of nature embodied in the smell of wild-currant blossoms, the heat of sunlight on skin, and the feel of worn flat rock underfoot (*MA* 18; *PH* 239, 249–50). Through this sensuous immersion in the natural landscape, Tom Outland models the attitude with which Cather hoped future visitors would approach Mesa Verde. Rather than merely sightseeing or souvenir hunting, Tom becomes an exemplary nature tourist, transmuting embodied experience into a reverence for nature that Cather, like Muir, conceives as "a religious emotion" (*PH* 250).

By sharing his experiences with the Professor—and, by extension, with Cather's readers—Outland also acts as an exemplary nature *writer.* Like Muir or Cather herself, Outland ventures into the vital landscape of nature and then shapes his experiences into a first-person narrative filled with evocative description of ecological detail. As Glen Love has argued, Outland's story does not merely interrupt the novel's third-person narrative, but transforms it: exemplifying both Cather's aesthetics of simplification and her passion for the natural landscape, "Tom Outland's Story" is the turning point in the novel's movement away from the psychological dramas and "overfurnished" sentences of "The Family" toward the radical simplicity of the novel's final section (*Profes-*

sor's House 306). By pointing out this movement toward short, incantatory sentences that evoke "a virtually wordless, sensory existence," Love suggests that Outland's story facilitates a new relationship to the natural world as well as a modernist prose style.[13] Like Thea Kronborg, whose sojourn in Panther Canyon involves lying "hour after hour in the sun" until "her power to think seem[s] converted into a power of sustained sensation," Godfrey St. Peter develops "a new sense" that enables him to "lie on his sand-spit by the lake for hours and watch the seven motionless pines drink up the sun" (*SL* 269–70; *PH* 263). Falling temporarily out of language as well as out of "domestic and human relations," the Professor becomes "a primitive," interested only in "earth and woods and water" and the awareness that he "was earth, and would return to earth" (*PH* 275, 265). By taking Outland's story to heart, St. Peter sees past the commodified clutter of modern life to the "Truth under all truths" of our creaturely participation in material nature—both through our mortality and through the material life of the senses.[14]

Cather's novel thus enacts the nature movement's utopian hope that, as Muir put it in 1901, national park tourism would inspire "thousands of tired, nerve-shaken, over-civilized people" to awaken from "the stupefying effects of the vice of over-industry and the deadly apathy of luxury" and begin "to mix and enrich their own little ongoings with those of Nature" (*National Parks* 1). To those whose senses are awakened, Muir writes, "it will hardly seem necessary to cross the continent in search of wild beauty, . . . for they find it in abundance wherever they chance to be" (2–3). Inspired by Outland's example, the Professor travels to the Southwest to experience that remote landscape for himself, but he also becomes more attentive to natural objects near at hand: white clouds over the lake, "pine-trees [turning] red in the declining sun," a "curly root that thrust itself across his path," and "maple-leaves along the street" in the very town that stands for modern commercialism and alienation (*PH* 265–66). In 1927, agreeing with Muir that "It is Nature, even though it be but a vacant lot," American Museum of Natural History curator Frank E. Lutz added that "Nature becomes a part of and fills out our lives if some friend introduces us to her and we become really acquainted" (377). By "mixing and enriching" the Professor's story with that of his adventurous and emblematic friend, Cather shows how even the ordinary landscape of modernity might provide the revitalizing contact with nature that is represented more dramatically by the distant landscape of the national park—a reading that might explain why embracing "a world full of Augustas," a modern world circumscribed by domestic rituals attuned to the "sadnesses of nature," can be described as being "outward bound" (*PH* 281).

Like Muir, however, *The Professor's House* insists that such local epiphanies depend on the preservation, and indeed the production, of nature in the form of national parks, remote "world[s] above the world," reservoirs of a mysterious "kind of value" that cannot be translated into "chemicals and dollars and cents" (239, 244, 130). When Cather writes about Mesa Verde in "Tom Outland's Story," she minimizes the traces of the modern national park that she herself encountered in 1915 and presents instead a romantic tale of wilderness adventure and original discovery. But by embedding "Tom Outland's Story" in *The Professor's House,* she constructs a narrative that is highly self-conscious about its own embeddedness in the material culture of nature tourism. By making the Blue Mesa an exotic interlude rather than integrating its landscape into the larger narrative (as she had in *O Pioneers!* or even *The Song of the Lark*), Cather constructs nature as a space set apart, its value located explicitly in its distance from the prosperous farms of *O Pioneers!* and the "heaped-up, machine-made materialism" that prosperity had produced ("Nebraska" 238). The novel's structure thus mirrors John Muir's famous vision of the national parks as pristine temples, sanctuaries from the "raging commercialism" of modern society (*Yosemite* 202). Instead of moving backward in time to the landscape of the pioneer past, this novel moves spatially, relocating the space of nature from the working landscape of the agrarian frontier to the aestheticized space of the modern national park—a space at once removed from and integral to the landscape of modernity, designed and produced for urban tourists like Godfrey St. Peter and Cather herself.

Oddly, however, St. Peter's vision of "Outland's country" as a land of "sculptured peaks and impassable mountain passes" sounds much more like Rocky Mountain National Park in northern Colorado than the canyons and tablelands of Mesa Verde (*PH* 270). Anxious about his family's attachment to material possessions and seduced by the "glittering idea" of nature as landscape enshrined in national park posters and brochures, the Professor disavows the fact that Mesa Verde is the only national park created to preserve, *not* "rugged topography and scenic wonders," but archaeological remains (Smith ix). Objects, not landscape, are the reason for this particular national park's existence; and despite the novel's affirmation of landscape, objects are also central to Tom Outland's project of nature education. What Outland discovers on the mesa is not, as St. Peter claims, a "rugged, untamed vista," but a domestic scene that resembles nothing so much as a traditional still life painting adapted to New World ecology: clay jars and bowls, dried beans and ears of corn, "strings of pumpkin seeds, and plum seeds, and a cupboard full of little implements made of turkey bones" (*PH* 270, 208). Intimate rather than sublime in scale, this literalized still life presents the products of local nature brought within the proximal space of the body, evoking modes of production and consumption more responsive to ecological specificities than the modern capitalist economy of mobile commodities and mass-produced consumer goods.[15] Read this way, "Tom Outland's Story" does not so much sweep readers into a pure expanse of nature as resituate them in an alternative domestic space, one whose value lies in its distance from the modern capitalist economy and its evocation of an earlier way of life based on handicrafts and subsistence agriculture—in other words, the primitivist utopia that Cather and other white visitors saw in the living cultures of the Hopi and Zuni Pueblos.

Outland's fascination with these Pueblo artifacts, and his desire to see them preserved in a national museum, should remind us that Cather herself experienced what she called "the cliff-dweller thrill" not only in the Southwest, but also in New York City, at an exhibit of cliff-dweller remains at the American Museum of Natural History (qtd. in Butcher 9). According to Elizabeth Shepley Sergeant, this urban encounter with ancient Pueblo pottery was for Cather a rapturous and revitalizing experience. Despite having been dug up, pieced together, transported and arranged by "hard-boiled archaeologists," these resonant objects still "conjure[d] up" both the Pueblo women who made them *and* "the burning sun of Arizona; the cry of the cicada in the great silence of a cliff city; the aromatic odor of yellow flowers growing in rocky crevices" in a land whose "rock walls challenged one to climb" (Sergeant 132–33). For Cather, Pueblo artifacts could serve as metonyms for nature because they were a "human expression" of their natural environment, products of a culture whose "national purpose," Cather believed, was to observe and express a "religion [that] was largely a personal recognition and interpretation of nature" ("Mesa Verde" 332–33). Sergeant's anecdote testifies to the success of the museum's strategy of presenting nature as still life: for these two visitors at least, these displaced and displayed objects served as highly effective metonyms for both the prehistoric culture of the cliff-dwellers and the living landscape of nature.

Accordingly, Tom Outland becomes not only the imaginary founder of a national park, but also a prototype of the modern museum educator. Cather takes pains to distinguish Outland's interest in objects from that of the mercenary pot-hunter or acquisitive connoisseur.[16] Unlike many of the pot-hunters, dealers, and collectors who capitalized on the booming trade in Southwestern artifacts, he is committed to the careful documentation that gives objects scientific value;[17] rather than simply digging up objects to sell or keep, he keeps a record of "each day's work among the ruins," sketching and describing each object and noting "where and in what condition [he] had found it, and what [he] thought it had been used for" (*PH* 262, 210). Moreover, unlike Roddy Blake, who first appears like an emblem of the vice of luxury in a Dutch genre painting, with gold spilling from his pockets, Outland aspires to "[have] in his pocket" only "the secrets which old trails and stones and watercourses tell" (Yongue, "Genre Painting" 161; *PH* 259). Recognizing this proximal knowledge of nature as his most valuable "possession," Tom hopes neither to sell nor to own the clay pots, tools, and turquoises, but to distribute them as representatives of both the ancient cliff-dwellers' intimacy with nature and his own "feeling of being *on the mesa*" (*PH* 250, 239). The connection is most clear in the case of the turquoise of the novel's epigraph. The image of Tom's "muscular, many-lined palm . . . with the blue stones lying in it" reverses the novel's dizzying sweep outward from cluttered domestic interior to the unbounded natural space of "that summer, high and blue." Here, the pure, bare space of the Blue Mesa is distilled into a solid object that can be transported and held in the hand (*PH* 119, 252).[18] Outland's desire to share these objects (first with the Smithsonian, then with the St. Peter family) echoes the museum educator's optimistic faith that firsthand contact with material objects, however removed from their original surroundings, could inspire "nature-sympathy" in even the most "over-civilized" of urban dwellers.

The trouble with objects, however, is their potential to be mistaken for mere commodities (as when Blake sells the artifacts to a German collector) or personal possessions (as when Cather, as she later guiltily confessed, took some ancient potsherds from Walnut Canyon and kept them for herself [Sergeant 133]). In order to be read as metonyms for nature, the objects must be incorporated into exhibits that make visible their interconnectedness with their original environment. This is why the middle section of *The Professor's House* is not Tom Outland's diary, but his oral account of his experiences on the mesa. Unlike the diary, which catalogues and describes the artifacts themselves, "Tom Outland's Story" functions like a museum diorama; its goal is to bring not just isolated objects but "whole living sections of nature within its walls" by situating the artifacts within a scenic background so perfect that it seems to transport its audience bodily into the landscape it represents.[19] The objects serve as compellingly tactile vehicles of transmission, but it is the landscape of nature—here, crafted in words rather than paint and plaster—that most fully resists their misinterpretation as mere commodities or possessions.

Given Cather's respect for Pueblo culture, one might expect this diorama to be an anthropological one, a "life group" like those designed by Franz Boas for the American Museum of Natural History. But the real subject of Cather's literary diorama is neither Colorado wildlife nor Pueblo culture, but Outland himself. Rather than replicas of ancient Pueblo people "engaged in some characteristic work or art illustrative of their life," Cather showcases the daily life of the nature tourist turned museum educator who collects and interprets their remains.[20] Cather thus creates a highly self-referential kind of diorama, one whose subject is the very curatorial work that produces such technologies of nature education. That self-consciousness makes "Tom Outland's Story" very different from the Panther Canyon episode in *The Song of the Lark*, which also presents a modern encounter with cliff-dweller artifacts. In the earlier novel, Thea Kronborg experiences her own body as a medium through which the spirits of long-dead Pueblo women return to life: she "walk[s] as they must have walked, with a feeling in her feet and knees and loins which she had never known before," and "feel[s] the weight of an Indian baby hanging to her back" (271). In contrast, Outland encounters these so-called "grandmothers" not as living presences, but as archaeological specimens (*PH* 242). Like Thea, Tom is moved by the knowledge that the trail he walks on was "worn by their moccasin feet coming and going for generations," and says that "their old pots, with the fire-black on them" make the cliff-dwellers "real to [him]" (*PH* 117–18). Here, however, any desire to identify with the ancient Pueblo people is disrupted by the literal, material presence of "one of the original inhabitants" in the form of "a dried human body, a woman" (*PH* 212). Like the deliberately artificial-looking mannequins Boas preferred for his "life groups,"[21] the mute, mummified body of "Mother Eve" arrests identification, underscoring the difference between the dead cliff-dwellers and the modern scientists and tourists—Outland, Cather, the reader—who study their remains.

In calling Mother Eve "a dried human body, a woman," Cather emphasizes both the humanity of this long-dead Pueblo woman and her present status as inert object and archaeological specimen. The odd phrasing contrasts strongly not only with *The Song of the Lark*'s lyrical evocation of imagined Native Americans, but also with Cather's 1916 essay on Mesa Verde, in which she emphasizes the continuity between the ancient cliff-dwellers and the living Indians who still inhabit the pueblos of the Southwest ("Mesa Verde" 333). Given Cather's satirical treatment of Smithsonian archaeologists in *The Professor's House*, this reduction of Pueblo culture to a single "dried human body" might be read as an ironic critique of Outland's objectifying scientific attitude, evidence of his masculine desire to master and possess the mesa by "dig[ging] out all its secrets" and inserting his own scientific document in place of the displaced body that represents most implacably the mesa's original inhabitants (*PH* 223, 221).[22] Given the cliff-dwellers' intimacy with their natural environment and the traditional image of nature as a female body, the marks of a violent death that scar this particular female body might also be read as a critique of the scientific objectification and penetration of mother nature herself.[23] In this reading, the fact that Mother Eve's body falls into the canyon on its way to being shipped to a German collector does not, as Roddy claims, represent the mummy's familial loyalty to the amateur archaeologists who claim her as their "grandmother," but rather a silent reproach to those who would disrupt the mesa's ecological integrity by removing her and the other artifacts from their natural habitat, whether for profit or for the edification of urban museum-goers (*PH* 244).

By returning Mother Eve to her natural environment rather than allowing her to circulate as either commodity or museum exhibit, Cather removes her from modernity and history and consigns her, along with the Native American cultures she represents, to a natural world imagined as a transcendent and timeless space. Read this way, Mother Eve's return to the canyon reinforces the primitivist stereotype of Native Americans as natural rather than cultural beings, and paradoxically also replicates the expulsion of Native Americans from the national parks so that those parks could be redefined as "pure nature" and made accessible to white urban tourists. Such removals were integral to the establishment of wilderness parks like Yellowstone and Yosemite; even at Mesa Verde, that most obviously acculturated of nature preserves, white Americans assumed that establishing a national park would require wresting the land surrounding the cliff dwellings from the Ute Indians who owned it and divesting them of their right to graze cattle there.[24] Rather than an escape from objectification as a scientific specimen, Mother Eve's fall would then represent the expulsion of living Native Americans from the modern gardens of Eden that conservationists like Muir sought to construct for the benefit of the white urban public. According to Elsie Sergeant, Cather was uninterested in the question of Indian rights that preoccupied many of her friends during the 1920s; pressed to consider what the Pueblo Indians' relation should be to a democratic American society, Cather "laughed and moved on to her major interests: landscape, the perspectives of history, the cliff dwellings" (Sergeant 174–75). In this novel as in the national park, the point of the story ultimately is not the fate of Native Americans, living or dead, but the salutary effects that Outland's project of nature education has on urban dwellers like Professor St. Peter.

On the other hand, it is also possible to read the objectification and loss of Mother Eve as an ambivalent repudiation of Cather's own earlier appropriation of Pueblo culture. By defining Outland's relationship to "his" Pueblo "grandmothers" as an inheritance of objects rather than a corporeal and spiritual identification, *The Professor's House* tacitly acknowledges, as *The Song of the Lark* does not, the difference between

Euro-American and Native American cultures that Cather would explore more fully in *Death Comes for the Archbishop* (1927), and so unsettles the fantasy that white urban dwellers can develop a more authentic relation to nature simply by "playing Indian" (Dilworth 7–8). By framing the body of "Mother Eve" as an archaeological specimen rather than incorporating it into a primitivist fantasy of spiritual merging, Cather does not so much objectify Pueblo culture as consider the possibility that the modern scientist, properly conceived, might provide a more appropriate model for meaningful contact with nature under the conditions of modernity. Outland's work on the mesa exemplifies what Cornell biologist and nature-study advocate Liberty Hyde Bailey called "nature-sympathy": a democratic mode of inquiry whose "essence is spirit" rather than disciplinary rigor and whose methods are "as free as its subject-matter, as far removed from the museum and the cabinet as the living animal is from the skeleton" (28). Rather than trying to replicate an "Indian Garden of Eden," Cather's literary diorama showcases a modern approach to the natural world that valorizes individual "use of the senses in acquiring knowledge," attends to the site-specific relationships between human culture and natural environment, and is not so focused on individual specimens as to risk "los[ing] the whole in the parts" (Bailey 18; *PH* 251).

Cather's decision to make "Tom Outland's Story" a diorama about Tom Outland rather than about Pueblo culture also represents an ambivalent repudiation of her own complicity in the fetishization of Native American culture within the discursive economy of nature tourism. In her 1916 travel essay on Mesa Verde, Cather presents the living culture of early twentieth-century Pueblo Indians in a way that echoes precisely a 1905 tourist pamphlet produced by the Fred Harvey Company to advertise "A New Hotel at Grand Canyon of Arizona." The Harvey pamphlet invites travelers to admire the spectacle of "quaintly-garbed [Hopi] Indians on the housetop," "the most primitive Indians in America, with ceremonies several centuries old" (qtd. in Dilworth 89–90). Cather's article, aptly titled "Mesa Verde Wonderland Is Easy to Reach," similarly draws attention to the "old Indians [who] come out in their white burnouses and take their accustomed grave positions on the housetops," concurring with Harvey's copy writer that "one has only to go down into Hopiland to find the same life going on today" as in the time of the ancient cliff-dwellers (86). Anticipating Cather's association of the cliff dwellings with Dutch still life, the same pamphlet also describes the interior of a Hopi dwelling as being "as cleanly as a Dutch kitchen." However, the dwelling in question is in fact "Hopi House," a tourist attraction featuring ethnographic exhibits (including an Indian family hired to inhabit the house as a kind of living diorama of Hopi home life), Hopi artisans at work, and a souvenir shop where tourists could buy Indian craft items similar to the ones in the ethnographic display (Dilworth 88–90). Conflating nature tourism, museum science, and commodity exchange, such attractions are likely the subtext of Cather's insistence that Mesa Verde is "not, as many people think, an inconveniently situated museum" ("Mesa Verde" 333). In this context, her decision to jettison Mother Eve from "Outland's country" suggests, if not a serious effort to engage with living Native American people, then at least a discomfort with her own complicity in the promotion of Pueblo culture as a tourist attraction.[25]

It is tempting, though anachronistic, to read Mother Eve's fall into the canyon as a gesture of resistance and despair similar to that of the heroines' plunge into the Grand Canyon at the end of the film *Thelma and Louise* (1991). Faced with the multiple contradictions involved in the intersection of nature education with anthropology and tourism, Cather seems to have thrown up her hands and let the Pueblo woman disappear into the "untamed vistas" of nature rather than attempting to imagine a future for her within the modern project of nature education. In insisting that the "real story" of Mesa Verde is not the one in archaeologists' "scientific books" but the one told to her by "the brother of Dick Wetherell [*sic*]," whose 1888 sighting of the cliff dwellings was the model for Tom Outland's, Cather also overlooks another story that she might have chosen to tell: that of the Colorado club women who had tried to negotiate an agreement with the Ute Indians that would establish a park at Mesa Verde without divesting the Utes of their grazing rights (*OW* 32).[26] That omission is perhaps indirectly addressed at the end of *Death Comes for the Archbishop*, where Father Latour belatedly acknowledges his own guilt for not intervening on behalf of the Navajos when the U.S. government drove them from their homeland (294–95). In *The Professor's House*, the omission is also marked indirectly in Cather's inability to imagine any role for the Professor's daughters other than that of consumer and in the Professor's ambiguous resolve to "live without delight" (282). If Cather's dislike of club women and their "causes" led her to privilege the "glittering idea" of wilderness preservation rather than a more complicated story of intercultural negotiations over the meaning and use of "nature," the silent fall of "Mother Eve" and the Professor's subdued resolve point—though tentatively and perhaps unconsciously—toward a difficult "letting go with the heart" of the primitivist fantasies that had fueled her own imagination and that of a generation of nature tourists and modernist writers.

Notes

1. I borrow this phrase from Fisher, *Hard Facts: Setting and Form in the American Novel.*

2. See the illuminating history of the department store in Leach, *Land of Desire.*

3. Arguing that Cather's 1915 visit to Mesa Verde "had a profound effect on the shape of her fiction and on her aesthetic sensibilities," Urgo shows how even *My Ántonia,* a novel so apparently removed from the Southwest and from any national park, is centrally informed by the ideals of the wilderness preservation movement ("National Parks" 58). In Urgo's view, both *My Ántonia* and *The Professor's House* reflect Cather's desire, shared with the national parks movement, to "preserve the American wilderness experience as an art form" and to ensure that a few carefully selected "emblems of national wildlands would be available forever" as "sites of heightened experience" (49, 61). Here, I explore how *The Professor's House* at once shares and unsettles that serene preservationist vision by exposing, through its unresolved conflicts and evocative silences, the practical and moral difficulties involved in making this highly constructed "nature" accessible and meaningful to modern urban dwellers.

4. For other readings of *The Professor's House* as a celebration rather than a critique of the modern scientist, see Love, "The Cowboy in the Laboratory," Bender, and Reynolds.

5. This goal was shared by many National Park Service officials and museum scientists; see, for example, Bryant and Atwood, Lutz, and Sherwood; also, Pitcaithley and Wonders.

6. "Superintendents' Resolution on Overdevelopment," National Park Service Conference, 1922 (qtd. in Pitcaithley).

7. Many white Americans in the early twentieth century viewed Southwestern pueblo cultures as models for imagining a human civilization more in harmony with the nonhuman world. See Hönnighausen, Dilworth, and the essays in Norwood and Monk.

8. "Natural Science for the Every-day Man," *Outlook,* May 1908 (qtd. in Wonders 109).

9. The resemblance between museum dioramas and department store windows is not coincidental. Hoping to attract larger audiences and more private funding, many museum professionals consciously followed the lead of department store retailers who were replacing haphazard assortments of objects with artfully arranged displays (Leach, *Land of Desires* 164–73). Newark Museum founder John Cotton Dana argued that department stores were the spaces most "closely associated with the life of the people" and thus the best model for progressive nature education; for Steward Culin, curator of ethnology at the Brooklyn Museum, department stores were "the greatest influence for culture and taste that exist today" (qtd. in Leach 168, 167).

10. See Yongue, "Genre Painting," for a discussion of this shift in the context of the seventeenth-century Dutch art with which Cather was probably familiar.

11. Cather consulted both of these scientific authorities as part of her research for *The Professor's House.* See Cather, "On *The Professor's House*" (*OW* 30–32) and Harrell.

12. On the connection between recreation and work in the national parks, see White.

13. In noting how the novel moves toward utterances that do not predicate but simply point toward material objects ("That is right," St. Peter says, looking at the natural objects in his path, "That is it" [*PH* 266]), Love interestingly parallels Douglas Mao's argument that in *Mrs. Dalloway* Virginia Woolf questions the human urge to transform the natural world and proposes as an alternative a relationship of "ostension," marked in conversations stripped down to indexical utterances like "Listen . . ." and "There!" (Mao 80).

14. In a recent re-reading of *The Professor's House,* Love shows how this moment, which might be viewed as a simple case of romantic primitivism, takes on new significance when read through an interpretive framework drawn from evolutionary biology and phenomenology. See Love, "Nature and Human Nature."

15. I am indebted here to Bryson's reading of Dutch still life in *Looking at the Overlooked.*

16. On the booming trade in Southwestern artifacts in the early twentieth century, see Wade and Dilworth.

17. On the importance of documentation to the professionalization of museum science, see Jacknis, "Patrons" 161.

18. The image of the turquoises in Tom's hand thus resonates with Bryson's reading of the distilled, centripetal space of Dutch still life and with Mao's argument that the desire to distill the flux of experience into "solid objects" is central to Anglo-American modernism.

19. "Scientific Taxidermy for Museums," *Report of the U.S. National Museum, 1892*, qtd. in Wonders 126.

20. Anthropologist Frederick Ward Putnam, qtd. in Jacknis, "Franz Boas" 100.

21. Boas argued that "No figure, however well it may have been gotten up, will look like man himself. . . . When the figure is absolutely lifelike the lack of motion causes a ghastly impression such as we notice in wax-figures. For this reason the artistic effect will be better when we bear in mind this fact and do not attempt too close an approach to nature; that is to say, since there is a line of demarcation between nature and plastic art, it is better to draw the line consciously than to try to hide it" (qtd. in Jacknis, "Franz Boas" 102).

22. See, for example, Lindemann, *Queering America* 102–9.

23. Although Cather herself rarely, if ever, directly referred to the Earth as female, images of the Earth as a fertile female body clearly inform her early pioneer novels, though not without ambivalence. For an influential critique of the image of science as a penetration of the body of Mother Earth, see Merchant.

24. On national parks and Indian removal, see Spence; on the Utes and Mesa Verde in particular, see Keller and Turek, and Burnham.

25. A similar self-consciousness is evident in William Carlos Williams's *In the American Grain*, published the same year as *The Professor's House*. Williams compresses into a single sentence the movement from desire to self-recriminating irony to rupture and repudiation that also characterizes Cather's novel: "The land! Don't you feel it? Doesn't it make you want to go out and lift dead Indians tenderly from their graves, to steal from them—as if it must be clinging even to their corpses—some authenticity, that which—Here not there" (74).

26. See Burnham, Keller and Turek, and Kaufman.

6

"An Orgy of Acquisition"

The Female Consumer, Infidelity, and Commodity Culture in *A Lost Lady* and *The Professor's House*

HONOR MCKITRICK WALLACE

In "The Novel Démeublé," Willa Cather asks a presumably rhetorical question: "Is the story of a banker who is unfaithful to his wife and who ruins himself by speculation in trying to gratify the caprices of his mistresses, at all reinforced by a masterly exposition of banking, our whole system of credits, the methods of the Stock Exchange?" (*OW* 37). In the context of her own works, this question becomes more ironic. Is the story of an engineer who is unfaithful to his wife at all reinforced by an exposition of bridge building—as in *Alexander's Bridge*? Is the story of a developer's wife who is unfaithful to him reinforced by placing that story in the context of the development of the West—as in *A Lost Lady*? While no one will accuse Cather of bogging her tales down in naturalistic detail, material objects and economic conditions are vital to her plots.

Early Cather critics took her perhaps too much at her word when she said that "economics and art are strangers" ("Escapism," *OW* 27). Marxist scholars of the 1930s such as Granville Hicks, for instance, notoriously charged Cather with "a refusal to examine life as it is" (147). More recently, however, critics have shown her approach toward material culture to be more complex. For instance, John Hilgart's analysis of commodity culture in *Death Comes for the Archbishop* and *The Professor's House* sees "a friction . . . between Cather's aesthetic model and her stance regarding mass culture" insofar as her "fiction is dotted . . . with special objects" (380). In *Willa Cather in Context: Progress, Race, Empire*, Guy Reynolds examines *The Professor's House* in terms of the theories of Thorstein Veblen, and Michael Spindler has also briefly written on this topic. Additionally, Janis Stout has argued in *Willa Cather: The Writer and Her World* that "the concern with money and the gaining or losing of wealth is another characteristic that distinguishes *A Lost Lady*, along with *The Professor's House* and *My Mortal Enemy*, from Cather's work more generally. . . . [They] had a great deal to do with the effects of money management and asset gathering, and not a little with the processes themselves" (189). This essay seeks to develop such analyses of material culture in Cather's later work by reading Marian Forrester and Rosamond Marsellus in the context of 1920s advertising culture's representation of women. My argument is that Cather connects eroticism, consumption, and technology to a critique of commodity culture and that, moreover, we can ultimately see Cather's oft-cited turning away from modernity as a rejection of the modern female consumer in favor of premodern ideals of femininity.

I want to situate my examination of these novels within what Lawrence Birkin has identified as the broad shift around the turn of the century from a culture emphasizing production and property to one emphasizing consumption and spending. As Birkin points out, this shift was not merely economic; studies of sexuality conducted by thinkers from Darwin and Freud to Havelock Ellis associated consumption and spending with a feminized notion of desire. Thus, he suggests, "in the course of the twentieth century, desire has begun to replace property as the symbolic badge of individualism" (12). While such a transition has had the effect of recognizing women and children as subjects, the advance of this idea seems to have been more readily accepted in science, psychoanalysis, and sexuality than in the culture more broadly, where the connection between consumption and a feminized desire was often greeted with suspicion. Since at least the beginning of the industrial revolution, women have long been in the role of consumers, as many critics have pointed out.[1] But whereas in the nineteenth century such consumption was confined to the home and was contained by ideas of self-regulation and restraint of desire, what Lubar refers to as the "second consumer revolution," occurring around the turn of the century and up through the 1920s, moved consumption into the public sphere and asked women to remove restraints upon their desire and to give in to impulse, play, and dreams.

Such an opening up of the separate spheres, and such an unleashing of female desire, did not always go over smoothly, and Cather is only one of many social critics to condemn the results of the tying of women's desire to consumption.[2] The rise in consumer culture brought with it an increased divorce rate and fears that technology and materialism would corrupt the virtue of women. It was understandably difficult for critics of consumption to separate perceived moral decline from changing patterns of consumption, since the two ideas were so closely interrelated—as Herbie DiFonzi argues in his study of the popular culture of divorce during this period.

> While the Victorian home had fancied itself a moral haven, the emerging modern home of the 1920s served as a consumption center. With materialism, ironically, came romance. The rigidity of the former generation's moral rules was undone, not by any desperate desire for licentiousness, but rather by the shifting social patterns brought on by a rising tide of disposable income. (16)

In the novels I will be examining, Cather deals with two sites of consumption—the telephone and the store—that were especially perceived as conflating the public and the private and their attendant desires. The former is an example of what Lubar describes as a "gray area" between production and consumption, while the latter was undergoing alterations in order to better mix consumption with desire. Cather's response to these sites identifies them not only with female desire, but also with infidelity and promiscuity.

The change that Birkin identifies as taking place in political, scientific, and sexological discourse was of course acknowledged and exploited by consumer culture itself. In the 1920s, the advertising industry began to create a discourse that implicitly acknowledged female sexuality—legitimate or otherwise—and tied it to what was represented as a wholly legitimate desire for commodities. According to Roland Marchand in *Advertising the American Dream: Making Way for Modernity, 1920–1940*, an article in *Printer's Ink* advised that "most American women lead rather monotonous and humdrum lives. . . . Such women need romance.

They crave glamour and color. . . . [Advertising should be] the magical carpets on which they may ride out to love [and] . . . see themselves as *femme* [*sic*] *fatales,* as Cleopatra or Helen of Troy" (67). The female consumer of the late twenties was thus encouraged to dream ways "out" of the house and to style herself after dangerous, seductive adulteresses who destroy both homes and empires. In keeping with this image, for instance, a favorite advertising strategy of the late twenties emulated the lurid headlines of *True Story,* hinting at adultery with such statements as "I Deceived My Husband and I'm Proud of it!" and "Some Wives Do It, but I Wouldn't Dare" (56). Such tactics portrayed the female consumer as a potential adulteress and the adulteress as the ultimate consumer.

A Lost Lady acknowledges this association in Marian Forrester's use of the telephone. For most of the telephone's history up until the twenties, it was regarded purely as a business tool, not for frivolous use. Marchand cites an advertising commonplace, for instance, in which a man stood next to a vast desk topped with an imposing phone, looking out a window of epic proportion. Marchand explains that, in this early iconography of the telephone,

> Both the telephone and the window-with-a-view symbolized prestige and power. Their combined presence adequately distinguished the executive . . . from the mere salesman. . . . The telephone itself, as AT&T ads constantly emphasized, symbolized control, the ability to "multiply" one's personality and issue commands at a distance. (238–39)

Carolyn Marvin has similarly argued for the telephone's masculine connotations in *When Old Technologies Were New: Thinking about Electric Communication in the Late Nineteenth Century.* Women were largely to be excluded from using the telephone, both by the insistence that the telephone be a business tool and by the suggestion that they were incapable of understanding the technology. Hence, women were often the butt of jokes in trade journals, demonstrating their technical incompetence by, for instance, forgetting to ring before talking.

In the face of this patriarchal reading of the telephone, however, a competing discourse began to associate it with women and with pleasure. The threat of this association had existed since the inception of the telephone, and many measures had been taken to contain its potential danger. In *America Calling: A Social History of the Telephone to 1940*, Claude Fischer notes that telephone "industry men . . . had misgivings about such conversations in the nineteenth century. Some worried that the telephone permitted inappropriate or dangerous discussions, such as illicit wooing" (79). Marvin cites an example of such fears in which "upon discovering that his residential telephone was engaged whenever he called home, a suspicious husband had the phone tapped and discovered that his wife was having a love affair" (69), and according to Henry M. Boettinger, "The imagination of early moralists was so fevered by prurient thoughts that one suggested laws prohibiting telephone installation in bedrooms" (203). In the face of the threat that women would master this new technology *too* well, Marvin argues that the figure of the technologically inept woman became a figure of virtue.

> [T]echnical ignorance as a form of worldly ignorance was a virtue of "good" women. . . . Unlike men, women in the stories related by professional journals rarely learned from their mistakes in using technology. . . . They were sheltered from all such practical demands by an old and sturdy code of chivalry that required the protection of their ignorance by men. (23)

Moreover, Marvin argues, the new technologies threatened the integrity of the very foundation of middle-class society: the family. Marvin suggests that "the picture that emerges . . . is one of the bourgeois family under attack. New forms of communication put communities like the family under stress by making contacts between its members and outsiders difficult to supervise. They permitted the circulation of intimate secrets and fostered irregular association" (69).

Cather herself seems to have shared her culture's ambivalence about technology and about the telephone in particular. As Stout points out, Cather "was trying to get one and could not, she would not have one because it interrupted her work, she would go out and use a telephone elsewhere in the afternoon, she was having it disconnected for the summer to save money, she was keeping her telephone number secret, and so on" (194). According to John March, in 1899 the Nebraska Telephone Company installed a system in Red Cloud, the model for *A Lost Lady*'s

Sweet Water. The response in Red Cloud anticipates the way telephony threatened the integrity of the family by publicizing private desires; March quotes the 20 January 1899 issue of the *Red Cloud Chief* as saying,

> Maybe we are mistaken but we understand that when a connection is made, the "hello girl" at central can, if she so desires, and is not too busy, listen to the conversation over any particular connection. If this is the case it might be advisable to know that the "hello girl" is one who has not been in the habit of telling all she hears. It might make business in the divorce courts take a boom. (751)

Such speculation suggests that Red Cloud shared the anxieties of the rest of the nation—fears about the virtue of women working in communication industries, as well as about the virtue of telephone users (specifically, those using the telephone for pleasure, rather than business).

A Lost Lady, then, reflects this ambivalence, particularly when Marian Forrester places a call to her erstwhile lover, Frank Ellinger, after discovering that he is married to another woman. Marian uses the telephone in Judge Pommeroy's office, against Niel's advice; Niel, who is more familiar with the technology, warns her that "central will hear every word you say" (*LL* 126). Despite this advice, Marian quickly loses control—but Niel has preemptively "saved her. The moment that quivering passion of hatred and wrong leaped into her voice, he had . . . cut the insulated wire behind the desk" (*LL* 128). Here we see first of all that the telephone is still situated firmly in the place of business; Marian must place her call from the judge's office, and, notably, Ellinger returns the placed call, not from his hotel room, but from the "office booth," presumably of the hotel. The telephone is still in the arena of male expertise and authority. But Marian's use of the telephone threatens to feminize and eroticize the telephone. Two gendered stereotypes are at work here—technology enables Marian to bring her intensely private concerns into public space and discourse, and at the same time that technology amplifies the possibility for a second gendered "misuse" of the telephone: using it, as Mrs. Beasley will, as a source of gossip. These threats, however, are at least partially nullified by the reassertion of male technical ability and protective spirit. The danger that Marian's erotic use of the telephone threatens is contained both by her incompetence and by Niel's superior (and chivalric) understanding of technology.

The many ambiguities in this scene reflect the larger concerns of the novel with progress and sexuality. For Niel, as for characters such as Adolph Blum, Marian signifies an almost feudal past; at the same time, however, she allies herself with figures symbolizing rampant progress, such as Ivy Peters. How, in this context, are we to evaluate her sexuality? Evelyn Helmick has argued that the Captain and his friends, including Frank, represent a medieval "band of brothers" who protect Marian and the values of the old West. Is Marian's portrait therefore that of a medieval lady, wooed and won with the tacit consent of her husband; is the novel, as Helmick has said, "an Arthurian romance in which courtly love is the subject" (40)? Or is Marian's desire that of a contemporary consumer and her infidelity thus a betrayal of the code of the past? The answer to these questions lies, I believe, in the order of the narrative in the telephone scene; we are allowed to imagine for a moment that Marian *has* betrayed the private and has revealed her indiscretions to the gossips. Only retroactively do we realize that Niel has silenced her in time, restoring the older chivalric order, preserving her status as "lady," at least for the time being. The potential problem with Marian's adultery, then, is not infidelity itself, so long as her desires remain confined to the Captain and his circle. As long as Marian continues to be chivalrously "rescued" from commodity culture, she retains her status as a sign of the past's noble order. Once her desires become part of a public commodity culture, as when she becomes both sexually and commercially complicit with Ivy Peters, she is indeed lost.

Five years after the publication of *A Lost Lady*, the association of women, pleasure, and telephony won out when AT&T's Arthur Page strove to convince consumers that the telephone was not a necessity, intended for emergencies only, but rather a convenience meant to facilitate pleasurable exchange. According to Marchand, "what Page proposed, and what the entire advertising and merchandising world of the late 1920s appeared to affirm, was that business should cast off its sober, utilitarian outlook in favor of a new, more pleasure-minded, consumption ethic. The idea had persisted for too long that the telephone should not be used for 'frivolous conversation'" (118). The shift in telephone advertising, then, mirrors a larger shift in advertising culture. As Michael Tratner notes, "economic and sexual discourses in the mid-twentieth century moved far from the nineteenth-century logic of saving, replacing it with the logic of circulation" (3). And just as the shift to a commodity culture necessitated an emphasis on consumption as virtue, advertisers began to encourage sexual desire rather than restraint. Whereas the nineteenth-century bourgeois woman's function was, in Nancy Armstrong's words, to "self-regulate" desire, in the twentieth century desire became not only legitimate, but necessary for the continued expansion of American capitalism. And just as the nineteenth-century bourgeois social order relied on *women* behaving well, so twentieth-century commodity culture relied on women buying well. Like Page, advertisers were recognizing that women were America's chief consumers and were altering their messages to emphasize pleasure over practicality.

Cather critiques this shift in her portrayal of Rosamond Marsellus in *The Professor's House* as the female consumer.

Rosamond, as her father describes her, is a "consummate consumer" with a "faultless purchasing manner" (*PH* 153). The narrator frequently and sardonically comments on her attitudes toward money, noting that, for instance, "now that she was Tom Outland's heir, [she] detested to hear sums of money mentioned, especially small sums" (*PH* 46). When Louie claims that "she doesn't like anything showy, you know, and she doesn't care about intrinsic values" (*PH* 106), the irony is heavy indeed. And yet there may be some question as to what exactly is wrong with Rosamond's habits of consumption. After all, her father is something of an epicure, and while Outland himself may represent the appeal of the rustic, the so-called "primitive" civilization is clearly devoted to the aesthetic and the comfortable. Nor can it be said that Rosamond lacks taste or that she is guilty of the consumption of mass-produced items that, as John Hilgart carefully details, Cather tended to condemn; she prefers the antique and the handmade, and she avails herself of experts such as her own father to confirm the uniqueness of her finds. Rosamond, Outland, and the Professor alike share an admiration for what Hilgart describes as "special objects," "enduring things of beauty and meaning, most often connoting 'culture' in a rather vague way . . . of course, the antithesis of the commodity form so hated by Cather" (380). The difference, I contend, between good consumption and bad is twofold and in both cases gender-specific. First, Rosamond's buying power emphasizes display and promiscuity, violating earlier norms of feminine frugality and restraint. Second, Rosamond exemplifies the central role the consuming woman was beginning to take in capitalism, and as such reworks the model of feminine desire and male provision for that desire.

In his study of the department store from 1890 to 1925, William Leach suggests that the changes in the display of goods during this time period "marked a critical moment in the formation of a new culture of consumption" and that "the desire to show things off helped loosen the resistance to personal sexual display and performance in public that had hitherto distinguished American social behavior" (325). Shopping, like the telephone, threatened to open the domestic up to the economic, and as Leach notes, "[d]epartment stores did little to prevent or to control the loosening of sensual boundaries; indeed, they promoted it, even in the face of much opposition from purity and reform groups" (328). Because "store windows showed everything from bedroom sets to teacups, from lingerie to evening gowns" (328–29), they emphasized the sensuality of goods marked for intimate, private consumption. In this light, Rosamond's expedition for a "painted Spanish bedroom set" (*PH* 152) indicates a willingness to make public the consumption of a private object; not only is the bed a signifier of sex, but insofar as it is "painted" and "Spanish" it connotes exotic sexuality and painted women. When the Professor describes Rosamond's furniture shopping trip to Chicago as "an orgy of acquisition" (152), he conflates her material greed with sexual lasciviousness. The profusion of "pretty" bedroom sets which so oppresses the Professor suggests that Rosamond's "orgy" is as much about sexual as consumer excess.

Rosamond, of course, is not literally an adulteress. However, she is repeatedly viewed as betraying Tom Outland's memory *through* her consumption, and the text is littered with implicit questions about her integrity. Louie, for example, refers to her as having been "young Outland's fiancée . . . virtually his widow" (*PH* 42), leading Scott to speculate to his wife, "Now what the hell is a virtual widow? Does he mean a virtuous widow, or the reverseous?" (*PH* 46). Scott's reversal of Rosamond's supposed virtue undermines Louie's attempt to suggest that her inheritance was obtained through a legally enshrined notion of widowhood, casting doubt on the morality of thc transaction the inheritance represents.[3] If Rosamond is not really a widow, after all, the marital domesticity that legitimates such transactions is removed. In the context of the central narrative, "Tom Outland's Story," these hints about Rosamond take on added urgency. Tom's mother is apparently so devoted to his father that seeing him drown is too much for her already weakened health, and she dies shortly thereafter. Tom is assisted in Washington by "Virginia Ward," a "tiny little thing" with "gentle ways" (*PH* 226) whose very name, as Jean Schwind suggests, "is the product of a patriarchal culture predicated on female chastity and subordination" (74). And, of course, the Native American mummy at the heart of Tom's story, Mother Eve, is speculatively classified as an adulteress punished: Father Duchene thinks that "perhaps her husband thought it worth while to return unannounced from the farms some night, and found her in improper company. . . . In primitive society the husband is allowed to punish an unfaithful wife with death" (*PH* 222). In Tom's world, fidelity is a core value; Rosamond's continual betrayal of what he stood for, then, takes on added significance.

Moreover, Rosamond, destined to be a confirmation of Tom Outland's worth, becomes an agent, rather than an object, of consumption. Her husband Louie is likewise diminished to being a co-consumer instead of a man worthy of a beautiful woman. According to this reading, Rosamond and Louie, as the modern consuming couple, present a warped notion of male-female relations. While Outland was the masculine provider, Louie is demoted to fellow shopper. As Rosamond "proudly" tells her father, Louie "selects all my things for me" (*PH* 82), and while discussing plans for their shopping trips in France, Louie is "alarmed" that his wife might go without him, stating "it's to be understood that I always shop with you. I adore the shops in Paris" (*PH* 156). And yet, in "Tom Outland's Story," Tom notes that his landlord "took his lunch hour to go shopping with his wife and choose the satin. That seemed to me very strange. In New Mexico the Indian boys sometimes went to a trader's with their wives and bought shawls or calico, and we thought it rather contemptible" (*PH* 231). Rather than providing for his wife, Louie merely facilitates the unleashing of her consumer desires.

In the works following *The Professor's House*, Cather follows up on this rejection of the contemporary consuming woman. Even toward the end of *The Professor's House* we receive a clue of her preferred model of femininity when the Professor thinks to himself "that he would rather have Augusta with him just now than anyone he could think of. Seasoned and sound and on the solid earth she surely was, and, for all her matter-of-factness and hardhandedness, kind and loyal" (*PH* 281). Helmick notes, interestingly, that "perhaps of all the secular medieval virtues, loyalty must be deemed preeminent" (43). "Loyal" is also the word Cecile's dying mother uses to describe Cecile in *Shadows on the Rock.* Although both Cecile and her mother are as devoted to objects, comfort, and the aesthetic as Rosamond claims to be, they are *preservers* of a tradition, and Cather describes their "fine moral qualities" in terms of constancy: "the mother's unswerving fidelity to certain traditions, and the daughter's loyalty to her mother's wish" (*SR* 26). Whereas Marian and Rosamond fail both to restrain their desires according to the nineteenth-century model and to perform as expressions of men's greatness according to the feudal model, subsequent heroines succeed in combining femininity and materialism in a way Cather views as appropriate.

Far from being unattuned to the economic conditions around her and their cultural impact, then, Cather seems to have understood clearly the shift to late capitalism. Writing during a time when consumer culture was establishing itself fully, when capitalism was placing less and less stress on the validity of family ties, and when female sexual desire was being conflated with female consumer appetite, Cather appears to have turned her back on this vision of postmodern femininity, focusing much of her remaining work on premodern feminine fidelity.

Notes

1. See, for example, Mary Ryan, Nancy Armstrong, and Steven Lubar.

2. Several critics, most notably Cathy N. Davidson, have critiqued the very notion of separate spheres. While I share Davidson's suspicion of efforts to create a utopic domestic feminine space apart from the economic sphere, it should be clear from the following analysis that even though lines between the spheres are blurred in significant ways, the distinction nevertheless retains an ideological function and thus cannot be ignored.

3. Of course, Scott's own wife echoes Rosamond's consumption, but in attenuated form. Kitty's consumer desire, however, takes the form of envy—desiring what Rosamond desires—rather than a loosening of her own desires. The threat represented here stems from Rosamond and the possibility that she will corrupt her sister.

7

"Fragments of Their Desire"

Willa Cather and the Alternative Aesthetic Tradition of Native American Women

Deborah Lindsay Williams

Standing naked at the bottom of Panther Canyon, water streaming off her body as she bathes in a mountain stream, Thea Kronborg, heroine of Willa Cather's *The Song of the Lark* (1915), has an epiphany about art: "What was any art but an effort to make a sheath, a mould in which to imprison for a moment the shining, elusive element which is life itself" (*SL* 273). Realizing this, she suddenly understands something about her own voice and her efforts to become an opera singer: "In singing, one made a vessel of one's throat and nostrils and held it on one's breath, caught the stream in a scale of natural intervals." Thea's realizations, sparked by the natural beauty of Panther Canyon and her appreciation of the Native American artifacts she finds there, give her the courage to go to Germany and study voice: she will take her New World epiphany to the Old World and return an American diva. In the figure of Thea, Cather literally embodies female creative power—one of the few such figures in American literature.

During her stay in Panther Canyon, Thea spends a great deal of time thinking about the Native American artifacts that she finds there. Although she guiltily secretes a few pottery fragments in her cabin, for the most part she is content merely to look at the artifacts in the cave-lodges where she finds them. The remnants of the pueblo dweller's society—carbon flakes on a cave roof, potsherds, bowls—convey to Thea a powerful set of messages about the hardship of women's lives and about the beauty with which these women nevertheless surrounded themselves. The objects give her imagination something to seize onto and allow her to think about the lives lived out long before she ever arrived:

> she began to have intuitions about the women who had worn the path [that she is walking on], and who had spent so great a part of their lives going up and down it. She found herself trying to walk as they must have walked, with a feeling in her feet and knees and loins which she had never known before—which must have come up to her out of the accustomed dust of that rocky trail. She could feel the weight of an Indian baby hanging to her back as she climbed. (*SL* 271)

Her physical, even visceral appreciation of the past enables her to move forward, helps her to find new ways of thinking about opera, about art, about herself. Most important for her artistic epiphany, however, is the fact that these beautiful objects were made by *women:* female artists whose work "not only expressed their desire but . . . expressed it as beautifully as they could" (*SL* 274).

Sharon O'Brien has perceptively argued that Cather found in the figure of the opera diva an "example of women's creativity. The soprano's voice suggested to [Cather] that femininity and creativity might be naturally—if not socially—compatible" (*Emerging* 173). At the same time, however, O'Brien also observes that women performers were also "remote models for a woman writer. . . . Operas require sopranos . . . but American letters has no preordained place for women writers" (173). Both for this reason and because of her extensive acquaintance with singers such as Olive Fremstadt, it is not surprising that Thea Kronborg, opera diva, would represent Cather's successful imagining of female creative power. But it is no accident that Thea's artistic epiphany occurs as a result of the time she spends in the ruins of Panther Canyon. The artifacts that Thea tries not to displace represent another model of female artistry; they come from a tradition rooted in the Americas rather than in Europe and begin as humble, domestic utensils created from material readily at hand. Ironically, these domestic objects have survived longer than the society that produced them—the society that almost certainly oppressed their creators.

In the pueblos of the southwestern United States, Cather finds the remains of female artisanship that provide the source for Thea's inspiration. Twenty years later, Cather returns to these same pueblos in her essay "Escapism" (1936), in which she positions the work of these Native American women as the wellspring of an alternative aesthetic tradition in the United States. This shift in importance, from inspiration to foundation, occurs as a result of Cather's increased sense of working in a hostile environment—the literary scene of the late 1920s and 1930s—and her need to inscribe herself, however subtly, into a tradition of female creative power and endurance, emblematized by the material remains of these desert cultures. Feeling herself under attack by critics who dismissed her work as out of touch, overly romantic, and elegiac,[1] Cather opens her essay with a salvo that asserts a powerful female creativity: "Hundreds of years ago, before European civilization had touched this continent, the Indian women in the old rock-perched pueblos of the Southwest were painting geometrical patterns on the jars in which they carried water up from the streams." These women often "shaped their graceful cooking pots when they had nothing to cook in them" and clearly "experimented with form and colour to gratify something that had no concern with food and shelter" (*OW* 19). "Escapism" is often thought of as an example of Cather at her most reactionary, railing against mass culture and rampant consumerism, and indeed some of her observations seem quite conservative: her claim, for example, that all art "will be the same until all the values of human life have changed" (*OW* 28). But the fact that she uses the work of Native American women—the oppressed members of an oppressed culture—to make her point adds a radical, challenging subtext to the essay that belies its surface conservatism. When we pay closer attention to the material remains of Native American culture that Cather describes in "Escapism" and in her two "mesa" novels, *The Song of the Lark* and *The Professor's House*, we see that these artifacts and the landscape that contains them not only energize her creative imagination but also provide the impetus for her characters to escape the confines of social convention. "Escapism" merely codifies what has been happening in the novels written earlier: in typically subtle fashion, Cather finds and celebrates an aesthetic tradition rooted in the work of women who belonged to cultures that were destroyed by mainstream U.S. culture. And—again typically for Cather—her efforts in this direction have been generally overlooked.

In recent years, Cather's representations of the American Southwest have come under scrutiny by critics who argue that her "romantic racial portraits" (M. Fischer 42) of non-whites (including Native Americans and African Americans) contribute to a cultural amnesia about the treatment these people have received at the hands of the U.S. government. Elizabeth Ammons, for example, has written that "Cather longed for . . . the return of hegemonic, white, patriarchal control, the return, that is, of Western European global dominance" ("Cather" 258). Walter Benn Michaels has sounded a similar note, arguing that in Cather's Southwestern novels, particularly *The Professor's House*, "the only good Indian is a dead Indian" (52). What Michaels and others do not discuss, however, is the attention that Cather pays to the work that women within these cultures produced. One of the reasons that she extols these "vanished" tribal cultures, it seems, is that women had the opportunity to create objects of lasting value that were beautiful, essential objects of everyday life. Certainly Cather's politics were much more conservative than many of us in the academy would like to acknowledge, but to see her work solely as another manifestation of white cultural imperialism seems as much a misreading as those pronouncements made in the 1930s that declared her work to be simplistic, romantic, and old-fashioned. Always, Cather forces us to read with both hands, as it were: on the one hand, conservative, even stereotypical racial portraits exist in her work, such as the lampoonish representation of Blind D'Arnault, the black piano player in *My Ántonia*. At the same time, however, her work also challenges conventional stereotypes and attitudes. In *Death Comes for the Archbishop* (1927), for example, Father Latour takes pleasure in knowing that there is "Moorish silver" in the bell tolling the Angelus over his parish and that the very tradition of ringing the bell is "an adaptation of a Moslem custom" (48)—a rather unexpected perspective for a Catholic missionary.[2] And in the depictions of Southwestern pueblos that are so central to *The Song of the Lark* and *The Professor's House* rests a quietly feminist argument about the centrality of women—native women, at that—to the history of art in the United States. These are hardly the statements of someone "longing" for the return of the patriarchy.

Although Cather may have been more interested in vanished cultures than living communities, her appreciation of domestic artifacts—and her repeated depiction of these artifacts in her novels—provides insight to Cather's own sense of herself as an American artist, a woman who writes "entirely for myself" about "old neighbours . . . heavy farming people" (*OW* 94) and from these materials attempts to create something of lasting value. Her focus on these ordinary people at a time when such subjects were thought déclassé demonstrates her interest in examining the various cultures that meet on American soil and alter it in the process. The provenance of the material objects that make such an impact on her characters further reflects this interest, as well as her awareness of the complex cultural exchanges that shape both history and art: the Catholic bell comes from "infidels"; the high art of Dostoyevsky shares an aesthetic spirit with Native American women; an opera diva triumphs because of a lesson learned at the bottom of an Arizona canyon.[3] Once we see this complexity, a connection emerges between female artistry and a flexible, nuanced worldview that is not threatened by difference but is instead challenged by it, altered because of it: a cosmopolitan perspective. David Hollinger in *Postethnic America* (1995) describes the cosmopolitan view as sharing "with all varieties of universalism a profound suspicion of enclosures, but [itself] . . . defined by an additional element not essential to universalism itself: recognition, acceptance, and eager exploration of diversity. . . . For cosmopolitans, the diversity of humankind is a fact; for universalists, it is a potential problem" (84). Thus to see Cather's depictions of Native American culture as a kind of benign imperialism obscures an important function performed by these representations: they become a kind of shorthand with which she offers a counternarrative to the totalizing, often destructive narrative imposed by mainstream U.S. cultural history—without opening herself to the labels of "feminist" or "political."[4]

The images that Thea Kronborg creates for herself as she looks at the pueblo ruins of Panther Canyon bring these Native American women's lives into brief snapshot focus: she walks like them, feels the same pressure in her loins, even imagines a child on her back—which for the childless Thea is indeed an intuitive leap. It is not a romantic portrait but a simple sketch of a woman's daily routine, summoned into Thea's mind by the path she walks on, the pottery she holds in her hands, the lore told to her by Henry Biltmer, the Ottenburgs' caretaker. Walking in the footsteps of these women, living in their cave-lodges, makes Thea aware of "older and higher obligations" that she must fulfill, rather than "draw[ing] the plough under the rod of parental guidance" (*SL* 276). Despite the fact that her own father finds her passion for music to be "indecorous," she will go to Germany to study, secure in her knowledge that she can withstand "the hostility of comfortable, self-satisfied people toward any serious effort" (276). She tells Fred that what she loves is "the feeling that your life is your own and your strength is your own, and your talent is your own; that you're all there, and there's no sag in you" (284–85).[5]

In Panther Canyon, free from the judgments of these "comfortable" people, Thea behaves as she pleases: swims nude in the creek, doesn't wear corsets, leads the way in her hikes with Fred along the precarious cliffside paths. This freedom will continue when she leaves the canyon: she travels with Fred to Mexico but refuses to be "kept" by him and then journeys to Germany on her own. Her firm rejection of Moonstone, Colorado, becomes clear when she chooses to remain in Dresden to make her debut rather than return to stay by her mother's sickbed. Her decision enacts what Cather asks at the beginning of "Escapism": "what has art ever been but escape?" (*OW* 18). For Thea, art and the lessons she learns about art in Panther Canyon enable her to flee the stifling world of Moonstone and its unreflective respectability.[6]

The rejuvenation that Thea feels in Panther Canyon finds a corollary in the exhilaration Cather herself felt during her visits to the Southwest and when she went to an exhibit of artifacts at the Natural History Museum in New York City. Elizabeth Sergeant, in her memoir about Cather, notes that when the two women arrived at the museum Cather was "tense and low-spirited" but that as she looked through the exhibit she became "rapturously unaware of her physical depletion" (123). Cather tells Sergeant that it seems like "sacrilege to take anything for oneself from those cliff dwellings" but that she had nevertheless rather "shamefacedly" brought some potsherds back with her from her travels. Sergeant, like Thea (and evidently like Cather herself), easily imagines the creators of the artifacts she is looking at: she was "able to conjure up the women who, under conditions of incredible difficulty and fear of enemies, had still designed and molded [the pots], 'dreamed' the fine geometry of the designs, and made beautiful objects for daily use out of river-bottom clay" (123). Again, it is women who have this powerfully transformative energy, who can take "river-bottom clay" and turn it into something of lasting value, who see the value—the necessity—of making objects for domestic use into objects of beauty. In these artifacts Cather and Sergeant see the desire of the artisans, not just the objects themselves; it is the artistic desire about which Cather writes the most fiercely. And for Thea, who sees these objects in their natural setting, the potsherds *are* artistic desire in ceramic form: although the artists have disappeared from Panther Canyon "there still glittered in the sun the bits of their frail clay vessels, fragments of their desire" (*SL* 288).

Thea feels uneasy taking any potsherds from their resting place; she is willing instead to be simply an observer, soaking in the emotions and sensations that seem to saturate Panther Canyon. The few things she does take back to her cabin with her she feels guilty about, "as if she is being watched." She thinks of herself as "a guest in these houses, and ought to behave as such" (274). Instead of collecting artifacts, she rests on the rocks in the sun, like a blonde lizard, letting ideas and music wander in and out of her thoughts, feeling ever more connected to the ancient world around her. In her reveries she gains "a certain understanding of those old people [that] came up to her out of the rockshelf . . . not expressible in words" (272). She abandons taxonomies and hierarchies and allows impressions simply to wash over her; the power of thought becomes instead a "power of sustained sensation" (270). It is the power of that sustained sensation that enables her to become the diva "Kronborg."[7] In her ability to intuit, to see what is not actually there in front of her, Thea anticipates what Cather will write about a few years later in "The Novel Démeublé" (1922), in which she famously claimed that "whatever is felt upon the page without being specifically named there . . . the inexplicable presence of the thing not named, of the overtone divined by the ear but not heard by it . . . gives high quality to the novel" (*OW* 42). This is Cather's definition of "high art" but it is also a challenge—and a lesson—to her readers, who must learn how to read in this intuitive, impressionistic fashion if they want to understand Cather's own work. Thea's ability to read so much into, and get so much out of, the landscape of Panther Canyon demonstrates that she is finally ready to make art herself.

Thea's time in Panther Canyon anticipates, to some degree, Tom Outland's sojourn on the Blue Mesa in Cather's other "mesa" novel, *The Pro-*

fessor's House (1925). There are, however, significant differences between the two characters and the way they treat the landscape, differences that highlight Cather's desire to create for herself an indigenous female artistic tradition. Tom wants to excavate and catalog all that he finds, for example, but Thea "liked better to leave [the potsherds] in the dwellings where she found them" (*SL* 274). Thea thinks of herself as a guest in Panther Canyon; Tom thinks about the mesa in terms of "possession"—although he disingenuously tells Roddy Blake that the Cliff City belongs to "everyone." When the two novels are juxtaposed, what emerges is Cather's subtle condemnation of the desire to possess something as intangible as landscape—a critique of the colonizing impulse. A far cry from the optimism that runs through Thea's story, *The Professor's House* is a bitter novel, demonstrating, as Marilee Lindemann has persuasively argued, that its author knew she was "writing in a country that was rushing to push women writers to the margins of literary history" (*Queering* 114). Even as Tom attempts to take control of the past by "dig[ging] out all its secrets" (*PH* 223), however, the presence of the artifacts on the mesa serves as a countermeasure, a gesture on Cather's part to remind us, and possibly to remind herself, that women's art can prevail despite cultural pressures that attempt to belittle or destroy it.

The Professor's House offers experiments in both structure and content; it is one of Cather's least conventional novels. Structurally, the novel was Cather's attempt to "insert the *Nouvelle* into the *Roman*" (*OW* 30), and Tom's early days on the mesa, living in idyllic bliss with Roddy Blake, suggest an experiment in same-sex living that challenges conventional, heterosexual, representations of couple-dom. The domestic scenes between Tom and Roddy are, at least briefly, some of the happiest in all of Cather's fiction. Tom's time on the mesa is "like a dream" because of the beauty of the mesa itself and because of the joyous relationship he establishes with Blake. After Henry Atkins joins them as an aide-de-camp, life became "a holiday" and Tom says that "the three of us made a happy family" (*PH* 196). Just as Panther Canyon offers Thea an escape from poverty, conventionality, and spiritual deadness, so too does the mesa offer Tom a similar escape. And again like Thea, Tom is amazed by the beauty he finds in the ruins, from the "beautifully shaped water jars" to the frescoes that decorate living chambers, "one colour laid on another . . . [and] a painted border, little tents, like Indian tepees, in brilliant red" (*PH* 207, 211). Unlike Thea, however, Tom lacks the imagination to internalize the possibilities made available to him in his city above the world. Instead of becoming more certain about his desire to live outside of convention, ultimately he decides to live within convention, forcing Roddy off the mesa and then descending himself into the world of college, science, and that most conventional of deaths, wartime soldiering.

Not surprisingly, given what we have seen in *The Song of the Lark*, the world that Tom finds on the Blue Mesa is a woman's world. Most of the objects that Tom excavates and catalogs are domestic in origin: water jars, grinding stones, cloth, "little implements made of turkey bones" (*PH* 208). It is the world of the woman Tom calls "Mother Eve," the desiccated body discovered in one of the dwellings, with a scream frozen on her face and her ribs protruding from a wound in her side. The beauty of the mesa and the mystery presented by Eve and her vanished tribe spur the men to greater and greater efforts to understand—but in their efforts they also destroy and dismantle what it is they admire. Nor are their attempts to interpret the mysteries of the mesa very successful; Father Duchene's explanation for Mother Eve's death is a violent cliché, which he narrates "slyly": "perhaps her husband . . . found her in improper company. The young man may have escaped. In primitive society the husband is allowed to punish an unfaithful wife with death" (*PH* 222). His story functions as an assertion of male dominance over a body whose secrets cannot be known. Mother Eve, as John Swift has observed, "seems wholly outside of . . . familiar structures of religion, maternal origin, or erotic desire . . . [she] resists (and thus solicits) interpretation . . . but where one looks to understand her, one finds instead a vacancy, or at best a fragment" (17). Tom is oblivious to Father Duchene's clichés and records his story without comment. Hypothesizing about Eve's death is as close as Tom comes to imagining the lives of the Cliff Dwellers; he is more interested in the objects than in who made them. He sees himself as preparing the groundwork for an expert, an archaeologist, "someone who will revive this civilization in a scholarly work" (*PH* 220). When Tom leaves the mesa for Washington, it is with the dream of finding "men who would understand" the city on the cliff, who will "appreciate it and dig out all its secrets" (233). He links understanding with uncovering and ownership; knowing, for Tom, cannot happen without possession.[8]

Tom does not want his objects exposed to "vulgar curiosity" but only to those with the ability to appreciate what they represent—a set of meanings he hopes will be delivered to him by urban experts. It is clear, however, from his response to Blake's sale of the artifacts, that Tom has in fact already made up his mind about what these artifacts mean and his interpretation does not include a dollar value, which is the meaning that Blake has assigned to them. While Tom is in Washington, Blake sells the entire collection to a German collector of artifacts, which enrages Tom and results in the breakup of their relationship. Tom claims that Blake has sold things that "belonged to this country, to the State, and to all the people" and that he would "as soon sold [his] own grandmother as Mother Eve" (244). His nationalist, almost jingoist rhetoric is not lost on Blake, who calls his speechifying "Fourth of July talk" and points out Tom's hypocrisy: "I see now I was working for you like a hired man, and while you were away I sold your property" (245).[9] Although Tom claims this is not true, his emotions after Roddy leaves undercut his statement; alone on the mesa "something had happened," he explains, and "that process . . . brought with it great happiness. It was possession" (250). The artifacts are gone, Roddy is gone, and now Tom can do what he will with the city on the mesa; he can choose to interpret it in any way he sees fit.

In taking possession of the mesa, however, Tom loses the opportunity that the mesa and its artifacts present as a haven for alternative domesticity; he rejects Roddy and chooses instead social convention. Tom's desire to know all the secrets of the mesa is itself a convention, a typically masculine reaction to the unknowable, the mysterious, the sublime.[10] His conquest of the mesa—for certainly that is what it is, although Tom does not think of it as such—has at least two negative consequences. He will never comprehend the more cosmopolitan, fluid outlook of Thea Kronborg, and as a result, his actions have rendered the mesa unlivable by anyone other than himself. Were he able to accept the lessons offered by the mesa, he never would have needed the imprimatur of the Smithsonian Institution, never would have left Roddy, never would have dismantled their ménage. The niggling feelings of doubt Tom feels about his decision reveal themselves in the dark undercurrents that occasionally surface in the otherwise glorious language with which he describes his solitary days on the mesa: he has a vague sense that he was "heartless" when it came to Roddy's dismissal, that he will be "called to account" for what he's done (251–53). And although Thea, too, becomes a solitary figure in her pursuit of art, *The Professor's House* suggests that Tom may have made the wrong choice: he tried to possess something that cannot be possessed and in the process lost the one thing that gave his life meaning.

Not uncoincidentally, the artifacts that Roddy sells go to Germany with the collector Fechtig; we remember that Henry Biltmer plans to return to Germany with the artifacts he's taken from Panther Canyon, and Germany is where Thea goes with her Panther Canyon epiphany to study voice. Europe, it seems, is more hospitable to the tradition of women's art than is the United States and more aware of the importance of history in shaping both the present and the future. Tom's fervent avowal that the Cliff City belongs to everyone does not ring true in the end because Tom behaves from the beginning as if the Cliff City is his; the strong sense of kinship, even sisterhood, that Thea feels from the long-gone inhabitants of Panther Canyon does not exist for Tom (other than his feelings for Blake, which he refuses to acknowledge). Unlike Thea, Tom fails to learn the lessons being offered to him by the Cliff City; he wants to understand and excavate it in order to reveal secrets, not to learn about himself. His desire to record and index all the objects he finds on the mesa suggests his need for meanings to remain fixed, immutable, quite different from Thea's ability to feel "sustained sensation." Tom resists the alternative aesthetics and social structures being offered to him on the mesa; his resistance leads him back into a world that Lindemann characterizes as the world of "dutiful, depressed husbands and fathers [like] Godfrey St. Peter" (53). Thea's world becomes more cosmopolitan and more individualized as a result of her time in Panther Canyon; Tom's narrows. Although Thea is not herself an intellectual and Tom Outland is, it is Thea who embodies some of the ideas that Randolph Bourne, a literary critic and liberal intellectual, described in "Transnational America," written the year after *The Song of the Lark* was published.

> [T]he contribution of America will be an intellectual internationalism which goes far beyond the mere exchange of scientific ideas and discoveries and the cold recording of facts. It will be an intellectual sympathy which is not satisfied until it has got at the heart of the different cultural

> expressions, and felt as they feel. It may have immense preferences, but it will make understanding and not indignation its end. Such a sympathy will unite and not divide. (Bourne, n.p.)[11]

Thea, says her old friend Dr. Archie, "was born a cosmopolitan," which explains why she learned so much about music from the Mexicans who lived in her childhood town of Moonstone. The rest of the town, he observes, thought her friendships in "Mexican Town" were a "queer freak" (*SL* 606). The reciprocal nature of Thea's relationship continues when she performs at the Met as Sieglinde and Spanish Johnny, her friend from Mexican Town, is (unknown to her) in the audience. Unsophisticated, unlettered Spanish Johnny has the "only commensurate answer" to the passion displayed by Thea onstage, a "smile which embraced all the stream of life that passed him and the lighted towers that rose into the limpid blue of the evening sky" (411). His "*extasi*" reflects Thea's Panther Canyon epiphany. And it is precisely Thea's inborn cosmopolitanism that allows her to gather insight from the ghosts of pueblo women, instead of seeing merely artifacts to be collected and given as gifts, as Tom does: he gives Mrs. St. Peter one of the most beautiful water jars from the Cliff City.

Tom feels the power of the mesa when the objects that it once contained have been removed; the mesa becomes the *tabula rasa* on which he can write anything he wants. What he chooses to do is read all twelve books of Virgil's *Aeneid*, which he recasts in the Southwest: "When I look into the *Aeneid* now, I can always see two pictures: the one on the page and another one behind that: blue and purple rocks and yellow-green pinons with flat tops" (*PH* 252). His double vision of Virgil's epic seems on the one hand to be a creative act—he brings the classical tradition into the new world—but on the other hand, it is a creative act fueled by erasure and willful forgetting (the damage he has done to Blake and to the mesa itself). Thea, in contrast, imagines herself into the footprints of a vanished culture and uses her sensations of female strength to create something new for and of herself. Tom might be one of those people to whom Cather addressed herself in a letter she wrote about *Death Comes for the Archbishop* in which she said "I am amused that so many of the reviews of this book begin with the statement: 'This book is hard to classify.' Then why bother?" (*OW* 12). Instead of classifying his artifacts, Tom would do better to use them as fuel for his imagination, allowing the power of female creativity to help him reimagine his life.

In "The Novel Démeublé," Cather praises the way that Tolstoy uses material objects in his novels by saying that these things are "so much a part of the emotions of the people that . . . they seem to exist, not so much in the author's mind, as in the emotional penumbra of the characters themselves" (*OW* 40). As is the case throughout this essay, Cather is talking about writing but also instructing us in how to read her own work. In this instance, she offers a lesson about the significance of *things* in her fiction; it is less the object than the shadows cast by the object that are important. She returns to this image much later, in the unfinished "Light on Adobe Walls," where she points out that no artist can "paint those relations of light and shade—he can only paint some emotion they give him, some man-made arrangement of them that happens to give him personal delight—a conception of clouds over distant mesas" (*OW* 124). Even in this late essay, the Southwest still fuels her imagination—and instructs us in how to expand our own. And as always, Europe and the Southwest mingle, so that in her Southwestern adobe dwelling, Cather houses an array of European masters (Velasquez, Da Vinci, Shakespeare, Tolstoy), reminding us that there is an indigenous artistic tradition in the United States and that these early artists were women. Once we have read Cather's representations of the "thrill and tremble" (124) that the artifacts on the mesa caused in her, we realize that in her mind, the emotional penumbra of the Southwestern landscape casts a long shadow of female creativity across the history of art in the United States. It is for her a powerful countertradition that allows her to remind those who would silence the voice of the woman writer that things created by women last, whether it be water jars, cooking pots, or novels.

Notes

I am indebted to the responses I received when I presented an early draft of this essay at the American Literature Association conference in 2001, particularly to the questions asked by the convener of the panel, Janis Stout. I am, as always, grateful for the comments made by my husband, Cyrus R. K. Patell, which improved this essay immeasurably.

1. Sharon O'Brien discusses some of these reviews in her perceptive essay "Becoming Non-canonical: The Case Against Willa Cather." O'Brien argues that during the 1930s "the literary men who defined the canon . . . placed Willa Cather in the foothills of American literature—the appropriate landscape, many critics assumed, for a woman writer" (242). Lionel Trilling's review of *Shadows on the Rock* exemplifies O'Brien's point. After praising Cather's pioneer novels, Trilling disparages Cather's "mystical concern with pots and pans" and compares her work with the "gaudy domesticity of bourgeois accumulation glorified in *The Woman's Home Companion*" (qtd. in O'Connor 495). In *Shadows on the Rock* and other novels, however, the domestic objects that Trilling refers to so disdainfully hold a key to Cather's aesthetics and to her subtle assertions about female power and creative energy.

2. Father Latour, like Thea, is willing to see the world as fluid, as an exchange of differences that may never be resolved but that, in the exchange, present opportunities for knowledge and growth. Latour does not encounter Native American women's art in the way that Thea and Tom Outland do, but he does nevertheless experience the power of a female creativity, cloaked in ancient religious beliefs and antedating his Catholic faith by many centuries. Latour is both terrified and profoundly moved by these experiences, which fuel his cosmopolitan perspective. For a further discussion of Latour's aesthetics, see my essay "Losing Nothing, Comprehending Everything," in *Cather Studies 4*.

3. In his recently published essay "From Mesa Verde to Germany," Matthias Schubnell writes that "Cather saw aboriginal art as an important source for an American artistic tradition" (41). Although Schubnell's point is quite different from that made by Michaels and others, he too overlooks that what Cather saw in aboriginal art was a *female* American artistic tradition, an important distinction.

4. For a further discussion of Cather's strategies for avoiding labels and public controversy, see D. Williams, *Not in Sisterhood.*

5. In her recent biographical study *Willa Cather: The Writer and Her World,* Janis Stout observes that Thea's story "demonstrates both Cather's preoccupation with the problem of a woman's vocation and her willingness to think resistantly, in ways subversive of the norms that governed assumptions about women's lives" (144). Thea gains the strength for her subversive act—following her passion rather than social custom—from her time in Panther Canyon.

6. The novel suggests that Thea's choice is not without costs; she has become a cold woman and Doctor Archie feels that some integral part of Thea

has vanished. Sergeant comments that the novel "bore out much of what Willa had said to me about the desire, the passion which takes a woman of exceptional gifts away from the usual instinctive woman's lot of marriage and children to fulfill a directive that is altogether impersonal. Willa had experienced something of the sort" (134).

7. Fred, explaining Thea's operatic gifts to Doctor Archie, says that she "lets the musical pattern take care of her. The score pours her into all those lovely postures . . . lifts her and drops her. She lies on it, the way she used to lie on the Rhine music" (*SL* 367).

8. Even the act of naming the dead body Eve is itself an act of possession, as Janis Stout explained to me in a private letter. Naming the woman Eve incorporates the dead Pueblo woman into a belief system not her own; Tom's possessiveness extends even into death.

9. Marilee Lindemann makes a similar point in "Fear of a Queer Mesa," although she is concerned with constructions of citizenship and nationhood rather than aesthetics.

10. Roddy's decision to sell the artifacts may also be seen as a colonizing move, but the language with which he explains himself to Tom has more in common with that of an anxious mother who has tried to please her child—and failed utterly: "I took the best chance going, for both of us. . . . That money's in the bank this minute, in your name, and you're going to college on it. You're not going to be a day-labourer like me" (*PH* 243).

11. Although it is not known whether Cather read this piece of Bourne's, he was one of the literary critics whose opinion she respected and whose comments she took very much to heart.

8

Material Objects as Sites of Cultural Mediation in *Death Comes for the Archbishop*

Sarah Wilson

When Spanish colonial forces first pressed north into New Mexico, they carried crosses, prominently displayed in their parties, as symbols of their Catholic faith. The Pueblo Indians of the area responded strongly to these symbols, often greeting arriving forces with what appeared to be makeshift crosses of their own. Spanish missionaries rejoiced at these outward signs of receptivity to conversion. However, what was taking place was a far more complex cultural interaction. In *When Jesus Came, the Corn Mothers Went Away*, a study of colonial New Mexico, Ramón Gutiérrez details this interaction and points out the resemblance between the crosses carried by the Spanish and the prayer sticks used by the Pueblo peoples in their worship of the katsina. According to Gutiérrez, when these two populations met, the Pueblo Indians "apparently believed that the cross was a prayer-stick, and the Spaniards thought prayer-sticks were crosses" (82). The resemblance between the cross and the Pueblo prayer stick established a common material ground between the two cultures, a site where their very different interpretations of what was taking place could meet and negotiate.

This account of cultural interpenetration in colonial New Mexico is particularly suggestive with reference to Willa Cather's *Death Comes for the Archbishop*, whose narrative directly engages the intercultural dynamics of mid-nineteenth-century New Mexico. In her novel, Cather represents objects, often religious ones,[1] as just such sites for cultural negotiation and exchange. These objects reward close consideration because, as Gutiérrez has noted, they refuse the traditional interpretation of colonization as a one-sided imposition of cultural narratives. Within the specific materiality of the Southwestern santos tradition, grand narratives are overcome by the particularity of material experience. Cather's novel proposes the material object as a revolutionary site, wherein the cultural narratives of colonizer and colonized can engage in mutual reinterpretation and subversion, and multiple cultures can begin to accommodate each other's differences.

Recognizing the materialism of *Death Comes for the Archbishop* complicates the version of Catherian fiction put forward most famously by Cather herself in her declaration of artistic principles "The Novel Démeublé." In this essay Cather decried the "over-furnished" novel of her period, "the property-man . . . so busy on its pages, the importance of material objects and their vivid presentation . . . so stressed," and proposed to "throw all the furniture out of the window" (*OW* 35, 42). Against the "popular superstition that 'realism' asserts itself in the cataloguing of a great number of material objects, in explaining mechanical processes, the methods of operating manufactories and trades, and in minutely and unsparingly describing physical sensations," Cather counterpoised an art that is "bare" and yet real in the way that her own modernist masterpieces are (*OW* 37, 42). In the context of such statements, Cather might seem an unlikely candidate for an awareness of the eloquence of material culture (although two of her principal Anglo-American literary inspirations, Henry James and Sarah Orne Jewett, have recently been the subjects of studies that show their affinities for the object world).[2]

"The Novel Démeublé" does offer one productive ambiguity by which we can approach the important role accorded to objects in *Death Comes for the Archbishop*. Tolstoy, by Cather's account, while a great materialist, succeeds in creating vibrant and living literary works. Cather offers this explanation for his success at integrating the literary and the material:

> The clothes, the dishes, the haunting interiors of those old Moscow houses, are always so much a part of the emotions of the people that they are perfectly synthesized; they seem to exist . . . in the emotional penum-

> bra of the characters themselves. When it is fused like this, literalness ceases to be literalness—it is merely part of the experience. (*OW* 39–40)

Cather here recognizes a fundamental premise of material culture studies: that objects often express the culture that gave rise to them as eloquently as (or even more eloquently than) would any written record. According to the historian Jules Prown, "the great promise of material culture" for historical inquiry is that

> by undertaking cultural interpretation through artifacts, we engage the other culture in the first instance not with our minds, the seat of our cultural biases, but with our senses. Figuratively speaking, we put ourselves inside the bodies of the individuals who made or used these objects; we see with their eyes and touch with their hands. To identify with people from the past or from other places empathetically through the senses is clearly a different way of engaging them than abstractly through the reading of written words. Instead of our minds making intellectual contact with their minds, our senses make affective contact with their sensory experience. (17)

The similarity between Cather's terms and Prown's is striking. For both of these thinkers, materiality triggers a sensory empathy that acts as the first step toward even broader forms of cultural understanding. Cather's essay celebrates Tolstoy's novels as major achievements in the recording of what Prown terms material culture. Objects in Tolstoy's work are not the inessential markers of setting toted about by the "property-man" of "The Novel Démeublé." Rather, Tolstoy's objects clearly bear the traces of human investment and offer understandings of experience rather than the trappings of experience.[3] Cather's engagement with the object world—both in Tolstoy and elsewhere—conveys her interest in the communicative possibilities of material culture.

Death Comes for the Archbishop gives particularity to the fleeting concession to material awareness in Cather's discussion of Tolstoy's objects. According to Cather's published letter on *Archbishop*, the Southwest communicated powerfully to her through its very materiality. In the presence of the old mission churches, "the hand-carved beams and joists, the utterly unconventional frescoes, the countless fanciful figures of the saints" (*OW* 5), Cather

> soon felt that no record of them could be as real as they are themselves. They are their own story, and it is foolish convention that we must have everything interpreted for us in written language. There are other ways of telling what one feels, and the people who built and decorated those many, many little churches found their way and left their message. (*OW* 5–6)

Such a realization might well foreclose any novelistic project, and this sense of the limitations of language when faced with the culturally different is very much at play in *Death Comes for the Archbishop.* The missionary priest (and later archbishop) Father Latour, for one, "was quite willing to believe that behind Jacinto [a pueblo Indian] there was a long tradition, a story of experience, which no language could translate to him" (*DCA* 97). However, neither Cather nor Latour abandons the project of cross-cultural communication and understanding. They merely shift the emphasis from language to objects.

We can read *Death Comes for the Archbishop* as fundamentally structured by the materialist epiphany the old mission churches brought about in Cather. In its discontinuous form, made up of precisely textured scenes, objects become more than usually articulate. The very episodicity of the novel conduces well to reading it as a series of modernist "object lessons." Rather than proceeding sequentially, the novel appears to unfold out from a cluster of eloquent objects. Cather's technique is uniquely accommodating of the expressiveness of the material world. In this sense, Cather's experimental novel form should be understood as attempting to present the objects themselves, rather than the record of them that she knew could only be inadequate.

As Bill Brown has noted, "things just as they are, can disclose only the heterogeneity of the world" (*Sense* 85). In *Death Comes for the Archbishop,* the heterogeneity of the world is particularly evinced by the cultural heterogeneity of the American Southwest. The novel formally privileges objects because, while disclosing the heterogeneity of this world, they also serve as subtle mediators of the thoughts and beliefs of the many populations interacting in Father Latour's diocese. In their unassimilable heterogeneity, objects provide practice sites for those approaching the culturally unfamiliar. Objects propose forms of approach more flexible and innovative than the reflexive urge to assimilation.[4] For Cather, the new forms of understanding occasioned by objects have profound implications for intercultural contacts—those of her own age, and those of the nineteenth-century Southwestern scene that prefigured it. *Death Comes for the Archbishop* thus constitutes an important and underexplored expression of the materiality of Cather's engagement with questions of culture and cultures.

The first chapter opens with the main character of the novel, Father Latour, lost in a New Mexican desert. However, we know neither his identity nor that of the landscape until he fixes upon an unusual juniper tree, one that is growing in the shape of a cross. This tree does not help Latour find his way. Rather, it occasions a pause in which Latour's energy shifts from trying to find his way to the contemplation of the object before him. In this pause, the strange and unfamiliar man and landscape become knowable for the reader. When Father Latour kneels before the tree, he both performs and undergoes an act of imaginative translation. The tree is translated by him into a cross, and he is translated by the tree into a priest, for as he pauses before the tree, the narrative finally identifies, describes, and locates him. Admittedly, this is not a scene of intercultural contact (we have only a priest and a tree). However, I use the term "translation" to suggest the way in which this scene prefigures the synchrony with which objects will mediate between cultures in this novel. In the pause occasioned by the object, interpretive energies meet and mix.

Translation becomes possible in the cruciform tree episode because the very otherness of the object tempers the self-absorption of the individual who gazes upon it. The cruciform tree gathers Latour's energies and enables him to "blot . . . himself out of his own consciousness" (*DCA* 19). The religious implications of the symbol remind Latour that he is not the principal mover in this situation and, by disqualifying the idea of the self-sufficient individual, make the fruitlessness of self-directed motion apparent to Latour. This awareness is both profoundly Christian and profoundly narratological. Positioned at the very opening of the novel, the cruciform tree serves to underline the futility and wastefulness of paths taken merely to perpetuate an individual direction, or even as attempts to achieve an individual end. The object has more communal reach, more environmental sensitivity, than does any individual agenda. Like many other objects that we find in evidence in the narrative pauses of the novel, the cruciform tree is profoundly antiteleological. This proves indispensable in the object's assumption of the task of cultural mediation, for in this novel telos equates with limited access and limited perception. Communal accommodation and cross-cultural understanding are the goods that, in *Death Comes for the Archbishop,* are unavailable to the individual unwilling to lose his identity in the othernesses encompassed by a shared object.

From the early moment of the cruciform tree, then, both we and Father Latour are alerted to the reorienting of perspective possible through the mediation of material objects. As if in response to this insight, Latour gravitates to the mantels upon which his diocesans keep collections of wooden religious figures. This reflexive reference to local santos is particularly noteworthy because it constitutes one of Cather's alterations of the historical record. Archbishop Lamy, upon whom Latour is modeled, was in fact not supportive of the local santos; he is usually cited as the principal mover in the replacement of locally produced icons by factory produced icons (Farago 197). As Mary Chinery has recently argued, it was Cather herself who was familiar with and drew upon the Southwestern santos tradition. Cather's novel positions New Mexican santos as particularly valuable introductions to the specific cross-cultural pastiche of the mid-nineteenth-century American Southwest.

Early in his travels through the Southwest, Father Latour finds in an isolated Catholic home a figure of "a fierce little equestrian" (29) and is informed by a child that this figure represents Santiago. Latour identifies with this saint, for he like Santiago is a missionary, and he remarks upon the appropriateness of the figure's horse for the missionary of the Southwest. This comment meets with surprise. The horse is no charming embellishment; it is central to the figure's identity. The Southwestern Santiago is the saint of horses. The people's painstaking care in ornamenting the figure—he wears luxurious fabrics and ornate embroidery that no one in the settlement does—has extended to the embroidering of his very identity. Santiago is both "the same" as the St. Jacques with whom Latour identifies him, and not. The added dimension of the figure serves to upset Father Latour's expected relation to the community. Rather than simply ministering to supplicants, Latour finds himself learning of his religion from a local child. Ironically, the local revision of the saint also extends the reach of his religion. Even the local Indians pray to Santiago, since he blesses the mares and makes them fruitful. This wooden figure on a family's shelf gives Father Latour his first intimation of the range of Mexican and Indian beliefs and devotional practices. The object alerts Latour to the fact that there cannot be a simple transposition of religious belief from Europe to the American Southwest. What takes place in this zone is distinct, a reinvention informed by a multitude of cultural traditions. In this episode and others, it falls to the inanimate world to perform the intercultural translations that language cannot accomplish.

The material object depicts the cultural interpenetrations of the nineteenth-century Southwest so accurately because it can draw upon the experiences of those not usually involved in the crafting or advancing of official narratives.[5] Late one night, as he experiences a crisis of faith, Father Latour welcomes Sada, a disenfranchised old Mexican woman, into his church. This woman reminds Latour of the power, "for one who cannot read—or think—[of] the Image, the physical form of Love!" (*DCA* 229). Latour slights Sada's ability to think, but kneeling next to her he feels "the preciousness of the things of the altar to her who was without possessions; the tapers, the image of the Virgin, the figures of the saints, the Cross that took away indignity from suffering and made pain and poverty a means of fellowship with Christ" (*DCA* 228). The sacred objects reverse Latour's slighting of Sada, giving her access to, and a means to change, the understandings of a bishop.[6] Before this encounter, Latour has been feeling spiritually barren. Sada reinstructs him in the mystery and power of their shared religion, which in her hands becomes genuinely and equitably shared. No wonder that Sada reacts to the inanimate, according to Latour, "as if it were a living thing that had been kind to her" (229). As the inanimate is made alive through Sada, it too confirms her aliveness. In it she finds the traces of a community of devotion and shared symbolism, and to it she can add the traces of her own religious passion. In its accessibility and flexibility, the material world is uniquely available to the illiterate and the disempowered. Because it speaks to these populations, they in turn respond to it. The material object, invested with these responses, can express them with unprecedented authority.

This power is something that Father Vaillant has occasion to remind Latour about. The miraculous appearance and physical traces of the Virgin of Guadalupe provoke strong feeling in Vaillant: "All these poor Catholics who have been so long without instruction have at least the reassurance of that visitation. It is a household word with them that their Blessed Mother revealed Herself in their own country, to a poor convert. Doctrine is well enough for the wise, Jean; but the miracle is something we can hold in our hands and love" (*DCA* 53). That which can be held in the hands: Vaillant's metaphor is one of fundamental materiality, an experience that can be shared by all. Sharing is woven into the very fiber of Vaillant's metaphor, for that which is held in the hands is often either that just received or that about to be passed on.

Distinctively open to a range of cultures and a range of classes, objects embody the kind of cultural variety and métissage that is the fullest expression of Latour's diocese. Their history, and that of the region, is inscribed upon them. Like the old silver bell of San Miguel that Father Vaillant unearths, these objects speak of generations of cultural interpenetration, sometimes violent and exploitative, and other times more openly collaborative. When Father Latour wakes to the silvery sound of the bell of San Miguel, he first hears the voice of Rome, and then a more "Eastern" tone. Later, speaking to his vicar, Father Vaillant, Latour muses on the legacy of the silver bell: cast out of household silver and pledged to St. Joseph during the Spanish wars against the Moors, it, like all Spanish silverwork, draws upon the silverworking tradition of the Moors; imported to the New World, it figured in the instruction of silver working to the Mexicans, who then passed the skill to the Navajos. The bell is the object that makes this thread clear, through wars, enmities, and imperialisms. Each culture has its own vibrant tradition of silver working, but it also, within these objects, carries the traces of countless other influences. Although the cultures may remain estranged, as in the case of Roman Catholicism and Islam, the material objects with which they express the sacred also express the inevitability of interconnection. The bell expresses associations that the master narratives of religious difference and imperialism would quash. The necessary mobility of the material increases the reach of the community brokered by the material.

Father Vaillant experiences this object mobility during his travels in isolated areas of Arizona.

> Down near Tucson a Pima Indian convert once asked me to go off into the desert with him, as he had something to show me. He took me into a place so wild that a man less accustomed to these things might have mistrusted and feared for his life. We descended into a terrifying canyon of black rock, and there in the depths of a cave, he showed me a golden chalice, vestments and cruets, all the paraphernalia for celebrating Mass. His ancestors had hidden these sacred objects there when the Mission was sacked by Apaches, he did not know how many generations ago. The secret had been handed down in his family. (*DCA* 216)

With the missions sacked and crumbling, the missionaries either killed or fled and never replaced, the objects alone carry the symbolic weight of the Catholicism adopted by the Pima Indians. Father Vaillant's discovery serves to underline a preexisting condition of Catholic belief in the Southwest. Even before the Apache raids, the holy objects carried a disproportionate amount of the symbolic weight of Catholicism. In a study of the Pueblos published a year after *Death Comes for the Archbishop,* Leo Crane described religious festivals in which sacred objects were processed through villages and rested in public altars decorated by townspeople (41). According to Gutiérrez, "New Mexican churches, unlike their European counterparts, were rarely consecrated," while the holy objects ritually encoded their own "mobile quality" (59). The mobility of the holy objects accounts for their being salvageable from the Apache raids, but also suggests an accompanying symbolic mobility on their parts. In the remote reaches of this diocese, sacred relics, saved and honored for generations without outside influence, have not symbolically atrophied. Instead, in an accelerated version of what is taking place throughout the diocese, the holy objects of the Pima have developed independence from the Mass. They have developed affiliations with certain families. Their identity has incorporated some of the terrifying wildness of their new setting. They refer to past and future local events that do not figure in the symbolism of the Mass. Above all, these objects are something *shown to* Vaillant *by* their Pima Indian keeper. No mention is made of a transfer of guardianship. Responsibility for them is no longer Vaillant's to assume.

Material culture lends itself to such performance of communally achieved understandings. In other words, the mobility of material objects encourages the individual to adopt some such mobility. Through access to the objects, the Pima has found himself in the position of an interpreter of faith. Vaillant, on the other hand, experiences the objects as almost uncannily possessed by another culture. He is momentarily the outsider before the missionary. The Pima gains access to some of the historical texture behind Vaillant's relation with the objects, while Vaillant gains access to some of the innovativeness of the Pima's relation with the objects. Certainly neither performer's understanding of the other is complete. However, through the medium of the sacred objects the perspectives of the two men are no longer so carefully delineated.[7] They each begin to have access to the insights of the other.

The physical and symbolic mobility of the material object in *Death Comes for the Archbishop* is also made possible by the distinctive strain of cultural materialism Cather associates with the Southwest. A priest in Isleta tells Father Latour of the wampum, turquoises, and lives spent by the Pueblos of northern New Mexico in their attempts to procure parrots and their feathers from the South. This Indian trade does not seem motivated by personal gain so much as by the desire for the symbolically significant. Symbolic significance is a far more shifting standard of value than is the exchange value that motivates most of the white traders and settlers in Father Latour's diocese. Father Vaillant comments of the communities he works with that "These poor Christians are not thrifty like our country people at home; they have no veneration for property, no sense of material values. I stop a few hours in a village, I administer the sacraments and hear confessions, I leave in every house some little token, a rosary or a religious picture, and I go away feeling that I have conferred immeasurable happiness" (*DCA* 216). Father Vaillant's observation is more acute than his vocabulary here. The scene he describes requires that a distinction be made between a veneration of property and a sense of material values. The specific material values held by Euro-Americans do include a veneration of property and a focus on exchange value. Southwestern villagers, however, are responsive to the more fluid and unpredictable category of the symbolic value of the thing as thing. As a trader tells Father Latour about a group of Pecos men he once saw carrying a chest, "If I'd seen white men bringing in a chest after dark . . . I could have made a guess at what was in it; money, or whisky, or fire-arms. But seeing it was Indians, I can't say. It might have been only queer-shaped rocks their ancestors had taken a notion to. The things they value most are worth nothing to us" (*DCA* 143). The objects that the Indians value introduce standards of worth new to Euro-Americans.[8] The unpredictable basis of Indian valuation confuses the white trader but emphasizes the degree to which the significance of the material world defies limitation in Cather's Southwest.

The cultural clash of object valuation appears in its most extreme form through the behavior of an errant and excommunicated priest of the region, Father Lucero. Lucero is an infamous miser. His attitude sharply contrasts with the lack of "material values" that Father Vaillant notices in the area. In one sense, Lucero is the most extreme example of the local valuation of the material: he values money as material, for he hoards it and never capitalizes on its exchange value. On the other hand, his hoarding bespeaks a need to control his object. This need is so intense that it cannot allow the object to circulate and to partake of the shifting meanings brought by constant communal participation in, and reinvention of, the material.[9] Lucero's miserliness is an attempt to anchor the object in relation to one individual. The very isolation inherent in this attitude makes the communitarian materialism of the rest of the region stand out more strongly, as if in relief.

In a region where, despite Father Lucero's miserly efforts, so much remains (so productively) in flux, the culture best accommodates the itinerant priest that Father Vaillant wants to be, not the institutional cathedral with which Father Latour identifies. The priest who travels around the region must be receptive to each community's particularities of interpretation. Indeed, in the later moments of the narrative, when the two Fathers feel at home in the region, the effects of their time spent as itinerant priests become increasingly evident in the narrative. Their thinking begins to be punctuated by the wisdom (or even quiet inscrutability) of various local icons, whom they muse upon in all their distinctive materiality: the booted Santiago of Chimayo, the sternly well-dressed

Virgin of Santa Fé. In this respect Latour and Vaillant learn to act as Cather's pause-oriented compositional method dictates: "to touch and pass on" (*OW* 9). When one merely touches upon a village before passing on, belief systems too complex to be easily apprehended become represented by the treasured icon of the village. Fathers Latour and Vaillant are willing to engage occasional outright challenges to doctrine, but for the most part, simply seek to understand the materially inflected and contingent local Catholicism.

In this willingness to touch and pass on, the priests are rivaled only by the Indians of the area. Father Latour notes that "just as it was the white man's way to assert himself in any landscape, to change it, make it over a little (at least to leave some mark or memorial of his sojourn), it was the Indian's way to pass through a country without disturbing anything; to pass and leave no trace, like fish through the water, or birds through the air" (*DCA* 246). This hackneyed conception of Native American "environmentalism" extends Latour's insight from the cruciform tree episode. According to Latour's conceptualization, the Indian, accepting chance and unpredictability, does not attempt to halt the flux of the material world, to force the land into a signpost of his or her passage. The white man, on the other hand, attempts to assert individual mastery over either the physical or the cultural landscape in which he finds himself. For the white man, progress through the landscape is a conquest to be marked. Here, telos serves as explanation of the defacement—the "mark or memorial" left by the white traveler parallels Lucero's miserliness in that it attempts to monopolize interpretation of the material world. As we can recall from the cruciform tree episode, such a single-minded pursuit of progress through the landscape in the Southwest most often leads to limited and lost travelers.

Guy Reynolds has noted the ambivalence toward ideas of progress that characterizes *Death Comes for the Archbishop*. Cather's sense of the hostility between the forces of progress and the object is elaborated in her insistence, in her letter on the novel, that the "old homely images and decorations" of the mission churches not be replaced by "conventional, factory-made church furnishings from New York" (*OW* 6).[10] Progress threatens these precious objects by attempting to remove them to collections, in which they are set apart from the living energies that once gave them meaning. In this case Cather represents the threat of progress as personified by "the newer priests" (*OW* 6). These new priests, like Latour's prototypical white man traveling through the land, want to leave signposts of "progress." They represent individual attempts to dominate the communal processes of material identity formation. Factory-made religious icons speak of the Northeastern culture in which they were designed and manufactured, and of the priests who institute them. They enact an insidious erasure of the populations that have been interacting in the Southwest for centuries. The new icons are empty of the imaginative interpenetration by which the old icons enacted the Catholicization of the Southwest and the Southwesternization of Catholicism.[11] In proclaiming her attachment to the traditional icons of the Southwest, Cather articulates an awareness of an already deeply material culture and of the constellations of cultural narratives that meet in its objects.[12]

Rather than being attributed to Cather's notorious nostalgia, then, the attention that *Death Comes for the Archbishop* gives to the material culture of the mid-nineteenth-century Southwest must be understood as continuous with her campaign to protect cultural difference in the United States of her time. In an interview of 1924 Cather decried the erasure of cultural differences by progressive types across the United States, who try to turn immigrants "into stupid replicas of smug American citizens. This passion for Americanizing everything and everybody is a deadly disease with us. We do it the way we build houses. Speed, uniformity, dispatch, nothing else matters" (*WCIP* 71–72). These mass-produced Americans, like the mass-produced Catholic icons, are disturbing precisely because they communicate an assumed incompatibility between cultural variation and the kind of precipitate progress that characterized the United States of the early twentieth century. Cather would not have it be this way. After all, the mobility that *Death Comes for the Archbishop* associates with objects provides an alternative to both precipitate progress and nostalgic stasis. In this sense, the objects that *Archbishop* dwells upon have important contributions to make to the United States of Cather's day. They are not simply quaint artifacts to be celebrated by primitivist modernist art and folklore collections. Rather, they are material guides to the navigation of cultural difference. Cather's response to them and her construction of *Death Comes for the Archbishop* around them must be understood as evidence of her ongoing commitment to a culturally diverse America.

Notes

1. The central religious objects of *Death Comes for the Archbishop* are Catholic ones. Mary Chinery has recently provided an important historical and cultural contextualization of the specific Southwestern santos tradition that Cather's novel so often turns to. The Catholicism represented by these objects is significant, for Catholicism as a religion based upon proselytization has an interest in developing an aesthetic and ritualistic structure capable of accommodating a wide range of cultures. (See Reynolds for more on this.) Catholicism answers the challenge of flexible integration by dwelling on the material. The materialism that suffuses the symbolic system of Catholicism is thus a suggestive model for a writer attempting a more modernist multicultural aesthetic structure.

2. Bill Brown's *A Sense of Things: The Object Matter of American Literature* (2003) provides an indispensable background for the study of objects in early twentieth-century America; his chapters on Jewett and James (previously published in *American Literary History* and *The Henry James Review*) lead into a brief consideration of Cather's "The Novel Démeublé," *The Professor's House,* and "Paul's Case." For James's "object world," see also Agnew, "The Consuming Vision of Henry James." For Sarah Orne Jewett, see also Ammons, "Material Culture, Empire, and Jewett's *Country of the Pointed Firs.*"

3. In a 1921 interview Cather declared that an "old house built and furnished in miserable taste is more beautiful than a new house built and furnished in correct taste. The beauty lies in the associations that cluster around it, the way in which the house has fitted itself to the people" (*WCIP* 46). The ideas of "associations" and the "fit" of the house both assign agency to the object through its role as a site for the investment of human energies. This belief naturally develops into the eloquence of the material world in *Death Comes for the Archbishop.*

4. This role of objects is consistent with the modernist conceptualization of objects that Brown elsewhere identifies in Theodor Adorno's *Negative Dialectics* (1997). Brown argues that

> it is precisely by giving into—thinking or working through—reification and alienation, and by identifying a profounder separation (not of objects but of things), that Adorno came to re-identify ethical possibility: "If a man looks upon thingness as a radical evil . . . he tends to be hostile to otherness, to the alien thing that has lent its name to alienation, and not in vain" (*ND*, 191). . . . For Adorno, the problem [of modernity] has become the very will-to-assimilation. He designates the happiness of philosophy, over and against the "imperialism of annexing the alien," as residing "in the fact that the alien, in the proximity it is granted, remains what is distant and different." ("Secret Life of Things" 12)

5. Judith Fryer notes that Holbein's *Dance of Death,* which Cather claimed to have inspired the title of *Death Comes for the Archbishop,* is a series of woodcuts that "in form go back to the earliest modes of pictorial expression, the woodcarving and the line drawing. Their message, meant for people who could not read, was that death comes to all alike, emperor and peasant, judge and moneylender, physician and lover, old woman and worthy bishop" (311). The Holbein woodcuts offer a distinctly material experience that, evoked in the title of the novel, suggests leveling and the forging of unlikely community.

6. Reynolds also notes this moment.

7. In *Solid Objects: Modernism and the Test of Production,* Douglas Mao observes a similar (modernist) communicative materialism at work in the texts of Virginia Woolf, and even in the early writings of T. S. Eliot. According to Eliot's 1916 doctoral dissertation on F. H. Bradley, Mao explains, "we may fairly say that we know other subjectivities 'only through the mediation of objects'—that 'we have no knowledge of other souls except through their bodies' . . . and that indeed the 'platform of knowing . . . is the assertion of something to be known, something independent of me so far as knowing is concerned'" (Mao 52, citing Eliot, *Knowledge and Experience in the Philosophy of F. H. Bradley* [NY: Farrar, 1964] 151–52). Focusing on *Mrs. Dalloway* but also citing examples from Woolf's novels *The Voyage Out, Night and Day, Jacob's Room,* and *To the Lighthouse,* Mao builds a compelling argument about "intersubjective mediation by the object . . . in which . . . the object [often] negotiates loss or geographical separation as well as intersubjective distance" (54).

8. The priesthood offers Latour and Vaillant a relation to material objects that is unlike the typical one among Euro-Americans. Unlike the trader who

is stymied by Indian valuations of objects, by virtue of their calling the priests principally have a relation to the symbolic-expressive side of material objects as objects. They can, and must, appreciate objects in a multitude of different ways. As they are more alive to the kinds of energies that can be invested in an object, they serve as good intermediaries between cultures that largely appreciate objects as objects and cultures more preoccupied with the use value of objects.

9. Richard Millington positions Cather's "hostility to the novel" as akin to Benjamin's valorization (in "The Storyteller") of storytelling as "the animation of an ethic of communal exchange . . . as an alternative to the silence and solitude of private consumption" (692). My distinction between communal exchange via objects and solitary hoarding of them falls neatly into this pattern. In all likelihood, the object-centric episodicity of *Death Comes for the Archbishop* serves as resistance to the formal complicity of the novel with "solitary consumption" rather than the "communal exchange" that the novel locates in objects.

10. In a 1925 lecture at the University of Chicago, Cather deplored the prevalence of the "machine-made novel" in American letters. She particularly condemned "the importance attached to 'plot' in the modern novel" (*WCIP* 166). It seems appropriate, then, to connect the antiplot narrative experimentation of *Death Comes for the Archbishop* with her fascination with the material object that is *not* machine-made.

11. According to Colleen McDannell, "religious replication" of icons and shrines played a specific role in late-nineteenth- and early-twentieth-century American Catholicism: "Reproducing shrines told the Catholics of northern Indiana that they were not living in an undefined, wild space but that they were directly connected to the spiritual centers of Catholicity" (161). Cather's objection is to the use of mass-replicated religious objects to erase cultural distinctions; she celebrates the unique Catholicism that flourishes in its own particularity in "undefined, wild" spaces. Claire Farago suggests that in fact mass-produced religious objects, including print items, were incorporated into the improvisatory material Christianity of the late-nineteenth-century and early-twentieth-century Southwest.

12. Cather was not alone in apprehending the region in terms of its material culture. In his 1942 Pueblo novel *The Man Who Killed the Deer,* Frank Waters depicts as a particular power of Pueblo culture the ability to use the material world in order to divest oneself of one's individuality and achieve a fuller sense of community: Martiniano, a Pueblo Indian who reembraces traditional cul-

ture and ritual, exults in the experience of being "crowned at last with that symbol of the wild earth's nobility and his people's badge of immortality—a feather, if only a tuft of eagle-down. To have been one with me who for a time were not men but less than men and symbols of more than men" (296). In Oliver LaFarge's *Laughing Boy,* a novel published in 1929 (two years after *Death Comes for the Archbishop*) and greatly admired by Cather, the characters Laughing Boy and Slim Girl explicitly use material objects in order to perform Navajo cultural authenticity to Laughing Boy's family. Although the couple has been living in American society, traditional Navajo handicrafts such as blankets and silver jewelry serve as signals to the more traditional family members that Laughing Boy and Slim Girl desire continued participation in Navajo culture. In both of these cases, culturally mixed characters use objects to understand, and make themselves understood by, cultures with whom they have complex relations.

9

Gloves Full of Gold

Violations of the Gift Cycle in *My Mortal Enemy*

Robert K. Miller

An amethyst necklace. Austrian blankets. A fur hat with a garnet feather. And some of the sexiest curtains in American literature—curtains that are "long" and "heavy" in a "wonderful plum-colour, like ripe purple fruit . . . lined with that rich cream-colour that lies under the blue skin of ripe figs" (*MME* 23). These are among the material objects through which Myra Driscoll Henshawe constructs how she wishes to be seen by others. Readers of *My Mortal Enemy* may also recall other objects that attract or repel this complex woman, becoming gifts of different kinds. When Christmas shopping, for example, Myra chooses "a glistening holly-tree, full of red berries and pointed like a spire, easily the queen of its companions" (25) as a gift for Helena Modjeska—a gift that she enriches and complicates by sending with it a box of cakes of her own baking. Myra can also give away—without consultation—six of her husband's new dress shirts to the son of her janitor because she considers the cut unbecoming for a gentleman and her consort must fit the image she is determined to convey. Examining what Myra is willing to discard, either as a gift she bestows or as material she will abandon, can help us to understand why her life becomes so bleak.

The work of Marcel Mauss (1872–1950), a French anthropologist who was Cather's contemporary, provides a helpful structure for this examination. The nephew and student of Emile Durkheim, Mauss saw himself as a sociologist, but he is today considered one of the determinative figures in the development of anthropology as a scientific discipline. His work demonstrates extensive knowledge of myth, religion, economics, and law, as well as a serious interest in aesthetics. In recent years, scholars of literary theory have been most likely to learn about Mauss through Derrida's discussion of his work in *The Gift of Time*, which includes an assessment of Mauss's most famous work, *The Gift: The Form and Reason for Exchange in Archaic Societies*, or through Claude Lévi-Strauss, who compared Mauss to Moses "conducting his people all the way to a promised land" (54).[1] First published in 1923–1924, *The Gift* offers a cultural analysis that deserves greater attention in literary studies. Before applying Mauss to *My Mortal Enemy*, I will summarize those aspects of his findings that are most relevant to Myra's tale.

From close observation of Native American peoples in the Northwest, as well as peoples in Melanesia—observations that were informed by knowledge of ancient Indo and Germanic law—Mauss concluded that there are three common themes to multicultural rituals associated with the giving of material objects: "the obligation to give, the obligation to receive and [the obligation to] reciprocate" (39). To withhold or refuse a gift puts an individual or group of individuals (such as a family, tribe, or nation) at peril. The giving and receiving of gifts must be part of an unbroken cycle that binds people together, hence the importance of reciprocation. Because the ability to give gifts is closely associated with honor in archaic societies, reciprocation often required that a gift given in response to a gift received must be of greater value. In the most extreme case of this cycle discussed by Mauss, the potlatch of the Haïda people in the American Northwest, competitive gift giving can lead to the destruction of wealth when a party to the exchange of gifts is unable to reciprocate with a gift or gifts of greater value. The destruction (which took the form of breaking valuable objects and tossing others into the sea) demonstrated moral superiority grounded in sacrifice and thus allowed honor to be maintained. But such honor was achieved at great cost. Face had been preserved, but poverty and isolation were likely to follow. Unless new wealth could be discovered or generated, those who destroyed their material wealth could no longer participate in the gift-giving rituals that foster social ties. As the anthropologist Mary Douglas notes in her introduction to *The Gift*, "gift cycles engage persons in permanent commitments that articulate the dominant institutions" (ix). To give, to receive, and to reciprocate allows people to locate themselves within these cultural norms; to refuse any one of these obligations is to become a rebel or an outcast. In Mauss's words, "To refuse to give, to fail to invite, just as to refuse to accept, is tantamount to declaring war; it is to reject the bond of alliance and commonality" (13).

Moreover, there is a spiritual dimension to the gift cycle, not only because gifts must be given to the gods as well as to individuals, but also because "to make a gift of something to someone is to make a present of some part of oneself" (12). Gift giving thus involves self-sacrifice, not just the offering of material objects. Accordingly, honoring the gift cycle fosters both social and cosmic harmony. "Gifts to humans and to the gods also serve the purpose of buying peace between them both" (17).

Mauss points out that the Romans eventually moved away from an economy based on the exchange of gifts because a gift-based economy "was overexpensive and too sumptuous, *burdened with consideration for people* [emphasis mine], incompatible with the development of the market, commerce, and production, and, all in all, at that time was anti-economic" (54). Thus while an individual who breaks the gift cycle is at both social and spiritual risk, a culture can move away from that cycle if other forms of exchange seem to offer more opportunities at lower cost. Hence the movement from gift-economy to money-economy, which prepared the way for the emergence of capitalism: a sack of gold coins is easier to transport and can be used for a greater number of purposes than a pile of fish or vegetables.

If we read *My Mortal Enemy* with ideas such as these in mind, we can see that Myra's suffering, introduced during Nellie and Lydia's visit with her in New York City and emphasized in part 2 of the book, may be rooted in her violation of the gift cycle and her inability to find the means to enter back into it. She breaks the cycle by walking away from a fortune—refusing, in effect, her uncle's gifts. Knowing that she will be disinherited if she marries Oswald, she seeks honor through this "destruction" of her potential wealth but achieves only admiration—principally, the admiration of a sentimental friend who facilitates the act and a sentimental husband who is ultimately unable to satisfy her. In New York, she is restless in the homes of affluent business associates of her husband, accepting their hospitality ungraciously because she can outshine them in wit but not in wealth. And she is infuriated by

Oswald's acceptance of topaz sleeve buttons because she is perceptive enough by this point in her life to understand that there are no free gifts. These jewels are problematic not because they are expensive but because they cannot exist except as part of a gift cycle. They are either a gift to which Oswald must reciprocate (perhaps with romantic attention) or a gift given in reciprocation for some gift he has already bestowed. And because the identity of the gift-giver is not revealed—only that she is "a rich girl" who is "from a breezy Western city" (27)—Myra is unable to "pay her back." Although Myra is not the direct recipient of the gift, the jewelry has nevertheless entered her home. She can make Oswald "pay" by quarreling with him. But she cannot outshine her anonymous rival with a more sumptuous gift either to her husband or to the young woman, and Myra loves to have the last word or gesture.

Late in the novel, Myra describes herself as "a greedy, selfish, worldly woman" who wanted "success and a place in the world" (62–63), and there is certainly good reason to see her as a woman obsessed with material possessions. The sight of an acquaintance in a carriage of her own can spoil an afternoon for Myra, and even when she is dying she remains attached to "an ebony crucifix with an ivory cross" (75) and those Austrian blankets of hers, abandoning her plum-coloured curtains only when she is at the hour of her death. Much then can be said about how Cather uses Myra to explore issues relevant to both material culture and gift theory. But we can best see how these issues can be explored by focusing on one of the objects that Myra has been careful to retain in her possession and to which she directs Nellie's attention: "an old pair of long kid gloves, tied up like sacks," gloves that are filled with "ten- and twenty-dollar gold pieces" (*MME* 69). Cather's detailed description of these gloves, in a scene set in the early twentieth century, suggests that she wanted readers to reflect upon their significance.

The gloves in question are not only long and made of kid leather; they are also "yellow with age and tied at both ends with corset lacings" (69). Myra emphasizes that they were not her "wedding gloves, piously preserved." "No," she tells Nellie, "I went before a justice of the peace and married without gloves, so to speak!" (69). Lest we lose sight of these gloves, Cather subsequently makes an indirect reference to them in the note Myra leaves for Oswald when she escapes from their small apartment to die alone on a cliff overlooking the Pacific: "Dear Oswald:

my hour has come. Don't follow me. I wish to be alone. Nellie knows where there is money for masses" (79–80). The money is, of course, in those old kid gloves.

We know that Myra was still unmarried in 1876, because Nellie notes that date when reading to her from a volume of Heine inscribed "To Myra Driscoll from Oswald" (65). Myra is unlikely to have carried the gloves with her when she left her uncle's mansion, as we know that she was carrying only her muff and a small purse—and that Lydia packed some linen in another small bag. So the gloves were probably purchased in New York when Myra was a young married woman. Accordingly, I have used what was fashionable in 1880 when picturing Myra's gloves and how much money they could contain. Introduced in the sixteenth century and originally used by men when dueling ("History"), kid gloves were fashionable in 1880 and could be used as either day or evening apparel. Long ones in that year were worn tight and stopped one inch below the elbow—higher than they had been worn at midcentury, thanks in part to the influence of Sarah Bernhardt, one of Cather's favorite actors.[2]

How much gold could have fit in Myra's gloves? A twenty-dollar gold piece in circulation from 1838 to 1933—in other words, easily within the period in which *My Mortal Enemy* is set as well as when it was composed—measured 34 mm in diameter; a ten-dollar gold piece from this same period measured 27 mm in diameter, a relatively small difference. The most significant difference between the two coins was weight. At 34 grams, a twenty-dollar gold piece weighed twice as much as a ten-dollar piece, the difference determined primarily by thickness. Both coins would be wider and heavier than the half-dollar coins now in circulation. If we picture a half dollar, we will realize that ten- and twenty-dollar gold pieces could not possibly have fit within the fingers of a lady's glove. With this in mind, we can picture the fingers being tied off with corset strings, and note that the use of corset lacings adds to the sense that these gloves have been bound in a way that would distort and confine human flesh. Moreover, the gloves can almost be said to be made of Myra's own skin—reminding us of how Mauss argued that material objects could be an extension of the human self. Kid, after all, comes from the skin of young goat and Myra's hair is compared to "the fleece of a Persian goat" in the novel's opening scene (*MME* 5). A young goat no more, the kid is now "yellow with age." In other words, the leather has aged as Myra has aged, and if the gloves are "tied up" and distorted by the purpose for which they are now used, the same can be said of their owner, who is tied up and cut off by her pride, anger, and stubborn determination to resist change (Urgo, *Myth* 193–94).

With expert counsel,[3] I have determined that not counting the fingers and leaving one inch empty at the top of each glove so that they could be tied off, each of Myra's gloves would hold a volume of 43.5 cubic millimeters. Unlike sand, for example, gold coins would not completely fill this space, because the coins would rest in a pattern leaving small separations between many of them. This empty space, however, is easily offset by the fact that kid leather stretches over time and Myra's gloves are "old." Moreover, gold is one of the heaviest of metals, so there would have been considerable pressure on the kid to stretch. I am estimating Myra's size and operating on the assumption that each glove is 90% filled within the space that would not have been tied off. The ten- and twenty-dollar gold pieces pour out of the glove that is untied—suggesting balance between the denominations. So for the sake of argument, I have assumed that Myra has an equal number of ten- and twenty-dollar coins. With these assumptions in place—and I must emphasize that this is only an estimate of how much Myra has stashed away—each glove would have contained 217 coins if filled enough to look like "sacks" (69), to use Myra's word for them. If half of these coins were ten-dollar coins and half were twenty-dollar coins, each glove would hold $6,510 or a grand total of $13,020—not exactly spare change, even today. When adjusted for inflation, $6,510 in 1913 (when the Consumer Price Index began tracking the annual rate of inflation) would have the equivalent of $116,719.70 in purchasing power today. Multiply that by two, and we see that Myra, in her old age, has close to a quarter of a million dollars tucked away.

I want to move on to what the gloves and the gold signify, but I must pause here to emphasize that Myra really is withholding a significant fortune from her husband. Even if both gloves were only 25 percent full, Myra would have had the equivalent of $60,000 at hand. We should not envision an impoverished aristocrat who has piously preserved a small sum for acts of charity and devotion; instead, we must recognize that Myra is a miser who is still refusing to enter into the gift cycle that would free her from her self-imposed isolation by providing reciprocation to the husband who, whatever his faults, has nursed her in illness and almost certainly endured a fair amount of ridicule from the demanding woman he serves. Myra understands that the money would have comforted Oswald. As she tells Nellie, "We've often needed a hundred dollars or two so bitter bad" (70). But her use of the first-person plural in this case approaches the outrageous. While it recognizes her position as part of a couple who are bound together and have common needs, it also makes a spurious claim for sympathy. Oswald may have needed a couple of hundred dollars "bitter bad" to meet his responsibility to support the woman who had eloped to marry him. But Myra doesn't need a dime.

At first glance, the gloves seem to symbolize how Myra is, as she says, a "worldly woman." They are money gloves, not wedding gloves—and Myra's gratuitous announcement that they are not "wedding gloves, piously preserved" reinforces the sense that she has disassociated herself from social rituals marking kinship. What complicates the revelation of the gloves, however, is her declaration that the money hidden in them is reserved for "unearthly purposes" (70). Indeed, we first learn of this secret hoard when Myra wants Nellie to take a coin to Father Fay with the request that he use the money "to celebrate a mass . . . for the repose of Helena Modjeska, Countess Bozenta-Chlapowska" (70). This means that Nellie will be making a journey that Myra had been able to make for herself the previous year and which she could still probably make, judging from the determination she shows when leaving home to die. So one effect of Nellie's commission is to alert readers to the existence of gloves that might otherwise have remained unseen at the bottom of an old trunk.

While reflecting on the role of gloves in Cather's fiction, I have noted that gloves are often absent from scenes in which readers might expect to find them. On the cold day in Hanover when we first meet Emil, Alexandra, and Carl in *O Pioneers!*, none of these characters seems to be wearing gloves. Indeed, when Carl runs to the depot to fetch some spikes, he thrusts his hands into his pockets (*OP* 9) in order to keep them warm. And it's not as if Cather makes no reference to clothing in this well-known scene, for we learn about Alexandra's coat, hat, and veil and also learn that Carl had left his overcoat in the drug store. Similarly, on the cold day on which Lucy Gayheart goes skating for the last time, she is wearing a hat and coat (163) but no gloves, it seems, because her "hands trembled so that she could scarcely pull the leather laces taut and tie them" (167) when she puts on her skates. The only glove we see that day belongs to Harry Gordon, and it appears at the moment when, in misjudging Lucy, he betrays his friendship with her. Tired and cold, Lucy begs a ride from him, and he replies that he is too busy, touching "his *fur hat with his glove*" [emphasis mine] as he drives away (*LG* 166). When Thea Kronborg actually asks if she should wear gloves when singing, Mrs. Nathanmeyer responds, "No, I think not. Your arms are good, and you will feel freer without" (*SL* 252). In *My Mortal Enemy* Cather links gloves to fur and to suffering in the scene where Myra takes Nellie to a matinee. At the theater they recognize a popular writer who was once one of Myra's friends. In Nellie's words,

> For all the rest of the afternoon I could feel the bitterness working in her. I knew she was suffering. The scene on the stage was obliterated for her; the drama was in her mind. She was going over it all again: arguing, accusing, denouncing.
>
> As we left the theater she sighed: "Oh, Nellie, I wish you hadn't seen him! It's all very well to tell us to forgive our enemies: our enemies can never hurt us very much. But oh, what about forgiving our friends?"—*she beat on her fur collar with her two gloved hands*—[emphasis mine] "that's where the rub comes in!" (37)

The association of gloved hands with fur suggests that there is something bestial about this woman who beats herself: She has made herself less than fully human by withdrawing from the gift cycle fundamental to community. Although gloves and fur might seem to be a natural combination, for both are worn for warmth in the winter, the description of Myra at the theater evokes a glove scene Cather had published only three years earlier. When Frank Ellinger and Marian Forrester go off into the woods together in *A Lost Lady*, Ellinger is a wearer of gloves who, like Myra, is like an animal when passion is stirred. "Ellinger took off his glove with his teeth. His eyes, sweeping the winding road and the low, snow-covered bluffs, had something wolfish in them." At this very moment, Mrs. Forester cries out, "Be careful, Frank, My rings! You hurt

Fig. 7. Cather dressed for her Graduation Ball, 1895. (Nebraska State Historical Society)

me" (*LL* 62). The pattern in Cather's fiction seems clear: Nice people don't wear gloves, and those who do cannot be trusted.

The veteran of many Nebraska and New York winters, Cather must have worn gloves on many occasions—although, tellingly, she is rarely photographed in them. Indeed, in the only widely circulated picture of her in gloves, she appears to be wearing a costume that does not fit her emerging identity (fig. 7). So why are gloves so problematic in her fiction?

Although gloves can warm our hands, they also conceal them, turning what can seem open-handed into what can be taken as under-handed. At the very least, gloves keep us from feeling the warmth of another human hand—hence their association with broken relationships, as in the scene between Harry Gordon and Lucy Gayheart or the scene of Myra at the theater. Gloves are also associated with aggressive acts—such as slapping a man across the face with a glove when challenging him to a duel or throwing down the gauntlet when making a challenge of some kind. Frank Ellinger's gloves, which he bites off with his teeth before grabbing hold of Mrs. Forrester, are located within this latter tradition, as are Myra's. She challenges her uncle, her husband, Lydia, and Nellie among other characters. Moreover, like a gauntlet, Myra is associated with the *ancien régime*. And when she dramatically walks away from a large fortune on the night she leaves her uncle's house, she carries with her "nothing but her muff and her *porte-monnaie* in her hands" (13–14)—nothing but a small purse and an object that conceals her hands, one object associated with money and the other associated with gloves.

In short, there is reason to see something sinister about Myra's gloves. Long enough not only to be gauntlets but also blackjacklike weapons that could injure someone hit with them when they are filled with gold coins, they are clearly associated with hiding and hoarding rather than with warmth and utility. "Yellow with age" and all tied up, they have been hidden for a long time, and Myra makes a point of telling Nellie that Oswald does not know about the treasure they contain—indirectly instructing her to keep her mouth shut.

The gold coins within these gloves are also problematic. Coins are part of the market economy that replaced the gift economy of the archaic order with which Myra is linked. In an often-cited passage, Father Fay declares that Myra is "not at all modern in her make-up" (*MME* 76), and through the scene in which Myra listens to the *Casta Diva* aria in *Norma,* critics have linked Myra to both druids and ancient Rome (Woodress 387; Skaggs 92; Goldberg 83). By the early twentieth century, however, dollar bills (backed by a gold standard until 1933) were in wide circulation. So gold coins are both modern and premodern: they represent a money-based economy, but it is a money-based economy shaped by the value of a material object that can retain its value if a government prints out more paper money than it should. In other words, there is something "modern" about Myra's character, but it is as unmodern as she can make it. She will use coins, but they must be made of precious metals valued by archaic societies—and they must be kept out of general circulation, reserved for ceremonial occasions.

Myra uses a gold coin from one of her gloves to have a mass said for the "repose of the soul of Helena Modjeska . . . that noble artist, that beautiful and gracious woman" (*MME* 70). This line is ambiguous. Is

Modjeska a "noble artist" because of her fine spirit and high commitment to art, or is she a "noble artist" because, as Myra notes, she is Countess Bozenta-Chlapowska? In other words, is Myra honoring religion, art, or aristocracy? Characteristically, Cather leaves this question for readers to resolve on our own. Saving gold to honor the memory of Helena Modjeska could thus be taken as a sign of respect for high mass, high art, or high birth—all of which are "unearthly purposes" but purposes of different kinds.

Moreover, to spend ten or twenty dollars for a mass in Myra's lifetime would have been extravagant—and, as shown by Mauss, extravagance destabilizes personal relationships because reciprocation becomes more difficult. Although I have been unable to determine the average price for a mass card in 1913, I can report that the official rate for a mass in my own diocese is now $7—up from $2 in 1969, which was a good half-century after Myra paid for Madame Modjeska's mass.[4] Whatever the average price on the west coast of the United States may have been in 1913, Myra is certainly spending an extraordinarily large sum for the period in question. Rather than honoring a fee schedule designed to give priests some walking-around money without making the spiritually naïve conclude that the larger the sum, the better the mass, Myra is playing by her own rules. While there may be something magnificent about her gesture, it nevertheless reinforces how she consistently locates herself outside of a gift cycle that can help individuals overcome social and spiritual isolation.

Although highly prized by many peoples, both ancient and modern, gold itself is ambiguous. Widely associated with wealth, it can be dangerous for those who seek it, as in the Midas myth or for those native peoples who stood in the way of the imperial quest for gold. It is also worth noting that Myra's sarcasm made Nellie feel as if "touched by a metal so cold that one doesn't know whether one is burned or chilled" (6). This line from the very beginning of the book suggests that touching or receiving Myra's metal is likely to be injurious. Gold and silver are the only metals mentioned in *My Mortal Enemy*, and both are associated with Myra. On Christmas Eve during Nellie's visit to New York, Myra gives a silver dollar to the deliveryman who will take her gifts to Madame Modjeska, and she gives coins on several other occasions. I don't think it a stretch therefore to associate gold and silver with the touch of cold metal Nellie feels when Myra speaks sarcastically, and to consider that there may also be something cold about the ostensibly generous uses to which Myra puts this money. Furthermore, cold metal evokes for me the memory of the "shining metal" on Paul's dressing table in New York—the gun that he decides not to use when committing suicide ("Paul's Case" 259).

Despite the worldliness and grasping nature that Myra sees in herself (*MME* 62), it is her capacity to discard and to give rather than to receive or to reciprocate that is often emphasized. As noted earlier, she discards a large fortune and several friendships. She gives an expensive gift to Helena Modjeska, offers hospitality to those who please her, gives advice to people like Ewan Gray who choose to consult with her, and invests considerable energy in personal relationships. Nellie offers a memorable description of accompanying Myra on a visit to Anne Aylward, a poet dying of tuberculosis in her twenties, testifying that she had never seen Myra "so brilliant and so charming as she was in that sunlit study under the roofs" (35). This experience prompts Nellie to reflect that while her Aunt Lydia "often said that Myra was incorrigibly extravagant . . . I saw that her chief extravagance was in caring for so many people and in caring for them so much. When she but mentioned the name of someone whom she admired, one got an instant impression that the person must be wonderful, her voice invested the name with a sort of grace" (35).

A word like "grace," associated as it is in this scene with a woman who is dying, brings us back to the spiritual significance of using hidden gold for such unearthly purposes as a mass in honor of another friend who died. Is Myra practicing a kind of generosity that is ultimately redemptive, or is she playing out the part of the princess who once lived in what Nellie describes as "the Sleeping Beauty's palace" (15)?

To answer this question, we must come back to the scene with the gloves. "Oswald," Myra says, "does not know the extent of my resources" (70)—a line that is true in more than one sense. But these resources have almost surely been obtained *from* Oswald, accumulated over the years through housekeeping money. After all, Myra walked away from the Driscoll fortune and—so far as we are told—never earned an income of her own. She is supported by Oswald, who marries her only after he has begun to succeed in business and who is still supporting her, however modestly, at the end of her life. In other words, she is giving away what could be seen as money upon which Oswald could have a legitimate claim, or making a gift that is not in her sole power to give. But let us assume that Myra has acquired this money not only through careful saving but also through sacrificing comforts that she might otherwise have enjoyed. Let us even consider that the money could have been accumulated through gifts bestowed by John Driscoll during the years Myra lived in his home. The purse that Myra carries on the night of her elopement could have been filled with gold coins rather than with handkerchiefs and miscellaneous items of convenience, although I think this unlikely. Ultimately, the source of her money is less important than the manner in which she uses it—sparingly and yet extravagantly in a ritual that binds her to the dead rather than the living.

As in the archaic societies discussed by Mauss, gifts between relatives, friends, neighbors, and colleagues are often calculated in terms of value, and value, these days, is often associated with price. A ten-dollar gift calls for a ten-dollar counter-gift, although there are, to be sure, exceptions, such as homemade gifts that are difficult to price or special-interest items such as an inexpensive find at a garage sale that would enhance a friend's collection of ceramic dogs or movie memorabilia. To give a gift that is notably out of scale is to risk embarrassing the recipient or the presenter, unless there are extenuating circumstances. For example, a much-appreciated act of service could be recognized by a larger-than-normal counter-gift, for the counter-gift in this case would be in reciprocation of the service as well as for whatever object is handed over as part of the gift exchange. Each exchange is a kind of trade, and the sequence of trading that subsequently develops can be either delightful or burdensome. Even today, withdrawal from this system of exchange must be negotiated with care if one does not want to jeopardize a relationship. Thus, one would not simply stop giving a friend a gift at Christmas if the parties in question have been exchanging gifts for years unless one wants to give offense or signal displeasure of some kind. It would be more appropriate for friends to speak in advance of the holidays and agree not to exchange gifts any longer—an agreement that each party should then honor.

When Myra uses gold to pay for a mass in honor of Madame Modjeska she is providing a gift for which there can be no direct reciprocation—unlike the gift of the "glistening holly-tree" for which Modjeska reciprocates by attending Myra's New Year's Eve party and organizing an entertainment there. Dead for many years, Modjeska is in no position to buy Myra a mass of her own. But Myra's act is not exactly selfless. When making this gift in the past, she has gone to the church and announced her intentions. Now that she claims that she cannot hobble to the church any longer, she uses Nellie as her messenger—ensuring that Nellie witnesses the act of giving and sees the source from which the gift comes. She could have asked Father Fay to visit her and given him the money in person; after all, he is already familiar with this ritual of Myra's and within a few pages starts to visit frequently as Myra slips closer to death. But one witness, apparently, is not enough; Myra wants another—a person who will be free to tell this tale without violating professional ethics. In other words, she is ensuring that she will get some credit for what she perceives as a good deed. This scene thus becomes one of several in which Myra can be seen to be cultivating Nellie. Moreover, she may be cultivating the good opinion of Father Fay as well. We learn that she manages to impress him; indeed she does such a good job of this that he comes to see her resembling "some of the saints of the early Church" (76). And he comes to her when she is in need in a way that is not altogether dissimilar from the way her uncle "did not come to the church; the church went to him" (15).

There is certainly something self-interested about the other gifts Myra bestows. If she gives a deliveryman a silver dollar, she is likely to have her instructions followed carefully. An unusually large fee to a cabman allows her to recover her sense of self-worth after feeling humiliated by the sight of an acquaintance in her own carriage. The ten-dollar gold piece she gives to another cabman helps her to secure the privacy to die at a site of her own choice. Although these "gifts" can be seen as payment for service, they are out of scale and cannot be reciprocated by those upon whom they have been bestowed. Nor can the attentions Myra bestows upon Anne Aylward, who is an invalid of modest means. So Myra violates the gift-cycle described by Mauss not so much by operating altogether outside it but by operating selectively within it. She is more prepared to give than she is to receive, and her gifts must be given in a manner that draws attention to her and leaves others in her debt.

For the most part, then, Myra's gift giving is reflective of self-love rather than love for others. To return to those dress shirts that she gives to Willy Bunch, the son of the janitor in her New York apartment building. Willy may be pleased to wear them to "an Iroquois ball" (7)—one of many archaic references in the text—but how can he reciprocate? By whipping off his cap with greater alacrity when his patroness passes by? No, it is unlikely that Myra expects anything from poor Willy. He is simply the recipient of a gift that enables Myra to punish her husband. Gifts of this sort may well be poisonous, and it is useful to remember that *gift* means "poison" in German, signifying the problematic nature of the gift as a "present," for *gift* in English and German derives from the same root. The principal exception to Myra's normal use of gift giving as a means to dominate others is the holly tree she sends Helena Modjeska. The tree is expensive, but it is valuable not because of what it cost but because it is alive and thus suggestive of the archaic belief that gifts carried with them an animate force. And despite my many reservations about Myra, I must admit that she does something fine when she sends with this tree a box of cakes of her own baking. To bake something for a friend requires an investment of time and care, which is very different from popping into a flower shop and choosing an expensive object. Moreover, these handmade cakes can be seen as an extension of the self, which Myra normally keeps firmly under control. As Mauss argues, "to make a gift of something to someone is to make a present of some part of oneself" (12), and in this poison-free gift, Myra offers a glimpse of her best self.

When Myra was a young woman, her uncle gave her expensive products from material culture: "dresses and jewels, a fine riding horse, a Steinway piano" (10) among them. Oswald later gives her a book of poems. But gifts from material culture seem to have ended when she married. It is likely that Oswald gave her gifts on her birthday and at Christmas, and friends may have bestowed other objects upon her. But we never see this happening in the book. Instead, Cather draws attention to gifts received by others—such as the holly tree, the "flowers and plants and baskets of fruit that had been sent . . . [to Anne Aylward] for Christmas" (35), and, of course, the topaz sleeve buttons of questionable provenance that Lydia pretends to give Oswald. Although Myra clearly enjoys the comforts of material culture, material gifts go to others but not to her, emphasizing not only how she has been disinherited, but how she insists upon maintaining the role of the girl to whom tributes no longer come—with the exception of the flowers and baked goods that she accepts from Nellie (which are reminiscent of the tree and the cakes Myra had once given Modjeska). But when she reaches into her trunk, she offers no counter-gift to Nellie. On the contrary, she soon punishes Nellie, violating the gift cycle yet again. And when Nellie eventually does receive a gift of Myra's—the amethyst necklace that casts a chill over her heart (84)—it comes from Oswald, not from Myra.

Myra likes to give rather than to receive because this role is consistent with her desire for control.[5] She gives extravagantly, rather than generously, because she is as eager to make an impression as her uncle was when he bought silver instruments for the town band. The gifts in question call attention to themselves, making them aggressive rather than loving. How good, after all, is music played on a silver clarinet, and how sacred is the music at a mass paid for on a scale that evokes the only mass described in the book, the funeral mass for John Driscoll, when "the high altar blazed with hundreds of candles" while a *flock*—and yes, that is Cather's word—of priests bore up the coffin "on a river of colour and incense and organ-tone" (16)? I don't mean to suggest that there is something necessarily wrong with a lavish mass or with making a donation that exceeds what is expected. But I am troubled by economic and spiritual showmanship—the emphasis on spectacle, a spectacle that says, in effect, "I am ready for my close-up, Mr. DeMille"—while close family members, be they niece or husband, are pushed away and denied access to one's fortune.

Mauss emphasizes that the gift cycles he studied were not only economic but also social and spiritual, and the application of his gift-theory to *My Mortal Enemy* leads to three conclusions about this highly suggestive text.

First, there is no shame in enjoying the fruits of material culture. Like Myra Henshawe, we too can enjoy Austrian blankets and plum-colored curtains if we wish—because material objects are powerful. They locate us within a cycle of production and exchange, and when used properly foster relationships with other people. The shame comes from becoming so attached to objects that one is either unable to discard them or willing to give them away only under circumstances that foster tension rather than enduring relationships. Myra can discard at ease, but she can give only under specific conditions that she insists on defining.

Second, money, like objects, can also be a comfort. There's nothing intrinsically wrong in Myra's declaration, "I should have stayed with my uncle. It was money I needed" (62), for the money, in this case, is tied directly to the ability to sustain a close relationship. What matters, of course, is how we use the money that comes to us, and in her old age, if not sooner, Myra keeps her treasure for herself. To withhold money from a close relative is to commit the equivalent of an act of war, for this withholding is not only prideful but punishing. Destructive to others, it achieves only the temporary and morally questionable satisfaction of achieving honor at the expense of others. Toward the end of the book Myra tells Nellie that she would ask her uncle's pardon if she could, noting, "I know what it is to be old and lonely and disappointed. Yes, and because as we grow old we become more and more the stuff our forebears put into us. I can feel his savagery strengthen in me" (67). Myra, like her uncle, is a kind of savage, and her conduct echoes his own: If he withheld a fortune from Myra, Myra has withheld a fortune from her husband.

When she is ready to die, Myra finally transfers this fortune, but she does so indirectly and in a manner that characteristically allows for no reciprocation. Going off to die alone, she leaves Oswald a message that concludes, "Nellie knows where there is money for masses" (80). It is not likely that Nellie would have retrieved the gloves full of gold without Oswald's knowledge and used the entire fortune for masses. Most of the money must have been given to Oswald and used to help him begin a new life in Alaska. But this "gift," if it can be called that, is simply a variation on the pattern that Myra has followed for some time. Determined to avoid the social and spiritual ties that come through the receiving and reciprocating stages of the gift cycle, she gives for the most part when death promises to interrupt that cycle. She brings gifts to a dying poet, buys masses for a dead artist, and gives money to her husband in a manner that ensures that she will be dead before he gets access to it.[6] All of these "gifts" are ultimately one-sided. The only time in the novel when Myra allows for reciprocation is when Helena Modjeska becomes a celebrity-guest in the Henshawe home after receiving Christmas gifts from Myra. Myra's subsequent ritual of honoring her dead friend by paying for masses can be seen as a noble gesture. But it can also be seen as prideful, not only because the price she pays for these masses is so out of scale but because she seems determined to give the last gift.

Finally and most importantly, attention to the gift cycle can help us to understand why Myra Driscoll Henshawe becomes so bitter, so lonely, and so destructive despite having intelligence, imagination, and courage. Poverty cannot explain this, for Myra has a small fortune at her disposal even in old age. Romantic love, to be sure, has proven to be disappointing in the long term, as other readers of *My Mortal Enemy* have noted.[7] But many couples manage to negotiate the transition from passionate longing to domestic compatibility without believing that they have ruined their lives, and Myra has a husband who, whatever his limitations, remains attentive to her needs even in old age. I would not go so far as to argue that inability to enter into the gift cycle causes Myra's profound unhappiness, for human nature is complex and the sources of unhappiness diverse. Nevertheless, Myra's resistance to gifts from others as well as her determination to give gifts that cannot be reciprocated significantly contributes to the isolation from which she ultimately suffers. And the consistency with which she follows this pattern shrinks her world until she dies, as she has come to live, alone.

Notes

1. While recognizing the importance of Mauss's work, Lévi-Strauss laments that Mauss did not fully explore the implications of his findings. Here is how the text I excerpted reads in context: "Why did Mauss halt at the edge of those immense possibilities, like Moses conducting his people all the way to the promised land whose splendor he would never behold?" This strikes me as a bit like blaming Da Vinci for never getting an airplane off the ground, but the comment conveys how Mauss opened many new avenues of inquiry—and why Lévi-Strauss chose to build his own work on the foundation that Mauss had established.

2. According to "The History of the Opera Glove," evening gloves were usually wrist length in the mid-nineteenth century, "no more than 12 to 14 inches at most." This site describes Bernhardt as "one of the great glove-wearers of all time" and suggests that she favored long gloves as a means for covering thin arms. She toured the United States in the 1870s and drew considerable attention, which extended to her wardrobe.

3. A reference librarian at the Costume Institute of the Metropolitan Museum in New York helped me to determine the probable size of Myra's glove. Dr. Jeff McLean of the mathematics department at the University of St. Thomas provided information about the size and weight of ten- and twenty-dollar gold pieces. Dr. James Walsh of the mathematics department at Oberlin College calculated that each of Myra's gloves would have a total volume of 43.5 cubic millimeters. Because gold is heavy and its weight would cause each glove to stretch considerably over time, Dr. Walsh based his calculation on the assumption that each glove was 90 percent full in order for the glove to seem less full when stretched over time. Dr. Marsha Blumenthal of the economics department at the University of St. Thomas used the Consumer Price Index to calculate what $6,510 in 1913 would be worth in purchasing power in October 2001, when these calculations were made.

4. Drawing on their parish duties in the Archdiocese of St. Paul and Minneapolis, my colleagues the Rev. Dr. Robert Wellisch and the Rev. Dr. Martin Warren confirmed the mass rate for this archdiocese in 2002. Father Wellisch reported that the rate was $1 for a low mass when he was a boy and $5 for a high mass (or a mass that would have been sung). When he was ordained in 1969, the rate for a low mass had increased to $2 and "the weekday high mass was a thing of the past." Even if we assume that Myra had wanted a high mass sung for Madame Modjeska—although she does not specifically request one—a fee of ten or twenty dollars would have been extraordinary.

5. Merrill Skaggs notes, "To Myra the active seeker, love is appropriately her gift to those she selects to receive it. Having freely given (and thereby possessed her beloved), she cannot so freely receive (and thus relinquish control). The reversal offends her because receiving love creates dependency" (95).

6. This is the pattern that Myra follows within her own social class, where reciprocation would be most likely. She departs from this pattern when class differences allow her to patronize others—as when she overtips cab drivers or gives dress shirts to a janitor's son. Protected by a sense of class superiority, however false or fragile that may be, Myra apparently does not fear reciprocation from those she deems her inferiors.

7. Susan J. Rosowski's discussion of how *My Mortal Enemy* conveys the limitations of romantic love is especially compelling. See *The Voyage Perilous: Willa Cather's Romanticism*, 144–55.

10

Words To Do with Things

Reading about Willa Cather and Material Culture

Mary Ann O'Farrell

When Augusta, the seamstress in Cather's novel *The Professor's House,* finds Godfrey St. Peter (the titular professor) alone and unconscious in a closed room with a gassy stove, she seeks medical assistance, but tells the answering doctor only that he is needed and not what has happened. She is, Cather writes, "evidently embarrassed by the behaviour of the stove" (*PH* 278). The idea of holding an appliance to social account—or of not quite doing so, the better to save it from an acknowledgment of its failings—can only buttress those of us who make our sad apologies to the dressers we bump into, the coffee cups we shatter, the carpets over which we trip. Having thought ourselves—assisted in this by our mocking human neighbors—silly fetishists caught indulging a naive anthropomorphics, we might, with the help of Bill Brown's distinction between objects and things,[1] come to see ourselves instead as natural thing theorists—knocked by our bumpings and trippings into that realm in which the dresser and the carpet, the recalcitrant lock and the conniving key, the odd shoe and the violent bagel knife, demand to be seen not as *our objects* but as *their own things.*

Inviting us to read this volume, Janis Stout reminds us that Willa Cather has not usually been "regarded as a person or a writer for whom the material world held much importance,"[2] and indeed figuring out Cather's relation to things has historically been difficult, rendered so by Cather herself. The ascetic and rebarbative title of her famous essay, a call for "The Novel Démeublé," suggests a space stripped down and from which things have been banished, the novelist the remover who removes. But as the essays in this volume have so powerfully made clear, Cather's implication in material culture is not only inevitable but also profound. Working as a managing editor and as a writer for her living, Cather is seen here as a producer of works embedded in their locations (in magazines, in volumes and collections, on movie screens) and changed by their embeddedness, just as the artifacts and landscape of her beloved American Southwest are changed by their contextualization in the museum, the diorama, and the park. Involved with the world of commerce as editor, writer, and consumer, Cather is shown here, too, in her guise as commentator on consumptive habits and on the association—burgeoning even in the moment of her writing—of women with consumer culture. An author with a written commitment to the rites and rituals of the home (to patchwork and quilting, to the making of clear soups, and to the transmission of domestic skills), Cather is also, authors here remind us, a writer whose work was commodified as cinema with product tie-ins no less commercial for their now antiqued and collectible charm than the action figures and lunch boxes with which Hollywood advertises its films today. The Cather thus implicated in material culture is smart about that implication and its uses; as gifts and debts, as narratives, translations, and exchanges, objects are both constitutive and expressive of human and cultural relations, she knows, and they are able also to articulate a mediated relation between the worlds of nature and culture.

It is the persuasive consensus of these essays, then, to reject the emptying extremity of the *title* of Cather's essay in favor of the more moderate suggestion of the essay's *text* and of her writing's ample practice. Cather's novel démeublé is readable less as a room unfurnished than as a room sparsely furnished and in which if a *thing* is there to be found, it is there to work—to mean and to mean hard—as an object in the shadow of character. How many of these essays cite, to help us understand her use of material culture, Cather's preferential account of Tolstoy against Balzac: "But there is this determining difference: the clothes, the dishes, the haunting interiors of those old Moscow houses, are always so much a part of the emotions of the people that they are perfectly synthesized; they seem to exist, not so much in the author's mind, as in the emotional penumbra of the characters themselves" (39–40). For Tolstoy, *chez* Cather, the thing is subordinated to the humanity it expresses. And as Stout notes, in introducing our subject, "Concrete objects are both ingredients and traces of human identity, human history, and human culture." In seeing that bare stage into which the unfurnished room has morphed by the essay's conclusion as adorned, nevertheless, with a prop or two, readers of Cather's relation to material culture are good readers of Cather, whose novel-rooms are notably *not* unfurnished but are in fact so furnished that even the natural world within them is a nature furnished with things—the artifacts that, in Cather's sacralizing prose, become evidence of what Lionel Trilling (if he *could* be less dismissive, I would nevertheless have him no less astute) notoriously saw as Cather's "mystical concern with pots and pans" (Trilling, "Cather" 12).

Still, as the essays in this volume rightly suggest, Cather's relation to things must be a site of some ambivalence and tension. Against the moderation of the argument of "The Novel Démeublé," then, set again the extravagance of the entitling gesture. If things must be dismissed from the novel, removed from its considerations, it can only be because they are so alluring, distracting, seductive, demanding. Well-furnished, in fact, with things, Cather's novels and her novel-writing and novel-publishing practice register the claims and insistences of agential materiality: a magazine, its advertisements, and its demographics pressure a text with their needs; a turquoise bracelet demands appreciation (*PH*), as a string of amethysts chill their wearer out of luck (*MME*); an ambitious plow against the sky insists that the text it writes there must be read (*MA*); "a light engine," if it makes "no noise at all," turns a person into a body, materially facilitating the start of a career (*SL*); a broken jar, imagined whole, models for throat and body the shape in which they can best make and contain art and life as vessels (*SL*); the willfully mortifying heater teases life with the prospect of death (*PH*); the heavy weight of coins displaces the blood warmth of a hand, filling out a glove in its place (*MME*). Trilling's pots and pans—the cultural remnants that, after all, disrupt as much as constitute a human relation (Tom Outland's to Roddy Blake)—acquire their uncanny mysticism through Cather's fantastic and appetitive regard, which reimagines in the artifactual evidence of past civilization a kind of natural material culture: things somehow made and resonant with their making, yet found undarkened by the human penumbra. Cather's imaginary unfurnished room—the novel as a closet—is that space queer theory and shopping have together taught us to understand as the space where renunciation and desire work at once, where the good riddance of things is precisely what makes space for them as desiderata.

I wonder, that is, if Cather isn't also interested in things insofar as they might seem to escape the shadow of characters and persons, and, doing so, might seem as well to offer, to that which is human, resistances and agencies that thwart human desire even as they call it forth. Of one of the forms in the attic study of the professor's house (the torsos on which Augusta, the seamstress, is accustomed to fit the gowns for the professor's wife and daughters), Cather writes:

> Though this figure looked so ample and billowy (as if you might lay your head upon its deep-breathing softness and rest safe forever), if you touched it you suffered a severe shock, no matter how many times you touched it before. It presented the most unsympathetic surface imaginable. Its hardness was not that of wood, which responds to concussion with living vibration and is stimulating to the hand, nor that of felt, which drinks something from the fingers. It was a dead, opaque, lumpy solidity, like chunks of putty, or tightly packed sawdust—very disappointing to the tactile sense, yet somehow always fooling you again. For no matter how often you bumped up against that torso, you could never believe that contact with it would be as bad as it was. (*PH* 18–19)

The attic forms are readable as versions of femininity, whether as the models by which Godfrey St. Peter measures his dissatisfactions with the variously dissatisfying women in his life, whether as the harsh figures to which culture fits and cuts such women, or whether as experiential reminders of the real bodies of the real women in the novel whose "dead, opaque, lumpy solidity" always unsympathetically disappoints St. Peter before it lives to invite his would-be sympathetic touch again. As Bill Brown has most recently written of the attic figures: "despite the capacity of these objects to summon up past pleasures, one of them also—in its very physicality—seems to manifest the problems that the professor currently faces" (Brown, *Sense of Things* 128). Brown continues, "This is to say that within the novel, this form—or, more precisely, the substance of this form—prefigures the increasingly distant, unperceptive relations St. Peter has with the women in his life, especially his wife and his older daughter Rosamond, whose lack of sympathy and of generosity are always worse than he believes they will be" (128). A figure of the shocking, teasing, unresponsive "substance" of feminine resistance, the attic form is also absolute materiality, itself figured as a disappointing figure—the lumpen tease whose shape is imagined to promise sex and comfort but, unyielding even when you can do anything with it, refuses to register the impression of human desire. What if, then, unyielding substance here were not merely the vehicle for thinking out a phobic, frightened, allured, and disappointed relation to femininity? What if, instead, St. Peter's shocked and disappointed experience of a stupid and vampiric femininity modeled the encounter (we have such every day) between material humanity and a thingly materiality that, though it "drinks something from the fingers," still cannot be construed to want to touch them back. The tactile fluency revealed by Cather's language (it distinguishes hardnesses, registers stimulations, knows wood and felt and sawdust and putty) is telling of things often touched and of a sweet optimism about them ("you could never believe that contact . . . would be as bad as it was") endangered by numbing or embittering material rebuffs. Trilling again, still crabby, still astute:

> Willa Cather is not in my opinion a very intelligent or subtle mind, but she did show in her novels an understanding of the European attachment to *things* and how it differed from the American attachment. The elaborate fuss that she made about cuisine, about wine, and salads, and bread, and copper pots, was an expression of her sense of the unfeeling universe; cookery was a ritual in which the material world, some tiny part of it, could be made to serve human ends, could be made human. (Trilling, "That Smile" 349)

Trilling's comments appear in an essay on George Santayana, at a point at which a comparison of Santayana's materialism with Cather's is useful for Trilling's argument. Cather's materialism is European for Trilling insofar as it entails a "confrontation with the abyss" (349); the European/American distinction here is a gussied-up version of the practiced distinction between the knowing and the naive. Cooking and ritual link to

Cather's interest in Catholicism, for Trilling—a hopeful response, by his account, to an unflinching look at the abyss. Still, as the writing of the attic forms suggests, Cather's complex relation to materiality is more extensive than Trilling allows. Where he would see Cather shoring hope against the abyss, Cather instead describes a constant oscillation between naive belief in the responsiveness of things and the knowledge that, though you'll try them every time, every time they'll be found unfeeling, opaque, and hard. No wonder she toyed with kicking them out of the house. No wonder ("you might rest safe forever") in desire she kept them around.

What does it mean, though, really, for a novel to be furnished with things, for its condition to be anything but materially stripped down? The call for a novel démeublé can *only* succeed (every novel is démeublé) if we understand writing in the way it sometimes has been understood: as the very site of thinglessness, a space without spatiality, in which—because there can be no rooms—all rooms are unfurnished. Work in book culture has taught us to remember the materiality of the text, and our own work as authors and readers cannot help but remind us that writing is a process derived from the ink and the page, the keyboard and the screen, the arching or bending or aching of the back. But *this* thinglyness of writing is yet not the thinglyness we mean when we talk of Cather's pots and pans, her beads and gloves and earrings, her telephone, the santos and the pianos of which her writing speaks. These are representable but unreproducible in writing, which can only reproduce itself. And this is the condition and challenge that confronts writing: how, immaterially, to include the materiality with which it is enamored.

And yet, given that the novel's generic reputation as a celebration of things is well established, some tricks of novel writing must have been so efficacious in producing material effects that Cather's call for the elimination of things may seem to us a strong and fit response to the historical development of the novel; yet even as we have this response (thing-enamored ourselves) we may also be glad to find that call moderated in Cather's work. Let us look again at Cather's own writing, not in a novel but in the essay that has been so much the question in our essays. Despite its repudiation of the catalog (a "popular suspicion," she tells us, avers that realism "asserts itself" in catalogs [*OW* 37]), "The Novel Démeublé" is readable as one—perhaps as the catalog by which the novel's impoverished owners will auction off their belongings. Some of the things Cather would banish, some of the material forms around which she constructs her notions of the novel: "the egg one eats for breakfast" and "the morning paper" (36); "Woolworth store windows," in fantasy displaying classical "Tanagra figurines" instead of "Kewpie brides" (36); "cheap soap or a cheap perfume, or cheap furniture" (36); figuratively, "red meat thrown into [a] scale to make the beam dip" (37); the "mass of brick and mortar and furniture and proceedings in bankruptcy" (38) beside "the manners and dress and interiors of Puritan society" (41); "the clothes, the dishes, the haunting interiors of those old Moscow houses" (39), along with "the actual city of Paris; the houses, the upholstery, the food, the wines, the game of pleasure, the game of business, the game of finance" (38). In the very moment, that is, of dispatching things from the novel, Cather cannot resist recalling them, and her writing itself shows that this is so. "The manners and dress and interiors of Puritan society"—as points do a plane, three items make a list, and lists produce the *meubles* with which "The Novel Démeublé" warms and furnishes what might have been the chilly spaces of a spare and dismissive aesthetic manifesto. Cather's multiple and gratuitous "and"s—there for the fun of it, for the joy of repetition and the pleasure of conjunction—prolong the very process she admires younger writers for rejecting in favor of suggestion: *enumeration* offers delights against which Cather's own prose cannot defend. "[S]eventeen times," "eight times," "thirteen times" (Bucker): like the author we discuss, many of us in this volume are lured by the pleasures of the list. Enumerating, cataloging the things with which Cather contends, we notice these: "clay jars and bowls, dried beans, and ears of corn," "fire-blackened pots, . . . surgical instruments and yucca moccasins" (Raine); the expense of "wampum, turquoises, and lives" (Wilson); "diamonds, 'fine shoes,' and 'fine gloves,' . . . hats, pianos, carriages" (Bradley); a marionette, a cigarette, the "Italian tortoiseshell box where [cigarettes] were kept" (Stout); doilies and Italian flagons and "a china nightingale that sang" (Stout again). My own lists have been plentiful, too. How impossible the consideration of things in words without the help of lists, we seem collectively to have decided. One among us slows us all down, using the speedbumps of a bumpier punctuation to make us linger over items in his list: "An amethyst necklace. Austrian blankets. A fur hat with a garnet feather. And some of the sexiest curtains in American literature" (Miller). By the logic of accumulation, maybe, or maybe by some imaginary spatial logic, lists can seem to be the way to surmount the immaterial challenge of writing, the way to have things in writing. As topographic guide, the list creates a material topography in writing in the form of a linguistic array. But (writing represents itself) lists substitute for things in the material world the promise, threatening breach, that words can take their places and *be things* themselves. How is it one can have things in writing? By making one's writing exploit the distracting, attracting, enumerable (or is it lumpy, exasperating, opaque?) thingyness of words. How many times might words appear? Words become things in their enumeration: "seventeen times," "eight times," "thirteen times." The list is that trick of writing by which writing can produce (as from a hat) the materiality of things in pointing toward the materiality of words (of the signifier that may be more important than the signified).

As Captain Forrester in Cather's *A Lost Lady* recovers from the first of his two strokes, his altered ability to speak effects in a different way the list's trick of emphasizing the signifier and making things of words. "Though he recovered his speech," Cather writes, "it was thick and clouded; some words he could not pronounce distinctly,—slid over them, dropped out a syllable" (*LL* 93). Making his words less communicative, literally nonsensical, the stroke also alters Captain Forrester's social persona and makes him less comfortable with speech. Because of his trouble with words, the narrator reports, "he avoided talking even more than was his habit" (93).[3] Later, a second stroke loosens Captain Forrester's tongue in a particular way, and Cather's protagonist, Niel Herbert, registers the Captain's acquired verbal habit:

> He had noticed that often when Mrs. Forrester was about her work, the Captain would call to her, "Maidy, Maidy," and she would reply "Yes, Mr. Forrester," from wherever she happened to be, but without coming to him,—as if she knew that when he called to her in that tone he was not asking for anything. He wanted to know if she were near, perhaps; or, perhaps, he merely liked to call her name and to hear her answer. (136)

Cather's description of the Captain's frequent double call, "Maidy, Maidy," offers different accounts of what these words are for him. If the Captain calls to his wife without wanting that call to mean that she should come to him, his "Maidy, Maidy" is a phatic communication; unmeaning, the words might still be understood as functional in their establishment of a social relation between the Captain and Mrs. Forrester, consisting of his call and her response. As if he understands the relation to dissolve with the vibrations of the words, Captain Forrester would remake it by calling again.

But "perhaps, he merely liked to call her name and to hear her answer" (136). As pure sound, the words that constitute the Captain's exchange with his wife become their wordy selves, instances of any word's potential for sonic self-assertion in the face of subordination to the human penumbra. "Maidy, Maidy." Like the syllable used in chanting—or like the looped and whispered word with which a child might half-torture/half-comfort herself or himself into sleep—the repeated word loses its reference and becomes a thing in repetition. But where chanters find in repetition an escape from the materiality of the body and levitation into transcendence, I would suggest that one might find instead that sonic hallucination by which the immateriality of words gives way to an insistently uttered, near-palpable materiality.

I think an apprehension of linguistic materiality is what Eve Kosofsky Sedgwick must have been able to access in elaborating upon "Berengaria" in her essay on *The Professor's House.* Discussing the words with which the novel ends ("*F*ace with *f*ortitude the *Berengaria* and the *f*uture" [Sedgwick 176; emphasis on the Fs is Sedgwick's]) as part of her discussion not only of Cather's novel but also of how one reads and listens to sexualities in writing, Sedgwick responds most forcefully to the name of the ship St. Peter contemplates, the *Berengaria.* I quote Sedgwick at some length:

> Underneath the grammatic f-f-fortitudes of the heterosexist ordering of marriage, there are audible in this alphabet the more purely semantic germs of any vital possibility: *Berengaria,* ship of women: the {green} {aria}, the {eager} {brain}, the {bearing} and the {bairn}, the {raring} {engine}, the {bargain} {binge}, the {ban} and the {bar}, the {garbage}, the {barrage} of {anger}, the {bare} {grin}, the {rage} to {err}, the {rare} {grab} for {being}, the {begin} and {rebegin} {again}. (176)

Chastising Sedgwick, among so many others, in her book *Willa Cather and the Politics of Criticism,* Joan Acocella writes of this paragraph that "this list of anagrams, which must have taken a while to work out, supposedly reveals the maelstrom of lesbian energies churning beneath *The Professor's House*" (that "supposedly" didn't take quite so long, I bet) and comments, of Sedgwick on the *Berengaria*, "She apparently does not know that it was the name of a real ship, a famous Cunard ocean liner, on which Cather had returned from Europe immediately before starting work on *The Professor's House*" (55–56). Acocella's argument about Sedgwick ends there ("it was the name of a real ship"), cutting enough, it seems to think itself, without needing to include the "just" (it's just a ship) that would make explicit the elimination of Sedgwick's list by reduction to material reference: the *Berengaria*, it's just a ship. The apparent materiality of the ship and of the fact of it trumps words, and we all know it, the abruption of Acocella's argument suggests; words are just words, and ships and facts, as things, will take the place of them. But Acocella's reading misses that Sedgwick's is an exuberant response to the thingyness of Cather's linguistic choice: the professor will meet the *Berengaria* rather than, say, the *Queen Mary* (also a ship, but one less likely to end in rebeginning again). In Sedgwick's list, the *Berengaria* is not just a ship but also a word made into a thing (Maidy, Maidy) and liable to be treated as such, to be handled and mishandled, manipulated.

Introducing our subject, Janis Stout reminds us of why we want (as those of us writing in this volume have wanted) to spend some of our intellectual time among things. Stout writes that "words have been attended to and studied for so long, and have been so privileged above material objects in the hierarchy of what is worthy of attention, that the more recent interest in objects, not merely as illustrations of meaning but as coequal conveyers of meaning, is a significant corrective," and she is right, of course. In ending here with words, I do not mean to correct our course back yet again toward words instead of things, but rather to consider what Cather's extravagant (if merely apparent) renunciation of things might remind us: no things, in the novel *démeublé*, but in words.

Notes

1. In his introduction to "Things," a special issue of *Critical Inquiry*, Brown quotes Leo Stein to help him make the distinction: "Things are what we encounter, ideas are what we project" (3). Brown writes that "[a]s they circulate

through our lives, we look *through* objects (to see what they disclose about history, society, nature, or culture—above all, what they disclose about *us*), but we only catch a glimpse of things" (4). Thing theory, as Brown conceives it, begins its work by attending to "[t]he story of objects asserting themselves as things" (4).

2. The Willa Cather Scholarly Edition published by the University of Nebraska Press, under the general editorship of Susan Rosowski (in the earlier volumes, Rosowski and James Woodress), has begun the work in this regard, attending to Cather's materialism in the textual commentary, explanatory notes, and historical essays that accompany her works in the edition.

3. In what seems an authorial kindness (to the character) that is nevertheless also an odd contradiction, Cather does not indicate this problem in the speech she writes for Captain Forrester in the passages that follow upon this first stroke. His speech as written does not record stumbling or error of the kind that Cather tells us characterizes it.

Bibliography

Acocella, Joan. *Willa Cather and the Politics of Criticism.* Lincoln: U of Nebraska P, 2000.

Agnew, Jean-Christophe. "The Consuming Vision of Henry James." In *The Culture of Consumption: Critical Essays in American History, 1880–1980,* edited by Richard Wrightman Fox and T. J. Jackson Lears, 65–100. New York: Pantheon, 1983.

Albertini, Virgil. "Willa Cather and the Bicycle." *Platte Valley Review,* Spring 1987, 12–22.

Ammons, Elizabeth. "Cather and the New Canon: 'The Old Beauty' and the Issue of Empire." In *Cather Studies,* vol. 3, edited by Susan J. Rosowski, 256–67. Lincoln, NE: U Nebraska P, 1996.

———. "Material Culture, Empire, and Jewett's *Country of the Pointed Firs.*" In *New Essays on "The Country of the Pointed Firs,"* edited by June Howard, 81–100. New York: Cambridge UP, 1994.

Armstrong, Nancy. *Desire and Domestic Fiction: A Political History of the Novel.* New York: Oxford UP, 1987.

Bailey, Liberty Hyde. *The Nature-Study Idea.* 1903. New York: Macmillan, 1909.

Beardslee, Mildred. See Willa Cather.

Bender, Eileen T. "Pioneer or Gadgeteer: Bergsonian Metaphor in the Work of Willa Cather." *Midwest Quarterly* 28 (1986): 130–40.

Bennett, Mildred R. "A Note on the White Bear Stories." *Willa Cather Pioneer Memorial Newsletter* 17 (Summer 1973): 4.

———. "Willa Cather in Pittsburgh." *Prairie Schooner* 33 (Spring 1959): 64–76.

———. *The World of Willa Cather.* New York: Dodd, Mead, 1951.

Bensen, Peter. "Willa Cather at *Home Monthly.*" *Biography,* Summer 1981, 227–48.

Berry, Sarah. *Screen Style: Fashion and Femininity in 1930s Hollywood.* Minneapolis: U Minnesota P, 2000.

Bintrim, Tim. "Recovering the Extraliterary: The Pittsburg Writing of Willa Cather." PhD diss., Duquesne U, 2002.

Birkin, Lawrence. *Consuming Desire: Sexual Science and the Emergence of a Culture of Abundance, 1871–1914*. Ithaca: Cornell UP, 1988.

Boettinger, Henry M. "Our Sixth-and-a-Half Sense." In *The Social Impact of the Telephone*, edited by Itheil de Sola Pool, 200–7. Cambridge: MIT Press, 1977.

Bohlke, L. Brent, ed. *Willa Cather in Person: Interviews, Speeches, and Letters.* Lincoln: U of Nebraska P, 1986.

Bok, Edward. *The Americanization of Edward Bok.* New York: Scribner's, 1921.

Bourne, Randolph. "Trans-national America." *Atlantic Monthly,* July 1916.

Brown, Bill. *A Sense of Things: The Object Matter of American Literature.* Chicago: U of Chicago P, 2003.

———. "The Secret Life of Things (Virginia Woolf and the Matter of Modernism)." *Modernism/Modernity* 6.2 (April 1999): 1–28.

———. "Thing Theory." *Critical Inquiry* 28.1 (2001): 1–22.

Brown, E. K., with Leon Edel. *Willa Cather: A Critical Biography.* New York: Knopf, 1953.

Bryant, Harold C., and Wallace W. Atwood. *Research and Education in the National Parks.* Washington, DC: U.S. Dept. of the Interior, National Park Service, 1936.

Bryson, Norman. *Looking at the Overlooked: Four Essays on Still Life Painting.* Cambridge, MA: Harvard UP, 1990.

Burnham, Philip. *Indian Country, God's Country: Native Americans and the National Parks.* Washington, DC: Island, 2000.

Butcher, Fanny. "Willa Cather Tells Purpose of New Novel." *Chicago Daily Tribune,* 12 Sept. 1925: 9.

Byrne, Kathleen D., and Richard C. Snyder. *Chrysalis: Willa Cather in Pittsburgh, 1896–1906.* Pittsburgh: Historical Society of Western Pennsylvania, 1980.

Cades, Hazel Rawson. "Long or Short, Everybody Likes Nice Hair." *Woman's Home Companion,* September 1928, 87.

———. "Look at Her Eyes." *Woman's Home Companion,* October 1928, 119.

Caffrey, Margaret M. *Ruth Benedict: Stranger in This Land.* Austin: U of Texas P, 1989.

Carruthers, Hayden. "Postscript." *Woman's Home Companion,* April 1930, 204.

Casson, Herbert. "The Wonders of Magazine Making." *Woman's Home Companion,* September 1904, 8–9.

Cather, Caroline. Letter to Mrs. Jo. G. Ayre. 7 Oct. 1873 (?). Nebraska State Historical Society.

Cather, Franc. Letter to Mrs. Jo. G. Ayre. 17 Feb. 1876. Nebraska State Historical Society.

Cather, Willa [Elizabeth L. Seymour, pseud.]. "The Burglar's Christmas." *Home Monthly,* December 1896, 8–10.

———. "The Count of Crow's Nest," Pts. 1 and 2. *Home Monthly,* September 1896, 9–11; October 1896, 12+.

——— [Mildred Beardslee, pseud.]. "Cycle Notes for Women." Fashionland. *Home Monthly,* August 1896, 17.

———. *Death Comes for the Archbishop.* 1927. Scholarly Edition. Historical essay and explanatory notes by John J. Murphy. Edited by Charles W. Mignon with Frederick M. Link and Kari Ronning. Lincoln: U of Nebraska P, 1999.

———. [Mildred Beardslee, pseud.]. Fashionland. *Home Monthly,* December 1896, 15; January 1897, 18; October 1896, 21.

———. Letters: to Rose Ackroyd, 16 May 1941 and 27 December 1941, Alderman Library, Univ. of Virginia; to Zoë Akins, [21 November 1922], 15 January 1931, 15 December 1936, ? February 1943, and 5 January 1945, Huntington Library; to Witter Bynner, 7 June 1905, Houghton Library, Harvard Univ.; to Mrs. C. F. Cather, 26 November [1921], Texas Woman's University; to Mrs. George P. Cather, 23 February 1913, Love Library, Univ. of Nebraska; to Dorothy Canfield Fisher, 14 October 1940, Bailey-Howe Library, Univ. of Vermont; to Mariel Gere, 6 August 1896, Gere Collection, Nebraska State Historical Society; to Ferris Greenslet, 18 November 1917, 11 Jul, 1918, 20 June [1920?], 13 March 1932, and 10 June 1940, Houghton Library, Harvard Univ.; to Blanche Knopf, [? December 1928], 10 July [1931], and 26 December 1931, Harry Ransom Humanities Research Center, Univ. of Texas; to Lydia, Pauline, and Mrs. Lambrecht, 19 January [1935], WCPM, Red Cloud, Nebraska; to Annie Pavelka, 19 May 1936, WCPM; to Viola Roseboro', 9 November 1940, Alderman Library, Univ. of Virginia; to Elizabeth Shepley Sergeant, 13 November [1916?], Pierpont Morgan Library, New York; to Carrie Miner Sherwood, 13 March 1918, 27 December [1921], [11 December 1932?], 18 September 1943, and 20 January 1945, Willa Cather Pioneer Memorial; to Helen [Sprague?], 22 March 1936, Willa Cather Pioneer Memorial; to Charlotte Stanfield, 12 June 1921, 10 June 1922, and 16 October 1926, Alderman Library, Univ. of Virginia; to Irene Miner Weisz, 4 February 1922, 12 February 1923, [16 March 1925], 11 January 1926, 29 October 1932, and 26 December 1942, Newberry Library, Chicago; to Alexander Woollcott, 8 February 1935, Houghton Library, Harvard Univ.

———. *A Lost Lady.* 1923. Scholarly Edition. Historical essay by Susan J. Rosowski with Kari A. Ronning. Explanatory notes by Kari A. Ronning. Edited by Charles W. Mignon and Frederick M. Link with Kari A. Ronning. Lincoln: U of Nebraska P, 1997.

———. *Lucy Gayheart.* 1935. New York: Vintage, 1995.

———. "Mesa Verde Wonderland Is Easy to Reach: Colorado Show Place as Authoress Sees It." *Denver Times,* 31 January 1916. Rpt. in *The Professor's House,* Scholarly Edition. 327–334.

———. *My Ántonia.* 1918. Scholarly Edition. Historical essay by James Woodress. Explanatory notes by James Woodress with Kari Ronning, Kathleen Danker, and Emily Levine. Edited by Charles Mignon with Kari Ronning. Lincoln: U of Nebraska P, 1994.

———. *My Mortal Enemy.* 1926. New York: Vintage, 1990.

———. "Nebraska: The End of the First Cycle." *Nation,* 5 September 1923, 236–38.

———. "Neighbor Rosicky." Pts. 1 and 2. *Woman's Home Companion,* April 1930; May 1930.

———. "Neighbour Rosicky," *Obscure Destinies.* New York: Knopf, 1932. 3–71.

——— [Elizabeth L. Seymour, pseud.]. "Nursing as a Profession for Women." *Home Monthly,* May 1897, 3–5.

———. *Obscure Destinies.* 1932. Scholarly Edition. Historical essay and explanatory notes by Kari A. Ronning. Edited by Frederick M. Link with Kari A. Ronning and Mark Kamrath. Lincoln: U of Nebraska P, 1998.

———. *One of Ours.* 1922. Boston: Houghton Mifflin, 1937.

———. *On Writing: Critical Studies on Writing as an Art.* 1949. Lincoln: U of Nebraska P, 1988.

———. *O Pioneers!* 1913. Scholarly Edition. Historical essay and explanatory notes by David Stouck. Edited by Susan J. Rosowski and Charles W. Mignon with Kathleen Danker. Lincoln: U of Nebraska P, 1992.

———. "Paul's Case." In *Collected Short Fiction 1892–1912.* Rev. ed. Edited by Virginia Faulkner. 243–261. Lincoln: U of Nebraska P, 1970.

———. *The Professor's House.* 1925. Scholarly Edition. Historical essay by James Woodress. Explanatory notes by James Woodress with Kari A. Ronning. Edited by Frederick M. Link. Lincoln: U of Nebraska P, 2002.

———. "A Resurrection." *Home Monthly,* April 1897, 4–8.

———. *Sapphira and the Slave Girl.* New York: Knopf, 1940.

———. *Shadows on the Rock.* 1931. New York: Vintage Books, 1971.

———. *The Song of the Lark.* 1915. Rev. ed. 1937. Rpt. Boston: Houghton Mifflin, 1988.

———. "Tommy, the Unsentimental." *Home Monthly,* August 1896, 6–7.

———. [Mary K. Hawley, pseud.]. "Two Women the World Is Watching." *Home Monthly,* September 1896, 4–5.

C. B. V. Letter to the editor. *Woman's Home Companion,* August 1930, 130.

Chinery, Mary. "Willa Cather and the Santos Tradition in *Death Comes for the Archbishop.*" In *Willa Cather and the American Southwest,* edited by John N. Swift and Joseph R. Urgo, 97–107. Lincoln: U of Nebraska P, 2002.

Clark, Ricky. "Mid-Nineteenth-Century Album and Friendship Quilts 1860–1920." In *Pieced by Mother: Symposium Papers,* edited by Jeanette Lasanky, 77–86. Lewisburg, PA: Union County Historical Society, 1988.

"Consuelo, Duchess of Marlborough." *Home Monthly,* February 1897, 12.

Crane, Joan. *Willa Cather: A Bibliography.* Lincoln: U of Nebraska P, 1982.

Crane, Leo. *Desert Drums: The Pueblo Indians of New Mexico 1540–1928.* 1928. Glorieta, NM: The Rio Grande Press, 1972.

Crews, Patricia Cox, and Ronald C. Naugle, eds. *Nebraska Quilts and Quiltmakers.* Lincoln: U of Nebraska P, 1991.

Daiches, David. *Willa Cather.* Ithaca, NY: Cornell UP, 1951.

Davidson, Cathy N. "Preface: No More Separate Spheres!" *American Literature* 70:3 (September 1998): 443–63.

Derrida, Jacques. *Given Time: I. Counterfeit Money.* Translated by Peggy Kamuf. Chicago: U of Chicago P, 1992.

"Description of Property." Appliqué Album Quilt (Hollingsworth). Winchester-Frederick County Historical Society, Winchester, VA.

DiFonzo, J. Herbie. *Beneath the Fault Line: The Popular and Legal Culture of Divorce in Twentieth-Century America.* Charlottesville: UP Virginia, 1997.

Dilworth, Leah. *Imagining Indians in the Southwest: Persistent Visions of a Primitive Past.* Washington, DC: Smithsonian, 1996.

Douglas, Mary. Foreword. *The Gift: The Form and Reason for Exchange in Archaic Societies,* by Marcel Mauss. New York: Norton, 1990.

Dreiser, Theodore. "The Real Sins of Hollywood." In *Authors on Film,* edited by Harry M. Geduld, 206–22. Bloomington: Indiana UP, 1972.

Farago, Claire. "Transforming Images: New Mexican Santos between Theory and History." In *The Visual Culture of American Religions,* edited by David Morgan and Sally M. Promey, 191–208. Berkeley: U of California P, 2001.

Ferrero, Pat, Elaine Hedges, and Julie Silber. *Hearts and Hands: The Influence of Women and Quilts on American Society.* San Francisco: Quilt Digest P, 1987.

Fischer, Claude. *America Calling: A Social History of the Telephone to 1940.* Berkeley: U of California Press, 1992.

Fischer, Mike. "Pastoralism and Its Discontents: Willa Cather and the Burden of Imperialism." *Mosiac* 23.1 (1990): 31–44.

Fisher, Philip. *Hard Facts: Setting and Form in the American Novel.* New York: Oxford UP, 1985.

Fitch, W. E. "Bicycle-Riding: Its Moral Effect upon Young Girls and Its Relation to Diseases of Women." *Georgia Journal of Medicine and Surgery* 4 (1899): 155–56.

F. N. O. "Athletics: The Racing Man, His Imitator, and His Machine." *Home Monthly,* September 1896, 17.

Fox, Richard Wightman, and T. J. Jackson Lears. *The Culture of Consumption: Critical Essays in American History, 1880–1980.* New York: Pantheon, 1983.

Fryer, Judith. *Felicitous Space: The Imaginative Structures of Edith Wharton and Willa Cather.* Chapel Hill: U of North Carolina P, 1986.

Garvey, Ellen Gruber. *The Adman in the Parlor: Magazines and the Gendering of Consumer Culture, 1880s to 1910s.* New York: Oxford UP, 1996.

Geduld, Harry M., ed. *Authors on Film.* Bloomington: Indiana UP, 1972.

Geismar, Maxwell. *The Last of the Provincials.* Boston: Houghton Mifflin, 1947.

Gifford, Denis. *Books and Plays in Films, 1896–1915.* New York: McFarland, 1991.

Goldberg, Jonathan. *Willa Cather and Others.* Durham, NC: Duke UP, 2001.

Gore, James Howard. *My Mother's Story: Despise Not the Day of Small Things.* Philadelphia: Judson P, 1923.

Greenslet, Ferris. Letter to Willa Cather, 22 January 1917, Houghton Library, Harvard Univ.

Gutiérrez, Ramón. *When Jesus Came, the Corn Mothers Went Away: Marriage, Sexuality, and Power in New Mexico, 1500–1846.* Stanford: Stanford UP, 1991.

Hall, Al, ed. *Petersen's Complete Guide to the Bicycle.* Los Angeles: Petersen, 1975.

Hall, Carrie A., and Rose G. Kretsinger. *The Romance of the Patchwork Quilt in America.* 1935. New York: Bonanza, n.d.

Harrell, David. *From Mesa Verde to "The Professor's House."* Albuquerque: U of New Mexico P, 1992.

Hawley, Mary K. See Willa Cather.

Helmick, Evelyn. "The Broken World: Medievalism in *A Lost Lady.*" *Renascence: Essays on Values in Literature* 28.1 (1975): 39–46.

Hicks, Granville. "The Case Against Willa Cather." *English Journal,* November 1993. Rpt. *Willa Cather and Her Critics,* edited by James Schroeter, 139–47. Ithaca: Cornell UP, 1967.

Hilgart, John. "Death Comes for the Aesthete: Commodity Culture and the Artifact in Cather's *The Professor's House.*" *Studies in the Novel* 30 (1998): 377–404.

The History of the Opera Glove: From Josephine to Shania. http://www.operagloves.com/history.html (accessed 2 September 2002).

Hoare, Philip. *Serious Pleasures: The Life of Stephen Tennant.* London: Hamish Hamilton, 1990.

Hollinger, David. *Postethnic America.* New York: Basic Books, 1995.

"The Home Monthly." Editorial. *Home Monthly,* August 1896, 12.

Hönnighausen, Lothar. "Landscape with Indians and Saints: The Modernist Discovery of Native American and Hispanic Folk-Culture." *Amerikastudien* 37 (1992): 299–323.

Hoover, Sharon, ed. *Willa Cather Remembered.* Lincoln: U of Nebraska P, 2002.

Jacknis, Ira. "Franz Boas and Exhibits: On the Limitations of the Museum Method of Anthropology." In *Objects and Others: Essays on Museums and Material Culture,* edited by George W. Stocking, 75–111. Madison: U of Wisconsin P, 1985.

———. "Patrons, Potters, and Painters." In *Collecting Native America 1870–1960,* edited by Shepard Krech and Barbara A. Hail, 139–71. Washington, DC: Smithsonian, 1999.

Jameson, Fredric. *Marxism and Form: Twentieth-Century Dialectical Theories of Literature.* Princeton: Princeton UP, 1971.

Kaufman, Polly Welts. *National Parks and the Woman's Voice: A History.* Albuquerque: U of New Mexico P, 1996.

Keller, Robert H. and Michael F. Turek. *American Indians and National Parks.* Tucson: U of Arizona P, 1998.

Kerns, Wilmer L. *Frederick County, Virginia: Settlement and Some First Families of Back Creek Valley 1730–1830.* Baltimore: Gateway P, 1995.

Kirakofe, Roderick. *The American Quilt.* New York: Clarkson Potter, 1993.

Knopf, Afred A. *Portrait of a Publisher: 1915–1965.* New York: The Typophiles, 1965.

Lathrop, JoAnna. *Willa Cather: A Checklist of Her Published Writings.* Lincoln: U of Nebraska P, 1975.

Laurence, Frank M. *Hemingway and the Movies.* Jackson: UP of Mississippi, 1981.

Leach, William R. *Land of Desire: Merchants, Power, and the Rise of a New American Culture.* New York: Pantheon, 1993.

———. "Transformations in a Culture of Consumption: Women and Department Stores, 1890–1925." *Journal of American History* 71.2 (1984): 319–42.

Lévi-Strauss, Claude. "Selections from *Introduction to the Work of Marcel Mauss.*" In *The Logic of the Gift: Toward an Ethic of Generosity,* edited by Alan D. Schrift, 45–69. New York: Routledge, 1997.

Lewis, Edith. *Willa Cather Living: A Personal Record.* New York: Knopf, 1953.

Lindemann, Marilee. "Fear of a Queer Mesa?: Faith, Friendship, and National Sexuality in 'Tom Outland's Story.'" In *Willa Cather and the American Southwest,* edited by John N. Swift and Joseph R. Urgo, 43–55. Lincoln: U Nebraska P, 2002.

———. *Willa Cather: Queering America.* New York: Columbia UP, 1999.

Lipsett, Linda Otto. *Pieced from Ellen's Quilt: Ellen Spaulding Reed's Letters and Story.* Dayton, OH: Halstead & Meadows P, 1991.

Loeb, Lori Anne. *Consuming Angels: Advertising and Victorian Women.* New York: Oxford UP, 1994.

Love, Glen A. "The Cowboy in the Laboratory: Willa Cather's Hesitant Moderns." In *New Americans: The Westerner and the Modern Experience in the American Novel,* 107–69. Lewisburg: Bucknell UP, 1982.

———. "Nature and Human Nature: Interdisciplinary Convergences on Cather's Blue Mesa." In *Willa Cather's Ecological Imagination,* Cather Studies vol. 5, edited by Susan J. Rosowski, 1–27.Lincoln: U of Nebraska P, 2003.

———. "*The Professor's House:* Cather, Hemingway, and the Chastening of American Prose Style." *Western American Literature* 24.4 (1990): 295–311.

Lubar, Steven. "Men/Women/Production/Consumption." In *His and Hers: Gender, Consumption, and Technology,* edited by Roger Horowitz and Arwen Mohun, 7–37. Charlottesville: UP of Virginia, 1998.

Lutz, Frank E. "The Still-Open Road." *Natural History* 27.4 (July–August 1927): 373–82.

Mao, Douglas. *Solid Objects: Modernism and the Test of Production.* Princeton, NJ: Princeton UP, 1998.

March, John. *A Reader's Companion to the Fiction of Willa Cather.* Edited by Marilyn Arnold with Debra Lynn Thornton. Westport, CT: Greenwood Press, 1993.

Marchand, Roland. *Advertising the American Dream: Making Way for Modernity, 1920–1940.* Berkeley: U of California P, 1985.

Marvin, Carolyn. *When Old Technologies Were New: Thinking about Electric Communication in the Late Nineteenth Century.* New York: Oxford UP, 1988.

Mayne, Judith. *Private Novels, Public Films.* Athens: U of Georgia P, 1988.

Mauss, Marcel. *The Gift: The Form and Reason for Exchange in Archaic Societies.* 1923–24. Translated by W. D. Halls. New York: Norton, 1990.

McDannell, Colleen. *Material Christianity: Religion and Popular Culture in America.* New Haven: Yale UP, 1995.

Merchant, Carolyn. *The Death of Nature: Women, Ecology, and the Scientific Revolution.* New York: HarperCollins, 1980.

Michaels, Walter Benn. *Our America: Nativism, Modernism, and Pluralism.* Durham: Duke UP, 1995.

Millington, Richard. "Where Is Cather's Quebec? Anthropological Modernism in *Shadows on the Rock.*" In *Willa Cather's Canadian and Old World Connections,* edited by Robert Thacker and Michael A. Peterman, 23–44. Lincoln: U of Nebraska P, 1999.

———. "Willa Cather and 'The Storyteller': Hostility to the Novel in *My Ántonia.*" *American Literature* 66.4 (1994): 689–717.

Mott, Frank Luther. *A History of American Magazines, 1885–1905*. Cambridge: Harvard UP, 1957.

Muir, John. *Our National Parks.* Boston: Houghton Mifflin, 1901.

———. *The Yosemite.* 1912. Garden City, NY: Anchor-Doubleday, 1962.

Nordenskiöld, Gustav. *The Cliff Dwellers of the Mesa Verde.* Translated by D. Lloyd Morgan. Stockholm: Norstedt & Söner, 1893.

Norwood, Vera and Janice Monk, eds. *The Desert Is No Lady: Southwestern Landscapes in Women's Writing and Art.* New Haven: Yale UP, 1987.

O'Brien, Sharon. "Becoming Noncanonical: The Case Against Willa Cather." In *Reading in America: Literature and Social History,* edited by Cathy N. Davidson, 240–258. Baltimore: Johns Hopkins UP, 1989.

———. *Willa Cather: The Emerging Voice.* Cambridge: Harvard UP, 1987.

O'Connor, Margaret Anne, ed. *Willa Cather: The Contemporary Reviews.* New York: Cambridge UP, 2001.

O'Keeffe, Georgia. *Georgia O'Keeffe.* New York: Viking, 1976.

Oklahoma Heritage Quilts. Paducah, KY: American Quilters' Society, 1990.

Page, E. D. "Women and the Bicycle." *Brooklyn Medical Journal* 11 (1897): 84.

Papers of Gertrude Battles Lane, Collections of the Manuscript Division, Library of Congress, Washington, DC

Peary, Gerald, and Roger Shatzkin, eds. *The Classic American Novel and the Movies.* New York: Frederick Ungar, 1977.

Pitcaithley, Dwight T. "National Parks and Education: The First Twenty Years." 2002. *History of the National Park Service.* National Park Service. http://www.cr.nps.gov/history/NPAE.HTM (accessed 21 July 2002).

Potter, David M. *People of Plenty: Economic Abundance and the American Character.* Chicago: U of Chicago P, 1954.

Power, Will S. "Cycling for Health and Pleasure." *Home Monthly,* August 1896, 13.

Presbrey, Frank. *The History and Development of Advertising.* New York: Doubleday, Doran, 1929.

Prown, Jules David. "The Truth of Material Culture: History or Fiction?" In *History from Things: Essays on Material Culture,* edited by Steven Lubar and W. David Kingery, 1–19. Washington, DC: Smithsonian, 1993.

Reed, David. *The Popular Magazine in Britain and the United States, 1880–1960*. Toronto: U of Toronto P, 1997.

Reynolds, Guy. *Willa Cather in Context: Progress, Race, Empire.* London: Macmillan; New York: St. Martin's, 1996.

R. M. Film Review. *New York Evening Post.* 5 Oct. 1934. Clipping from *A Lost Lady* Film Collection. University Archives and Special Collections, University of Nebraska-Lincoln.

Robinson, Phyllis C. *Willa: The Life of Willa Cather.* Garden City: Doubleday, 1983.

Romines, Ann. *The Home Plot: Women, Writing, and Domestic Ritual.* Amherst: U of Massachusetts P, 1992.

——. Interview with Charlene Hoschauer. Red Cloud, Nebraska, May 2001.

Rosowski, Susan. *The Voyage Perilous: Willa Cather's Romanticism.* Lincoln: U of Nebraska P, 1986.

Rosowski, Susan J., and Bernice Slote. "Willa Cather's 1916 Mesa Verde Essay: The Genesis of *The Professor's House.*" *Prairie Schooner* 58.4 (1984): 82–86.

Rowe, Dr. G. Allen. "Health Topics: Bicycling and 'Billiousness.'" *Home Monthly,* November 1896, 23.

Ryan, Mary P. *Womanhood in America: From Colonial Times to the Present.* New York: New Viewpoints, 1975.

Safford, Carleton L., and Robert Bishop. *America's Quilts and Coverlets.* New York: Dutton, 1972.

Scanlon, Jennifer. *Inarticulate Longings: "The Ladies' Home Journal," Gender, and the Promise of Consumer Culture.* New York: Routledge, 1995.

Scarry, Elaine. *The Body in Pain: The Making and Unmaking of the World.* New York: Oxford UP, 1985.

Schapiro, Meyer. "The Apples of Cézanne: An Essay on the Meaning of Still-life." *Art News* 34 (1967): 33–53.

Schlesinger, Arthur M. *Learning How to Behave: A Historical Study of American Etiquette Books.* 1946; rpt. New York: Cooper Square, 1968.

Schubnell, Matthias. "From Mesa Verde to Germany." In *Willa Cather and the American Southwest,* edited by John N. Swift and Joseph R. Urgo, 31–42. Lincoln: U Nebraska P, 2002.

Schwind, Jean. "This Is a Frame-Up: Mother Eve in *The Professor's House.*" In *Cather Studies* vol. 2, edited by Susan J. Rosowski, 72–91. Lincoln: U of Nebraska P, 1993.

Scott, Mrs. J. E. "An Element of Success." Mothers and the Nursery. *Home Monthly,* June 1897, 18–19.

——. "Needed Knowledge." Mothers and the Nursery. *Home Monthly,* August 1896, 18.

Sedgwick, Eve Kosofsky. "Willa Cather and Others." In *Tendencies,* 167–76. Durham: Duke University Press, 1993.

Sergeant, Elizabeth Shepley. *Willa Cather: A Memoir.* Philadelphia: Lippincott, 1953.

Seymour, Elizabeth L. See Willa Cather.

Sherwood, George H. "The Story of the Museum's Service to the Schools." *Natural History* 27.4 (1927): 315–38.

Skaggs, Merrill Maguire. *After the World Broke in Two: The Later Novels of Willa Cather.* Charlottesville: UP of Virginia, 1990.

Slote, Bernice. *The Kingdom of Art: Willa Cather's First Principles and Critical Statements 1893–1896.* Lincoln: U of Nebraska P, 1966.

Smith, Duane A. *Mesa Verde National Park: Shadows of the Centuries.* Lawrence, KS: UP of Kansas, 1988.

Spence, Mark David. *Dispossessing the Wilderness: Indian Removal and the Making of the National Parks.* New York: Oxford UP, 1999.

Spindler, Michael. "Cather's *The Professor's House.*" *Explicator* 51.1 (1992): 31–33.

Stout, Janis P., ed. *A Calendar of the Letters of Willa Cather.* Lincoln: U of Nebraska P, 2002.

———. *Willa Cather: The Writer and Her World.* Charlottesville: UP of Virginia, 2000.

Swift, John N. "Unwrapping the Mummy: Cather's Mother Eve and the Business of Desire." In *Willa Cather and the American Southwest,* edited by John N. Swift and Joseph R. Urgo, 13–22. Lincoln: U of Nebraska P, 2002.

Tebbel, John. *The American Magazine: A Compact History.* New York: Hawthorn, 1969.

Thelma and Louise. Directed by Ridley Scott. MGM, 1991.

Tratner, Michael. *Deficits and Desires: Economics and Sexuality in Twentieth-Century Literature.* Stanford, CA: Stanford UP, 2001.

Trilling, Lionel. "'That Smile of Parmenides Made Me Think.'" 1956. Rpt. in *The Moral Obligation to Be Intelligent: Selected Essays,* edited by Leon Wieseltier, 340–53. New York: Farrar, Straus and Giroux, 2000.

———. "Willa Cather." 1937. Rpt. in *Willa Cather: Modern Critical Views,* edited by Harold Bloom, 7–13. New York: Chelsea House Publishers, 1985.

Trout, Steven. *Memorial Fictions: Willa Cather and the First World War.* Lincoln: U of Nebraska P, 2002.

Turim, Marueen. "I Married a Doctor: *Main Street* Meets Hollywood." In *The Classic American Novel and the Movies.* Edited by Gerald Peary and Roger Shatzkin. Media History Project. University of Minnesota College of Journalism and Mass Communications. http://www.mediahistory.umn.edu

Ulrich, Laurel Thatcher. *The Age of Homespun: Objects and Stories in the Creation of an American Myth.* New York: Knopf, 2001.

Urgo, Joseph. "*My Ántonia* and the National Parks Movement." In *Willa Cather's Ecological Imagination.* Cather Studies vol. 5, edited by Susan J. Rosowski, 44–63. Lincoln: U of Nebraska P, 2003.

———. *Willa Cather and the Myth of American Migration.* Urbana: U of Illinois P, 1995.

Veblen, Thorstein. *The Theory of the Leisure Class.* 1899. New York: Dover, 1994.

Wade, Edwin L. "The Ethnic Art Market in the American Southwest 1880–1980." In *Objects and Others: Essays on Museums and Material Culture,* edited by George W. Stocking, 167–91. Madison: U of Wisconsin P, 1985.

Ward, Florence E., and Katherine Glover. "The Farm Woman Goes into Business." *Woman's Home Companion,* October 1926, 4.

Watts, Richard Jr. Review of *A Lost Lady* (Warner Brothers movie). *New York Herald Tribune.* 6 Oct. 1934. Clipping from *A Lost Lady* Film Collection. University Archives and Special Collections, University of Nebraska-Lincoln.

"The Way of the Reformer Is Hard." *Home Monthly,* May 1897, 12.

White, Richard. "Are You an Environmentalist or Do You Work for a Living?" In *Uncommon Ground: Rethinking the Human Place in Nature,* edited by William Cronon, 171–85. New York: Norton, 1996.

Williams, Deborah Lindsay. "Losing Nothing, Comprehending Everything: Learning to Read Both the Old World and the New in *Death Comes for the Archbishop*." *Cather Studies* vol. 4, edited by Robert Thacker and Michael A. Peterman, 80–97. Lincoln: U of Nebraska P, 1999.

———. *Not in Sisterhood: Willa Cather, Edith Wharton, Zona Gale, and the Politics of Female Authorship*. New York: Palgrave/St. Martin's, 2001.

Williams, William Carlos. *In the American Grain*. 1925. New York: New Directions, 1956.

Wilson, Erasmus. "A Boy and a Girl." *Home Monthly*, October 1896, 15.

———. "A Boy and a Girl." *Home Monthly*, September 1896, 13.

———. "And Now It Is Our Girl." *Home Monthly*, April 1897, 11.

Wonders, Karen. *Habitat Dioramas: Illusions of Wilderness in Museums of Natural History*. Uppsala, Sweden: Almqvist & Wiksell, 1993.

Woodress, James. *Willa Cather: A Literary Life*. Lincoln: U of Nebraska P, 1987.

Woolf, Virginia. "The Movies and Reality." In *Authors on Film*, edited by Harry M. Geduld, 86–91. Bloomington: Indiana UP, 1972.

Yaeger, Patricia. "White Dirt: The Surreal Racial Landscapes of Willa Cather's South." In *Willa Cather's Southern Connections: New Essays on Cather and the South*, edited by Ann Romines, 138–55. Charlottesville, VA: UP of Virginia, 2000.

Yongue, Patricia Lee. "Search and Research: Willa Cather in Quest of History." *Southwestern American Literature* 5 (1975): 27–39.

———. "Willa Cather's *The Professor's House* and Dutch Genre Painting." *Renascence* 31 (1979): 155–67.

"You Get Only What You Pay For." *Woman's Home Companion*, October 1930, 4.

Zuckerman, Mary Ellen. *A History of Popular Women's Magazines in the United States, 1792–1995*. Westport, CT: Greenwood P, 1998.

Contributors

JENNIFER BRADLEY is associate professor of English at Mercy College of Health Sciences. Her work has focused on Cather's participation in the discourse of etiquette and the democratization of manners. Her article "A Glimpse Inside Childhood: Willa Cather's Childhood Scrapbook" appeared in the Fall 2002 *Willa Cather Newsletter and Review.*

PARK BUCKER is an assistant professor of English at the University of South Carolina Sumter. He is coeditor with Matthew J. Bruccoli of "*To Loot My Life Clean*": *The Thomas Wolfe/Maxwell Perkins Correspondence* (University of South Carolina Press, 2000) and *Catch as Catch Can: The Collected Stories and Other Writings of Joseph Heller* (Simon & Schuster, 2003). Bruccoli and Bucker are also the coauthors of *Joseph Heller: A Descriptive Bibliography* (University of Pittsburgh Press/Oak Knoll, 2002).

ROBERT K. MILLER is a professor of English at the University of St. Thomas in St. Paul, Minnesota. In addition to editing *Great Short Works of Willa Cather* for HarperCollins, he has spoken and written about Cather on numerous occasions. Examples of his work can be found in *Cather Studies; Willa Cather: Family, Community, and History; Willa Cather's Southern Connections; Willa Cather's New York;* and the *WCPM Newsletter and Review.* He is currently completing a book on Cather and the nature of generosity.

Mary Ann O'Farrell is an associate professor of English at Texas A&M University. She is the author of *Telling Complexions: The Nineteenth-Century English Novel and the Blush* (Duke University Press, 1997) and coeditor of *Virtual Gender: Fantasies of Subjectivity and Embodiment* (University of Michigan Press, 1999). She is currently at work on "Jane Austen's Mafia, or the Force of Manners," a project that examines the recurrent and vigorous cultural interest in manners in a wide variety of texts.

Anne Raine is an assistant professor of English at the University of Ottawa. Her teaching and research interests center on the relationships among literature, public discourse, and the material environment. She has published articles on Marianne Moore, Mary Austin, and the visual artist Ana Mendieta, and is currently at work on a book project on American modernism and the early twentieth-century back-to-nature movement.

Ann Romines, a professor of English and the director of graduate studies in English at The George Washington University, is the author of many essays on American women's writing and cultures and of two books: *The Home Plot: Women, Writing and Domestic Ritual* and *Constructing the Little House: Gender, Culture and Laura Ingalls Wilder.* She is editor of *Willa Cather's Southern Connections: New Essays on Cather and the South,* of the *Willa Cather Newsletter and Review,* and of the forthcoming Nebraska Scholarly Edition of Cather's *Sapphira and the Slave Girl.* She is also a lifelong collector of American quilts.

Michael Schueth is a doctoral student at the University of Nebraska-Lincoln. He is currently working on his dissertation exploring Willa Cather and literary celebrity culture. Schueth edits *The Mowers' Tree,* the newsletter of the UNL Cather Colloquium, and has recently been published in the *Willa Cather Newsletter and Review.*

Janis P. Stout is a professor emerita of English at Texas A&M University. Among her books are *Katherine Anne Porter: A Sense of the Times* (1995), *Through the Window, Out the Door: Women's Narratives of Departure, from Austin and Cather to Tyler, Morrison, and Didion* (1998),

Willa Cather: The Writer and Her World (2000), and *A Calendar of the Letters of Willa Cather* (2002).

Honor McKitrick Wallace is a lecturer at the University of Tennessee, Knoxville. She has published articles in *Tulsa Studies in Women's Literature* and *Style*, and her current project examines the connections between production, property, and narrative form in American women's literature.

Deborah Lindsay Williams is an associate professor of English at Iona College, where she teaches American literature and women's studies. Her most recent book is *Not in Sisterhood: Edith Wharton, Willa Cather, Zona Gale, and the Politics of Female Authorship*. She is currently working on a book about Zona Gale and the cultural politics of the early twentieth century.

Sarah Wilson is an assistant professor of English at the University of Toronto. She is the author of an article on Cather published in *American Literature* in 2003 and of forthcoming articles on Henry James and Herman Melville. She is completing a book on Progressive-era modernists and the melting pot.

Index